Performing Israel's Faith

Performing Israel's Faith

Narrative and Law in Rabbinic Theology

Jacob Neusner

Baylor University Press
Waco, Texas USA

Cover Design: Pamela Poll; the quilt was handmade by Suzanne R.
              Neusner and used by permission.
Book Design: Diane Smith

Library of Congress Cataloging-in-Publication Data

Neusner, Jacob, 1932-
   Performing Israel's faith : narrative and law in rabbinic theology / Jacob
Neusner.
      p. cm.
   Includes bibliographical references and index.
   ISBN 1-932792-25-2 (pbk. : alk. paper)
   1. Covenants--Religious aspects--Judaism. 2. Gentiles in rabbinical lit-
erature. 3. Atonement (Judaism) 4. Jewish law. 5. Aggada--History and
criticism. 6. Rabbinical literature--History and criticism. I. Title.
   BM612.5.N48 2005
   296.3--dc22
                                                2005003245

Printed in the United States of America on acid-free paper

Contents

Preface

This book carries forward the argument of E. P. Sanders in *Paul and Palestinian Judaism*[1] that, "the fundamental nature of the covenant conception . . . largely accounts for the relative scarcity of appearances of the term 'covenant' in Rabbinic literature. The covenant was presupposed, and the Rabbinic discussions were largely directed toward the question of how to fulfill the covenantal obligations." This proposition is then meant to disprove the conviction ("all but universally held") that Judaism is a degeneration of the Old Testament view: "The once noble idea of covenant as offered by God's grace and obedience as the consequence of that gracious gift degenerated into the idea of petty legalism, according to which one had to earn the mercy of God by minute observance of irrelevant ordinances." Sanders invokes the language of "covenantal nomism."

In these pages I show how covenantal nomism works: how the norms of conduct set forth by the Halakhah (law) of Rabbinic Judaism realize the corresponding norms of conviction defined by the Aggadah (lore) of that same Judaism, so that the covenant is acted out, embodied in the social order of the Israelite community: "a kingdom of priests and a holy people."

All the translations are my own. The theological systematization of the Halakhah and the Aggadah derives from extensive work of mine, which I digest in these pages. Specifically, for my picture of the theology of the Aggadah I rely upon the following:

The Theology of the Oral Torah. Revealing the Justice of God. Kingston and Montreal: McGill-Queens University Press, 1999.

[1] London: SCM Press, 1977, xvii+627.

The theology of the Halakhah as set forth in the first six centuries C.E. in the Mishnah (200), Tosefta (300), Yerushalmi (400), and Bavli (600), is worked out in detail in the following:

The Halakhah: An Encyclopaedia of the Law of Judaism. The Brill Reference Library of Judaism. 5 Vols. Leiden: E. J. Brill, 1999.
The Theology of the Halakhah. The Brill Reference Library of Ancient Judaism. Leiden: E. J. Brill, 2001.
The Social Teaching of Rabbinic Judaism. The Brill Reference Library of Judaism. 3 Vols. Leiden: E. J. Brill, 2001.
Handbook of Rabbinic Theology: Language, System, Structure. Leiden: E. J. Brill, 2003.

In writing this book I consulted my colleague, Professor Bruce D. Chilton, Bard College, as well as Professors William Scott Green, University of Rochester, to whom I owe the title and much of the conception of the work, and Herbert Basser, Queen's University, upon whose instincts and judgment I rely in all things Rabbinic.

It is a genuine pleasure to present this exercise in the law and theology of Judaism through Baylor University Press under the directorship of Carey C. Newman—not the first book I have written in partnership with Dr. Newman, and I am confident, also not the last.

Jacob Neusner
Research Professor of Theology
Bard College

Introduction

The law of the Torah sets forth rules of normative conduct—acts of omission or acts of commission—that realize Israel's partnership with God in the repair of the world. Covenantal conduct is behavior that actualizes a freely entered-into agreement between God and humanity. Judaism, which rests upon the covenant between God and Israel made at Sinai in the Torah, expresses its theology (norms of conviction) in law (norms of conduct). The faithful Israelite, in keeping the law, acts out the theological truth of the Torah. This I take to represent that covenantal nomism of which E. P. Sanders writes, as noted in the Preface.

These are abstract claims, and they require concrete examples. Here I show in practical terms how, in Judaism, theology expresses itself in law, and how law embodies theology in everyday conduct—all in accord with the Torah revealed by God to Moses at Sinai.

Among many components of the law and theology of Judaism, where do we look? Here I answer that question in two ways: first in the paired chapters, chapters 1 and 2, then 3 and 4; second in chapter 5.

First, I deal with two large issues of theology and show how these are acted out in law. That is in chapters 1 and 2, on the doctrine of the gentiles, and chapters 3 and 4, on the doctrine of sin and atonement. In each case I first expound the theological definition of right belief as set forth in the exegetical and narrative writings of the ancient rabbis. Then I provide a systematic account of the details of the law as laid out in Scripture, then the Mishnah, Tosefta, Yerushalmi (a.k.a., Talmud of the Land of Israel, Talmud of Jerusalem), and Bavli (a.k.a., Talmud of Babylonia). In this way I show the correspondence, the synergism, of theology and law. To do so I expound

1

the way in which various exegeses and narratives of the Rabbinic canon spell out a coherent theological doctrine.

Chapters 1 and 3 provide the exposition of the theological norms. Then in chapters 2 and 4 I spell out the character of the law as set forth in the normative legal documents of Judaism, with a clear statement of how the law makes its theological statement through norms of conduct. The component of the covenant of which narrative speaks is embodied in the law that prescribes proper conduct in accord with the covenant.

That work of reconstruction sets the stage for chapter 5's more systematic survey of the specific meeting of law and lore, narrative and legal norm. Specifically, I show how these are integrated. Chapters 1 and 2, then 3 and 4, do not integrate law and theology but stand each on its own. That is why, in chapter 5, I provide a reading of law to show how law on its own realizes the theological narrative of Scripture. The law is shown to embody and respond to elements of the biblical narrative, thus once more: covenantal conduct.

The division between chapter 1 and chapter 2, chapter 3 and chapter 4—that is, between lore (exegesis, narrative) and law—follows the division in Judaism between norms of conviction and norms of conduct. Law and lore are called, in Hebrew, Halakhah, law, and Aggadah, lore. Halakhah is formed of the consonants that yield *halakh*, go, thus: the way." Aggadah is formed of those that yield *haged*—"tell, thus, narrative" and by extension, exegesis. Chapters 1 and 3 are constructed out of Aggadic documents and passages, chapters 2 and 4, Halakhic ones.

Scripture, particularly the Pentateuch, conveys both law and narrative. Where in Judaism beyond Scripture—in particular, Genesis, Exodus, Leviticus, Numbers, and Deuteronomy—do we find the Halakhah and Aggadah? The answer is, in the documents produced by Rabbinic sages in the formative age of what became normative Judaism, the first six centuries c.e. These fall into two classifications: law and lore, Halakhah and Aggadah, respectively.

The Halakhic definition of right behavior is defined by the legal documents: the Mishnah, a philosophical law code completed at ca. 200 C.E.; the Tosefta, a collection of complementary rules completed at ca. 300 C.E.; the Talmud of the Land of Israel and the Talmud of Babylonia, ca. 400 and 600 C.E., respectively, commentaries on the Mishnah and the Tosefta. The bulk of the law, organized in topical expositions, is in the Mishnah and the Tosefta. The bulk of the exegesis and analysis of the law is in the two Talmuds.

The narrative, exegesis, and generalization of which the theology is comprised is set forth principally in documents organized around Scripture as commentaries. The Aggadic portrayal of right belief takes shape in three ways. First, the Rabbinic sages produce exegeses of the Hebrew Scriptures, finding the sense and meaning of the received Torah. Second, they amplify the narratives of Scripture, so reshaping them as to yield new insight into Scripture's stories. Third, they generalize on Scripture, finding points in common among two or more stories to yield a sustaining truth. That is the source of their theology, which recapitulates in propositional terms the upshot of Scripture's narratives. The Aggadic documents of ancient times include commentaries to Genesis, Exodus, Leviticus, Numbers, Deuteronomy, Lamentations, Song of Songs, Ruth, and Esther. One Aggadic document is organized around the synagogue lections for special Sabbaths of the liturgical calendar. Aggadic compositions also find their way into the two Talmuds.

Although they work together to set forth covenantal conduct, the compilations of the Halakhah and those of the Aggadah represent distinct modes of writing. They are distinct not only in topic—practical rules of conduct versus theoretical conceptions of meaning—but also in form. Each unfolds in accord with its distinctive modes of thought, and each pursues a particular program of inquiry and exegesis. However, both in theory and in practice, the Aggadah and the Halakhah work out the logic of a single generative conviction. It is that the one and only one God is engaged in creating the world and sustaining a perfect world order based on justice, and that Israel shares in the task. In addition, the generations of loyal practitioners of Judaism, from antiquity forward, have received the Halakhah and the Aggadah as a single, seamless statement, in their own way according to those writings the title, "Judaism." So they represent one truth in two media. In Judaism, then, the faithful Israelite acts out truth.

But how the Halakhah and the Aggadah join together to make a coherent statement of covenantal conduct and conviction remains to be seen. Given their formidable, fundamental differences in genre and focus, in their rhetoric, logic of coherent discourse, and even their disparate topical programs, we cannot regard as obvious the answer to that question. To spell out the answer, I show what theological statement the Aggadah makes upon an urgent theological question of Rabbinic Judaism, and what corresponding actions the Halakhah frames in addressing that same urgent issue.

Clearly, this approach to the canonical documents of Judaism taken in these pages claims to discern large and coherent statements, statements that all together cohere in systematic and cogent constructions of law and theology. How to show that that proposition is not merely alleged and episodically illustrated but tested and systematically demonstrated? It is by setting forth the evidence—the way in which the Rabbinic writings in their own words and their own way register the large-scale propositions I discern in them.

To present the Halakhah, accordingly, I cite passages at length from the Mishnah and the Tosefta, where most of the topical exposition is worked out, as well as in a limited way the Yerushalmi and the Bavli. I know of no better way of affording access to the concrete law, in all its detail. Then my claim that the law embodies theology may be tested against the dense details of the Halakhah. The character of the Mishnah and its successor-documents of exegesis and analysis of law makes the work easy, since the entire legal corpus is topically organized in accord with the Mishnah's program. Hence I am able to take bodies of the law of relationships with idolatry and provide a precis of the law to show in detail the character of the rules. Then, in describing, analyzing, and interpreting the law, I make my point.

But the Aggadah presents a problem, for it is not topically organized. It generally is set forth in dialogue with Scripture, in exegetical form. It sometimes makes its points through narratives, both freestanding and amplifying those of Scripture. And just as Scripture provides data for theological generalization but no systematic statement of a theological character, so the Aggadic writings rarely set forth topical expositions. I explain how I know that the Aggadah addresses the very issues that I impute in these pages. My reconstruction of the Rabbinic system that animates the Aggadic compilations is what I recapitulate in chapters 1 and 3. Now, as people generally realize, the Aggadic compilations contain diverse, often conflicting opinion. I am not just picking and choosing illustrations of a proposition of my own devising. I do not bring to the texts a prefabricated theological system of my own. Constructive theology of Judaism, whether historical or contemporary, plays no role in this book.

The Aggadah contains its own signals of normativity. The logic of mythic monotheism—the monotheist narrative—dictates what is normative in the Aggadah, which can tolerate conflict in detail but which dictates dogmas of a theological character that are readily identified and never challenged. For example, no one can doubt that the normative dogmas of the Aggadah encompass the propositions that God is one, merciful and just, that God loves Israel and yearns for Israel's freely given love, that humanity sins when it disobeys God and the like. The two dogmas in play in these pages—the doctrine that the gentiles are those that worship idols and do not know God, and the doctrine that when Israel sins, it can repent and atone and be reconciled with God—form irrefutable norms of conviction and attitude. These are matched, as we see in chapters 2 and 4, by norms of conduct and action, thus once more, covenantal nomism—conduct that realizes the covenant of God and Israel. Readers will quickly see that the Aggadic theology and the Halakhic norms of law overlap yet retain each its own voice and message. How this is worked out will become clear in the transition from chapter 1 to chapter 2, and chapter 3 to chapter 4. The movement is jarring, yet the message is coherent.

Thus, to present the Aggadah and the Halakhah I provide sizable abstracts of the actual language of the canonical writings of the formative age. Here too, readers will test my generalizations—my claims concerning the theological conceptions I allege inhere in the narrative and exegetical and Halakhic writings—against the actualities of the Rabbinic writings. These texts are not widely familiar or accessible, so I have given a generous serving of the original texts in their own language, but in English translation. Having encountered the original texts, in a fairly literal translation, readers will see what it means to speak of conduct that conveys the truth of the covenant. Here God truly lives in the details.

Chapter 1

The Aggadic Theology of the Nations

A religious system defines itself by erecting boundaries between those that belong and those that do not. The character of these boundaries delivers the systemic message. Hellenistic Judaism, represented by Philo of Alexandria, differentiated Israelites from Egyptians and identified Israelite culture with that of Rome, for example.[1] Rabbinic Judaism, building on Scripture, encompassed all Israel and excluded all not-Israel. Knowledge of God made known in the Torah defined the Israelite, and rejection of God and the laws of the Torah characterized the outsiders, "the nations" or gentiles.

The Aggadic theology asks questions of theodicy: why do the gentiles reject God? How to account for God's election of Israel? The Halakhic actualization of that theology then translates into rules of conduct with idolaters and idolatry the norms of Israelite conduct.

The category, the gentiles or the nations, without elaborate differentiation, encompasses all who are not Israelites, that is, who do not belong to Israel and therefore do not know and serve God. These are called "idolaters," and the meaning of "the gentiles" is always and only, "idolaters."[2] That category takes on meaning only as complement and opposite to its generative counterpart, having no standing—self-defining characteristics—on its own. That is, since Israel encompasses the sector of humanity that knows, loves, and serves God by reason of God's self-manifestation in the Torah, the gentiles are comprised by everybody else: those placed by their own intention and active decision beyond the limits of God's revelation. Guided by the Torah Israel worships God. Without its illumination gentiles worship idols. At the outset, therefore, the main point registers: by "gentiles" the sages understand, God's enemies, and by "Israel" the sages understand, those who

7

know God as God has made himself known, which is, through the Torah. In no way does this account deal with secular categories, but with theological ones.

Defining Gentiles/Non-Israelites

Gentiles are idolators, and Israelites worship the one, true God, who has made himself known in the Torah. In the Oral Torah, that is the difference— the only consequential distinction—between Israel and the gentiles. Still, there is that and one other, Israel stands for life, the gentiles for death.

Before proceeding, let us consider a clear statement of why idolatry defines the boundary between Israel and everybody else. The reason is that idolatry—rebellious conduct, expressing arrogance against God—encompasses the entire Torah. The religious duty to avoid idolatry is primary; if one violates the religious duties, the Israelite breaks the yoke of commandments, and if he violates that single religious duty, he violates the entire Torah. Violating the prohibition against idolatry is equivalent to transgressing all Ten Commandments:

Sifré to Numbers CXI:I.1ff.
1. A. "But if you err and do not observe [all these commandments which the Lord has spoken to Moses]" (Num 15:22-26):
2. A. "But if you err and do not observe":
   B. Scripture speaks of idolatry.

Now one may test the proposition, as the sages commonly do, by proposing other readings of the evidence that is adduced besides the one offered as normative. Here is a sequence of options:

   C. You maintain that Scripture speaks of idolatry. But perhaps Scripture refers to any of the religious duties that are listed in the Torah?
   D. Scripture states, ". . . then if it was done unwittingly without the-knowledge of the congregation." Scripture thereby has singled out a particular religious duty unto itself, and what might that be? It is the prohibition against idolatry.
   E. You maintain that Scripture speaks of idolatry. But perhaps Scripture refers to any of the religious duties that are listed in the Torah?
   F. Scripture states, "But if you err and do not observe," indicating that all of the religious duties come together to give testimony concerning a single religious duty.
   G. Just as if someone violates all of the religious duties, he thereby breaks off the yoke [of the commandments] and wipes out the mark of the covenant and so treats the Torah impudently, so if one violates a single religious duty, he thereby breaks off the yoke [of the command-

ments] and wipes out the mark of the covenant and so treats the Torah impudently.

H. And what might that single religious duty be? It is idolatry, for it is said [in that regard], ". . . to violate his covenant" (Deut 17:2). [Thus the covenant refers in particular to the rule against idolatry, which then stands for the whole.]

I. "Covenant" moreover refers only to the Torah, as it is said, "These are the words of the covenant" (Deut 28:69).

The systematic proof having been completed, the exposition now pursues a different path to the same goal:

J. [Providing a different proof for the same proposition as D–I], Rabbi says, "Here the word 'all' is used, and elsewhere the word 'all' is used. Just as in the word 'all' used elsewhere Scripture refers to idolatry, so in the word 'all' used here Scripture refers to idolatry."

Now comes the demonstration that idolatry requires the denial of the Ten Commandments:

3. A. ". . . which the Lord has spoken to Moses":

B. How do you know that whoever confesses to belief in idolatry denies the Ten Commandments?

C. Scripture says, ". . . which the Lord has spoken to Moses," and elsewhere, "And God spoke all these words, saying" (Exod 20:1). "God spoke one word . . ." (Ps 62:12). "Are not my words like fire, says the Lord" (Jer 23:29). So too in respect to that concerning which Moses was commanded Scripture says, ". . . all that the Lord God commanded through the hand of Moses."

D. How do we know that that same rule applies also to all matters concerning which the prophets were commanded?

E. Scripture says, ". . . from the day that the Lord gave commandment [and onward throughout your generations]."

F. And how do we know that that is the case also concerning the commandments entrusted to the patriarchs?

G. Scripture says, ". . . and onward throughout your generations."

H. And whence did the Holy One, blessed be he, begin to entrust commandments to the patriarchs?

I. As it is said, "And the Lord God commanded Adam" (Gen 2:16).

J. Scripture thereby indicates that whoever confesses to belief in idolatry denies the Ten Commandments and rejects all of the commandments entrusted to Moses, the prophets, and the patriarchs.

K. And whoever denies idolatry confesses to belief in the entirety of the Torah.

Violating the religious duties in general means breaking the yoke of the commandments, but there is one that carries in its wake the violation of the entire

Torah or all Ten Commandments. Idolatry is that one. And that is what defines gentiles, that is, the whole of humanity that does not know God.

The gentiles hate Israel and therefore hate God. One wonders what accounts for the logic that links the one to the other. The answer to that question fully spells out the doctrine of the gentiles that the Oral Torah constructs, and everything else is commentary. What defines the gentiles—the lack of the Torah—explains also why their very character requires them to hate Israel, the people of the Torah. The gentiles' hatred of Israel came about because of the revelation of the Torah at Sinai:

> Bavli tractate Shabbat 9:3–4 I.45–6/89a
>
> A.   Said one of the Rabbis to R. Kahana, "Have you heard the meaning of the words 'Mount Sinai'?"
>
> B.   He said to him, "The mountain on which miracles [*nissim*] were done for Israel."
>
> C.   "But then the name should be, Mount Nisai."
>
> D.   "Rather, the mountain on which a good omen was done for Israel."
>
> E.   "But then the name should be, Mount Sinai."
>
> F.   He said to him, "So why don't you hang out at the household of R. Pappa and R. Huna b. R. Joshua, for they're the ones who really look into lore."
>
> G.   For both of them say, "What is the meaning of the name, Mount Sinai? It is the mountain from which hatred [*sinah*] descended for the gentiles."

The key to the entire system—the Torah—opens the lock at hand. Israel accepts the Torah, gentiles reject it, and everything follows from that single fact. Israel knows God, gentiles deny him, and relations between the two sectors of humanity are determined by that fact.

The Place of the Nations in the Theology of Israel

To reveal the justice of God, which is the purpose of the theological system of the Aggadah, the sages must devote a considerable account to the challenge to that justice represented by gentile power and prosperity, contrasted with Israel's subordination and penury. For if the metanarrative proclaims a justice that encompasses all creation, the chapter of gentile rule vastly disrupts the account. Gentile rule forms the point of tension, the source of conflict, attracting attention and demanding explanation. The idolaters should not dominate. The urgent question to which the system must respond is: What rationality of a world ordered through justice accounts for the world ruled by gentiles? And that explains why the systemic problematic focuses upon the question, how justice can be thought to order the world if the gentiles rule. That formulation furthermore forms the public counterpart to the private perplexity: Why the wicked prosper and the righteous suffer. It highlights two challenges to the conviction of the rule of moral rationality—gentile hegemony, matched by the prosperity of wicked persons. First, let us focus upon explaining the prosperity of the gentiles, defined as idolators.

The initial exposition of how things are, set forth in Genesis, tells how God made the world, recognized his failure in doing so, and corrected it. Abraham is Adam's match, and Sarah, Eve's. Through Abraham and Sarah a new humanity came into being, ultimately to meet God at Sinai and to record the meeting in the Torah. But then the question arises, what of the rest of humanity, the children of Noah but not of the sector of the family beginning with Abraham and Sarah, their son and grandson. The simple logic of the story responds: the rest of humanity, outside the holy family and beyond the commanding voice of Sinai, does not know God but worships idols. These are, today, the gentiles. And the gentiles, not Israel, govern the world. And how to resolve that tension imparts dynamism and movement to the story, which then is given an end, therefore also a beginning and a middle. That is Scripture's story, and that also is the story the sages tell in their own idiom and manner. Scripture resorts to a sustained narrative, such as people call "history," that proceeds from beginning to end. That is not how the sages describe and explain the world, for the sages think paradigmatically, rather than historically. They seek the moral rules that are implicit in the stories, rather than trying to find out what really happened on a particular day in a particular place. They identify patterns in events, the opposite of historical inquiry. So to tell the same tale Scripture does, they work out their ideas in a process of category-formation.

These are extreme propositions. How to be Israel is to live forever, and to be gentile is to die once and for all time, so that, at the end of days God will save Israel and destroy idolatry, remains to be explained. Here is one such formulation:

Bavli tractate Abodah Zarah 1:1 I:7–8, 10/4a

I.7 A. R. Hinena bar Pappa contrasted verses of Scripture: "It is written, 'As to the almighty, we do not find him exercising plenteous power' (Job 37:23), but by contrast, 'Great is our Lord and of abundant power' (Ps 147:5), and further, 'Your right hand, Lord, is glorious in power' (Exod 15:6).

B. "But there is no contradiction between the first and second and third statements, for the former speaks of the time of judgment [when justice is tempered with mercy, so God does not do what he could] and the latter two statements refer to a time of war [of God against his enemies]."

I.8   A.   R. Hama bar Hanina contrasted verses of Scripture: "It is written, 'Fury is not in me' (Isa 27:4) but also 'The Lord revenges and is furious' (Nah 1:2).

   B.   "But there is no contradiction between the first and second statements, for the former speaks of Israel, the latter of the gentiles."

   C.   R. Hinena bar Pappa said, "'Fury is not in me' (Isa 27:4), for I have already taken an oath: 'would that I had not so vowed, then as the briars and thorns in flame would I with one step burn it altogether.'"

I.10 A.   That is in line with what Raba said, "What is the meaning of the verse, 'Howbeit he will not stretch out a hand for a ruinous heap though they cry in his destruction' (Job 30:24)?

   B.   "Said the Holy One, blessed be He, to Israel, 'When I judge Israel, I shall not judge them as I do the gentiles, for it is written, "I will overturn, overturn, overturn it" (Ezek 21:32), rather, I shall exact punishment from them as a hen pecks.'

   C.   "Another matter: 'Even if the Israelites do not carry out a religious duty before me more than a hen pecking at a rubbish heap, I shall join together [all the little pecks] into a great sum: "although they pick little they are saved" (Job 30:24).'"

So one cannot overstress the given on which all else is built: to be a gentile is to practice idolatry and to die, and to be Israel is to serve the one true God and to rise from the grave to eternal life. That principle governs throughout. Everything else flows from it, and, in due course readers will see, upon that basis the present condition of the world is shown to cohere with the principle of the moral order of justice that prevails.

How this conviction plays itself out remains to be seen. That the world to come opens before Israel is explicit, as in the opening statement of the Mishnah-treatise on the subject, Mishnah-tractate Sanhedrin 11:1A:

> All Israelites have a share in the world to come, as it is said, "Your people also shall be all righteous, they shall inherit the land forever; the branch of my planting, the work of my hands, that I may be glorified" (Isa 60:21).

But in that very context readers recall, not even all Israel enters in. The ones who do not find definition in the logic of the Oral Torah viewed whole, those who deny the normative principles of the faith—that the Torah comes from heaven, that the teaching of the resurrection of the dead derives from the Torah—lose out. By their own word they do not know God, so, while remaining Israel, they join the gentiles before the very gate of the world to come. So too the principle of measure for measure furthermore applies:

those who deny resurrection as a principle of the Torah—the sole source of truth so far as the sages are concerned—also do not get it.

This brings us from the principles to the details of the sages' theology of the gentiles. What specifically is made known in the Torah about the gentiles, understood to mean "idolaters," emerges in chapter 2. First, all those prior to Noah simply are wiped out, do not get a share in the world to come, and do not stand in judgment. As to those after the flood, while they have no share in the world to come, they will stand in judgment. Justified, they still do not enter the world to come:

Mishnah-tractate Sanhedrin 11:3A–CC
A. The generation of the flood has no share in the world to come,
B. and they shall not stand in the judgment,
C. since it is written, "My spirit shall not judge with humanity forever" (Gen 6:3)
D. neither judgment nor spirit.

Once the generation of the flood enters, it draws in its wake the generation of the dispersion and the men of Sodom:

E. The generation of the dispersion has no share in the world to come,
F. since it is said, "So the Lord scattered them abroad from there upon the face of the whole earth" (Gen 11:8).
G. "So the Lord scattered them abroad"—in this world,
H. "and the Lord scattered them from there"—in the world to come.
I. The men of Sodom have no portion in the world to come,
J. since it is said, "Now the men of Sodom were wicked and sinners against the Lord exceedingly" (Gen 13:13)
K. "Wicked"—in this world,
L. "And sinners"—in the world to come.
M. But they will stand in judgment.
N. R. Nehemiah says, "Both these and those will not stand in judgment,
O. "for it is said, 'Therefore the wicked shall not stand in judgment [108A], nor sinners in the congregation of the righteous' (Ps 1:5)
P. 'Therefore the wicked shall not stand in judgment'—this refers to the generation of the flood.
Q. 'Nor sinners in the congregation of the righteous'—this refers to the men of Sodom."
R. They said to him, "They will not stand in the congregation of the righteous, but they will stand in the congregation of the sinners."

Now the exposition will shift to Israelite sinners, three classes of persons, with the same result: here too, some stand in judgment but will not enter the world to come. The spies who rejected the land, the generation of the golden calf, condemned to die in the wilderness, and the party of Korach define the

Israelites who lose out. They are those who rejected the restoration to the land do not reenter the land at the restoration that commences with resurrection, those who opted for an idol instead of God, and those who rejected the Torah of Moses. So these classes of Israelites match the gentiles, for they deny the three principal components of salvation and redemption: restoration, service of one God, and acceptance of the authority of the Torah of Sinai; some opinion differs, but the anonymous opinion represents the consensus of the sages, as always:

> S. The spies have no portion in the world to come,
> T as it is said, "Even those men who brought up an evil report of the land died by the plague before the Lord" (Num 14:37)
> U. "Died"—in this world.
> V. "By the plague"—in the world to come.
> W. "The generation of the wilderness has no portion in the world to come and will not stand in judgment,
> X. "for it is written, 'In this wilderness they shall be consumed and there they shall die' (Num 14:35)," The words of R. Aqiba.
> Y. R. Eliezer says, "Concerning them it says, 'Gather my saints together to me, those that have made a covenant with me by sacrifice' (Ps 50:5)."
> Z. "The party of Korach is not destined to rise up,
> AA. "for it is written, 'And the earth closed upon them'—in this world.
> BB. "'And they perished from among the assembly'—in the world to come," the words of R. Aqiba.
> CC. And R. Eliezer says, "Concerning them it says, 'The Lord kills and resurrects, brings down to Sheol and brings up again' (1 Sam 2:6)."

The Mishnah then takes up special cases of particular classes of gentiles singled out by Scripture.

What about gentiles in general? All depends upon their own actions. Since the point of differentiation is idolatry as against worship of the one God, gentiles may enter into the category of Israel, which is to say, they recognize the one God and come to serve him. That means, whether now or later, some, perhaps many, gentiles will enter Israel, being defined as other Israelites are defined: those who worship the one and only God. The gentiles include many righteous persons. But by the end of days these God will bring to Israel:

Yerushalmi Berakhot 2:8 I:2:
> A. When R. Hiyya bar Adda, the nephew of Bar Qappara, died Resh Laqish accepted [condolences] on his account because he [Resh Laqish] had been his teacher. We may say that [this action is justified because] a person's student is as beloved to him as his son.

B. And he [Resh Laqish] expounded concerning him [Hiyya] this verse: "My beloved has gone down to his garden, to the bed of spices, to pasture his flock in the gardens, and to gather lilies" [Song 6:2]. It is not necessary [for the verse to mention, 'To the bed of spices']. [It is redundant if you interpret the verse literally, for most gardens have spice beds.]

C. Rather [interpret the verse as follows:] My beloved—this is God; has gone down to his garden—this is the world; to the beds of spices—this is Israel; to pasture his flock in the gardens—these are the nations of the world; and to gather lilies—these are the righteous whom he takes from their midst.

Now a parable restates the proposition in narrative terms; having chosen a different mode of discourse from the narrative one that dominates in the Authorized History (Genesis through Kings) the sages reintroduce narrative for an other-than-historical purpose, as here:

D. They offer a parable [relevant to this subject]. To what may we compare this matter [of the tragic death of his student]? A king had a son who was very beloved to him. What did the king do? He planted an orchard for him.

E. As long as the son acted according to his father's will, he would search throughout the world to seek the beautiful saplings of the world, and to plant them in his orchard. And when his son angered him he went and cut down all his saplings.

F. Accordingly, so long as Israel acts according to God's will he searches throughout the world to seek the righteous persons of the nations of the world and bring them and join them to Israel, as he did with Jethro and Rahab. And when they [the Israelites] anger him he removes the righteous from their midst.

It follows that Israel bears a heavy burden of responsibility even for the gentiles. When Israel pleases God, the righteous among the gentiles are joined to them, and when not, not. So while gentiles as such cannot inherit the world to come, they, too, can enter the status of Israel, in which case they join Israel in the world to come.

This the gentiles will do in exactly the way that Israel attained that status to begin with, which is by knowing God through his self-manifestation in the Torah, therefore by accepting God's rule as set forth therein. In this way the theology of the Oral Torah maintains its perfect consistency and inner logic: the Torah determines all things. That point is made explicit: If a gentile keeps the Torah, he is saved. But by keeping the Torah, the gentile has ceased to be gentile and become Israelite, worth even of the high priesthood.

With so much depending on "being Israel," the question presents itself of how Israel comes into being. First comes the definition of how Israel becomes Israel, which is by accepting God's dominion in the Torah:

Sifra CXCIV:ii.1

1. A. "The Lord spoke to Moses saying, 'Speak to the Israelite people and say to them, I am the Lord your God'":
   B. R. Simeon b. Yohai says, "That is in line with what is said elsewhere: 'I am the Lord your God [who brought you out of the land of Egypt, out of the house of bondage]' (Exod 20:2).
   C. 'Am I the Lord, whose sovereignty you took upon yourself in Egypt?'
   D. "They said to him, 'Indeed.'
   E. "'Indeed you have accepted my dominion.'
   F. "'They accepted my decrees: "You will have no other gods before me."'
   G. "That is what is said here: 'I am the Lord your God,' meaning, 'Am I the one whose dominion you accepted at Sinai?'
   H. "They said to him, 'Indeed.'
   I. "'Indeed you have accepted my dominion.'
   J. "'They accepted my decrees: "You shall not copy the practices of the land of Egypt where you dwelt, or of the land of Canaan to which I am taking you; nor shall you follow their laws."'"

The passage underscores how matters are defined, which is by appeal to the Torah. Then the true state of affairs emerges when the same definition explicitly is brought to bear upon the gentiles. That definition, gentiles become Israel when they give up idolatry and serve and love God, yields the clear inference that gentiles have the power to join themselves to Israel as fully naturalized Israelites, so the Torah that defines their status also constitutes the ticket of admission to the world to come that Israel will enter in due course. The sages could not be more explicit than they are when they insist, the gentile ceases to be in the status of the gentile when he accepts God's rule in the Torah:

Sifra CXCIV:ii.15

15. A. ". . . by the pursuit of which humanity shall live":
    B. R. Jeremiah says, "How do I know that even a gentile who keeps the Torah, lo, he is like the high priest?
    C. "Scripture says, 'by the pursuit of which humanity shall live.'"
    D. And so he says, "'And this is the Torah of the priests, Levites, and Israelites,' is not what is said here, but rather, 'This is the Torah of the humanity, O Lord God' (2 Sam 7:19)."
    E. And so he says, "'open the gates and let priests, Levites, and Israelites will enter it' is not what is said, but rather, 'Open the gates and let the righteous nation, who keeps faith, enter it' (Isa 26:2)."

F.   And so he says, "'This is the gate of the Lord. Priests, Levites, and Israelites. . .' is not what is said, but rather, 'the righteous shall enter into it' (Ps 118:20)."

G.   And so he says, "'What is said is not, 'Rejoice, priests, Levites, and Israelites,' but rather, 'Rejoice, O righteous, in the Lord' (Ps 33:1)."

H.   And so he says, "It is not, 'Do good, O Lord, to the priests, Levites, and Israelites,' but rather, 'Do good, O Lord, to the good, to the upright in heart' (Ps 125:4)."

I.   "Thus, even a gentile who keeps the Torah, lo, he is like the high priest."

That is not to suggest God does not rule the gentiles. He does—whether they like it or not, acknowledge him or not. God responds, also, to the acts of merit taken by gentiles, as much as to those of Israel. The upshot is, "gentile" and "Israel" classify through the presence or absence of the same traits; they form taxonomic categories that can in the case of the gentile change when that which is classified requires reclassification.

The Basis of the Division Between Israel and the Nations

Nothing intrinsic distinguishes Israel from the gentiles, only their attitudes (or virtues) and actions: covenantal conduct. Opinion coalesces around the proposition that Israel and the gentiles do form a single genus, speciated by the relationship to God and the Torah. So in the end, a ferocious Israelite or a forbearing gentile represents mere anomalies, not categorical imperatives. Sufficient proof derives from the explicit statement that, when Israel acts like gentiles, it enters the classification of gentiles; if Israel conducts itself like the gentiles, Israel will be rejected and punished as were the gentiles, with special reference to Egypt and Canaan. This matter is spelled out in another formally perfect composition:

Sifra CXCIII:I.1–11

1   B.   "The Lord spoke to Moses saying, 'Speak to the Israelite people and say to them, I am the Lord your God'":

C.   "I am the Lord," for I spoke and the world came into being.

D.   "I am full of mercy.

E.   "I am Judge to exact punishment and faithful to pay recompense.

F   "I am the one who exacted punishment from the generation of the Flood and the men of Sodom and Egypt, and I shall exact punishment from you if you act like them."

First comes Egypt:

2. A. And how do we know that there was never any nation among all of the nations that practiced such abominations, more than did the Egyptians?

B. Scripture says, "You shall not copy the practices of the land of Egypt where you dwelt."

C. And how do we know that the last generation did more abhorrent things than all the rest of them?

D. Scripture says, "You shall not copy the practices of the land of Egypt."

E. And how do we know that the people in the last location in which the Israelites dwelt were more abhorrent than all the rest?

F. Scripture says, ". . . where you dwelt, you shall not do."

G. And how do we know that the fact that the Israelites dwelt there was the cause for all these deeds?

H. Scripture says, "You shall not copy . . . where you dwelt."

Now the account shifts to deal with the Canaanites, following the given form:

3. A. How do we know that there was never a nation among all the nations that did more abhorrent things than the Canaanites?

B. Scripture says, "You shall not copy the practices . . . of the land of Canaan [to which I am taking you; nor shall you follow their laws]."

C. And how do we know that the last generation did more abhorrent things than all the rest of them?

D. Scripture says, "You shall not copy the practices of the land of Canaan."

E. And how do we know that the people in the place to which the Israelites were coming for conquest were more abhorrent than all the rest?

F. Scripture says, ". . . to which I am taking you."

G. And how do we know that it is the arrival of the Israelites that caused them to do all these deeds?

H. Scripture says, "or of the land of Canaan to which I am taking you; nor shall you follow their laws."

Now the two cases are expounded in the same terms, and the specific type of laws that Israel is not to follow is defined:

7. A. If "You shall not copy the practices of the land of Egypt . . . or of the land of Canaan,"

B. might one think that they are not to build their buildings or plant vineyards as they did?

C. Scripture says, "nor shall you follow their laws:

D. "I have referred only to the rules that were made for them and for their fathers and their fathers' fathers."

E. And what would they do?

    F.   A man would marry a man, and a woman would marry a woman, a man would marry a woman and her daughter, a woman would be married to two men.

    G.   That is why it is said, "nor shall you follow their laws."

8. A.   ["My rules alone shall you observe and faithfully follow my laws":]

    B.   "my rules": this refers to laws.

    C.   ". . . my laws": this refers to the amplifications thereof.

    D.   ". . . shall you observe": this refers to repeating traditions.

    E.   ". . . and faithfully follow": this refers to concrete deed.

    F.   ". . . and faithfully follow my laws": it is not the repetition of traditions that is the important thing but doing them is the important thing.

At stake in differentiating Israel from the gentiles is life in the world to come; the gentiles offer only death:

9. A.   "You shall keep my laws and my rules, by the pursuit of which humanity [shall live]":

    B.   This formulation of matter serves to make keeping and doing into laws, and keeping and doing into rules.

10. A.   ". . . shall live":

    B.   in the world to come.

    C.   And should you wish to claim that the reference is to this world, is it not the fact that in the end one dies?

    D.   Lo, how am I to explain, ". . . shall live"?

    E.   It is with reference to the world to come.

11. A.   "I the Lord am your God":

    B.   faithful to pay a reward.

Here the entire doctrine of the gentiles is fully exposed. God judges Israel and the gentiles by a single rule of justice; to each is meted out measure for measure. Israel is not elect by reason of privilege; Israel is elect solely because Israel accepts the Torah and so knows God. All the nations were offered the Torah, God's grace extended to every one of them. But Israel alone accepted the Torah and its disciplines, not to murder, not to steal, not to commit adultery. All are equal before God. The same punishment exacted from the generation of the Flood, the Sodomites, the Egyptians, and all others will be exacted from Israel if Israel acts like them. At that point, Israel becomes gentile. It is the Torah that differentiates. And, at the end, the stakes are exactly what the reading of Mishnah-tractate Sanhedrin 10:1–2 sets forth implicitly: entry into the world to come.

    The focus is upon intention—how the idolater regards matters, rather than upon what he actually has done in making and worshipping the idol. The attitude of the idolater governs God's disposition of matters. God hates idolaters more than he hates the idol itself, for, all parties concur, in any case there is no substance in idolatry itself. The idolater rejects God and so makes the idol. So what is at issue in idolatry is the attitude of the idolater, that is, his rejection of the one true God, made manifest in the Torah. The idolater by his attitude and intention confers upon the idol a status that, on its own the idol cannot attain, being inanimate in any event. So the logic that governs distinguishes the actor from the acted upon, the cause from that which is caused, and the rest follows.

Having established that idolators subject themselves to God's hatred by reason of their attitudes and consequent actions, one must ask about the matter of fairness. To explain matters, this narrative must turn to an account of how things came about—a reason one should call historical but the sages would classify as paradigmatic. That is, the sages' explanation, framed in terms of a narrative of something that happened, turns out to be a picture of how things now are—a characterization of the established facts as these are realized under all circumstances and at any time, the tenses, past, present, or future, making no difference.

So when one asks why to begin with have gentiles entered the category of death, and why is it just that they should not enjoy life eternal, the answers are urgently needed. To find them the text must take up a tale that casts in mythic-narrative form what constitutes an analysis of characteristic traits. Not only so, but the narrative explicitly points to the enduring traits, not a given action, to explain the enduring condition of the gentiles: that is how they are, because that is how they wish to be.

Now the question becomes urgent. It concerns how this catastrophic differentiation has imposed itself between Israel and the gentiles, such that the gentiles, for all their glory in the here and now, won for themselves the grave, while Israel, for all its humiliation in the present age, inherits the world to come. And the answer is self-evident from all that has been said: the gentiles reject God, whom they could and should have known in the Torah. They rejected the Torah, and all else followed. The proposition then moves in these simple steps, which are now familiar: [1] Israel differs from the gentiles because Israel possesses the Torah and the gentiles do not; [2] because they do not possess the Torah, the gentiles also worship idols instead of God; and [3] therefore God rejects the gentiles and identifies with Israel.

And one asks where considerations of justice and fairness enter in. Here, at a critical turning, the system reaches back into its fundamental and generative conception, that the world is ordered by justice. The Oral Torah then has to demonstrate that the same justice that governs Israel and endows Israel with the Torah dictates the fate of the gentiles and denies them the Torah. And, predictably, that demonstration must further underscore the justice of the condition of the gentiles: measure for measure must play itself out especially here.

The gentiles deprived themselves of the Torah because they rejected it, and, showing the precision of justice, they rejected the Torah because the Torah deprived them of the very practices or traits that they deemed characteristic, essential to their being. That circularity marks the tale of how things were to begin with in fact describes how things always are; it is not historical but philosophical. The gentiles' own character, the shape of their conscience, then, now, and always, accounts for their condition—which, by an act of will, they can change. What they did not want, that of which they were by their own word unworthy, is denied them. And what they do want condemns them. So when each nation comes under judgment for rejecting the Torah, the indictment of each nation is spoken out of its own mouth, its own self-indictment then forms the core of the matter. Given what is known about the definition of Israel as those destined to live and the gentile as those not, one cannot find surprising that the entire account is set in that age to come to which the gentiles are denied entry.

When they protest the injustice of the decision that takes effect just then, they are shown the workings of the moral order, as the following systematic account of the governing pattern explains:

> Bavli tractate Abodah Zarah 1:1 I.2/2a–b:
>
> A. R. Hinena bar Pappa, and some say, R. Simlai, gave the following exposition [of the verse, "They that fashion a graven image are all of them vanity, and their delectable things shall not profit, and their own witnesses see not nor know" (Isa 44:9)]: "In the age to come the Holy One, blessed be He, will bring a scroll of the Torah and hold it in his bosom and say, 'Let him who has kept himself busy with it come and take his reward.' Then all the gentiles will crowd together: 'All of the nations are gathered together' (Isa 43:9). The Holy One, blessed be He, will say to them, 'Do not crowd together before me in a mob. But let each nation enter together with [2B] its scribes, 'and let the peoples be gathered together' (Isa 43:9), and the word 'people' means 'kingdom': 'and one kingdom shall be stronger than the other' (Gen 25:23).

The reader will note that the players are the principal participants in world history: the Romans first and foremost, then the Persians, the other world rulers of the age; it is as though China and India, the U.S.A. and Russia, were called to account for themselves before God:

> C. "The kingdom of Rome comes in first.
> H. "The Holy One, blessed be He, will say to them, 'How have you defined your chief occupation?'

I. "They will say before him, 'Lord of the world, a vast number of marketplaces have we set up, a vast number of bathhouses we have made, a vast amount of silver and gold have we accumulated. And all of these things we have done only in behalf of Israel, so that they may define as their chief occupation the study of the Torah.'

J. "The Holy One, blessed be He, will say to them, 'You complete idiots! Whatever you have done has been for your own convenience. You have set up a vast number of marketplaces to be sure, but that was so as to set up whorehouses in them. The bathhouses were for your own pleasure. Silver and gold belong to me anyhow: "Mine is the silver and mine is the gold, says the Lord of hosts" (Hag 2:8). Are there any among you who have been telling of "this," and "this" is only the Torah: "And this is the Torah that Moses set before the children of Israel' (Deut 4:44)." So they will make their exit, humiliated.

The claim of Rome—to support Israel in Torah-study—is rejected on grounds that the Romans did not exhibit virtue through the right conduct and, especially, through the right attitude, always a dynamic force in the theology. Then the other world rule enters in with its claim:

K. "When the kingdom of Rome has made its exit, the kingdom of Persia enters afterward.

M. "The Holy One, blessed be He, will say to them, 'How have you defined your chief occupation?'

N. "They will say before him, 'Lord of the world, We have thrown up a vast number of bridges, we have conquered a vast number of towns, we have made a vast number of wars, and all of them we did only for Israel, so that they may define as their chief occupation the study of the Torah.'

O. "The Holy One, blessed be He, will say to them, 'Whatever you have done has been for your own convenience. You have thrown up a vast number of bridges, to collect tolls, you have conquered a vast number of towns, to collect the corvée, and, as to making a vast number of wars, I am the one who makes wars: "The Lord is a humanity of war" (Exod 19:17). Are there any among you who have been telling of "this," and "this" is only the Torah: "And this is the Torah that Moses set before the children of Israel" (Deut 4:44).' So they will make their exit, humiliated.

R. "And so it will go with each and every nation."

As native categories, Rome and Persia are singled out, "all the other nations" play no role, for reasons with which readers are already familiar. Once more the theology reaches into its deepest thought on the power of intentionality, showing that what people want is what they get.

But matters cannot be limited to the two world empires of the present age, Rome and Iran, standing in judgment at the end of time. The theology values balance, proportion, it seeks complementary relationships, and therefore it treats beginnings along with endings, the one going over the ground of the other. Accordingly, a recapitulation of the same event—the gentiles' rejection of the Torah—chooses as its setting not the last judgment but the first encounter, that is, the giving of the Torah itself. In the timeless world constructed by the Oral Torah, what happens at the outset exemplifies how things always happen, and what happens at the end embodies what has always taken place. The basic thesis is identical—the gentiles cannot accept the Torah because to do so they would have to deny their very character. But the exposition retains its interest because it takes its own course.

Now the gentiles are not just Rome and Persia but others; and of special interest, the Torah is embodied in some of the Ten Commandments—not to murder, not to commit adultery, not to steal; then the gentiles are rejected for not keeping the seven commandments assigned to the children of Noah. The upshot is that the reason that the gentiles rejected the Torah is that the Torah prohibits deeds that the gentiles do by their very nature. Israel ultimately is changed by the Torah, so that Israel exhibits traits imparted by their encounter with the Torah. So too with the gentiles, by their nature they are what they are; the Torah has not changed their nature.

Once more a single standard applies to both components of humanity, but with opposite effect:

Sifré to Deuteronomy CCCXLIII:IV.1ff.
1. A. Another teaching concerning the phrase, "He said, 'The Lord came from Sinai'":
   B. When the Omnipresent appeared to give the Torah to Israel, it was not to Israel alone that he revealed himself but to every nation.
   C. First of all he came to the children of Esau. He said to them, "Will you accept the Torah?"
   D. They said to him, "What is written in it?"
   E. He said to them, "'You shall not murder' (Exod 20:13)."
   F. They said to him, "The very being of 'those men' [namely, us] and of their father is to murder, for it is said, 'But the hands are the hands of Esau'"(Gen 27:22). 'By your sword you shall live' (Gen 27:40)."

At this point the exposition proceeds to cover new ground: other classes of gentiles that reject the Torah; now the Torah's own narrative takes over, replacing the known facts of world politics, such as the earlier account sets forth, and instead supplying evidence out of Scripture as to the character of the gentile group under discussion:

   G. So he went to the children of Ammon and Moab and said to them, "Will you accept the Torah?"

  H.   They said to him, "What is written in it?"

  I.   He said to them, "'You shall not commit adultery' (Exod 20:13)."

  J.   They said to him, "The very essence of fornication belongs to them [us], for it is said, 'Thus were both the daughters of Lot with child by their fathers' (Gen 19:36)."

  K.   So he went to the children of Ishmael and said to them, "Will you accept the Torah?"

  L.   They said to him, "What is written in it?"

  M.   He said to them, "'You shall not steal' (Exod 20:13)."

  N.   They said to him, "The very essence of their [our] father is thievery, as it is said, 'And he shall be a wild ass of a man (Gen 16:12)."

  O.   And so it went. He went to every nation, asking them, "Will you accept the Torah?"

  P.   For so it is said, "All the kings of the earth shall give you thanks, O Lord, for they have heard the words of your mouth" (Ps 138:4).

  Q.   Might one suppose that they listened and accepted the Torah?

  R.   Scripture says, "And I will execute vengeance in anger and fury upon the nations, because they did not listen" (Mic 5:14).

Now one must turn back to the obligations that God has imposed upon the gentiles; these obligations have no bearing upon the acceptance of the Torah; they form part of the ground of being, the condition of existence, of the gentiles. Yet even here, the gentiles do not accept God's authority in matters of natural law:

  S.   And it is not enough for them that they did not listen, but even the seven religious duties that the children of Noah indeed accepted upon themselves they could not uphold before breaking them.

  T.   When the Holy One, blessed be He, saw that that is how things were, he gave them to Israel.

The same motif recurs: the gentiles rejected God, and that is why they worship idols. Now comes another parable, involving not a king but a common person:

2. A.   The matter may be compared to the case of a person who sent his ass and dog to the threshing floor and loaded up a *letekh* of grain on his ass and three *seahs* of grain on his dog. The ass went along, while the dog panted.

    B.   He took a *seah* of grain off the dog and put it on the ass, so with the second, so with the third.

    C.   Thus was Israel: they accepted the Torah, complete with all its secondary amplifications and minor details, even the seven religious duties that the children of Noah could not uphold without breaking them did the Israelites come along and accept.

D. That is why it is said, "The Lord came from Sinai; he shone upon them from Seir."

Along these same lines, the gentiles would like to make a common pact with Israel, but cannot have a share in God:

Sifré to Deuteronomy CCCXLIII:IX.2

A. Thus the nations of the world would ask Israel, saying to them, "'What is your beloved more than another beloved' (Song 5:9)? For you are willing to accept death on his account."

B. For so Scripture says, "Therefore they love you to death" (Song 1:3).

C. And further: "No, but for your sake are we killed all day long" (Ps 44:23).

Now comes the envy of the gentiles, their desire to amalgamate with Israel, and Israel's insistence upon remaining a holy people, a people apart by reason of adherence to the Torah:

D. [The nations continue,] "All of you are handsome, all of you are strong. Come and let us form a group in common."

E. And the Israelites answer, "We shall report to you part of the praise that is coming to him, and in that way you will discern him:

F. "'My beloved is white and ruddy . . . his head is as the most fine gold . . . his eyes are like doves beside the water-brooks . . . his cheeks are as a bed of spices . . . his hands are as rods of gold. . . . His legs are as pillars of marble. . . . His mouth is most sweet, yes, he is altogether sweet' (Song 5:10-16)."

G. When the nations of the world hear about the beauty and praiseworthy quality of the Holy One, blessed be He, they say to them, "Let us come with you."

H. For it is said, "Where has your beloved gone, O you fairest among women? Where has your beloved turned, that we may seek him with you" (Song 5:1).

Israel's is not the task of winning over the gentiles. That is God's task, and it will be done in God's own good time:

I. What do the Israelites answer them? "You have no share in him: 'I am my beloved's and my beloved is mine, who feeds among the lilies'" (Song 6:3).

The various gentile nations rejected the Torah for specific and reasonable considerations, concretely, because the Torah prohibited deeds essential to their being. This point is made in so many words, then amplified through a parable. Israel, by contrast, is prepared to give up life itself for the Torah.

The Contemporary Condition of Israel among the Nations:
God's Plan for the Gentiles

When readers recall that, within this theology, world history turns on Israel's destiny, they cannot find it surprising that the present arrangement of world politics responds to Israel's condition, specifically, its sinfulness. This simple proposition comes to expression in so many words in the following statement:

Esther Rabbah XI:i.11

    A.   Said R. Aibu, "It is written, 'For the kingdom is the Lord's and he is the ruler over the nations' (Ps 22:29).

    B.   "And yet you say here, 'when King Ahasuerus sat on his royal throne'?

    C.   "In the past dominion resigned in Israel, but when they sinned, its dominion was taken away from them and given to the nations of the world.

    D.   "That is in line with the following verse of Scripture: 'I will give the land over into the hand of evil men' (Ezek 30:12)."

    F.   [Continuing D:] "In the future, when the Israelites repent, the Holy One, blessed be He, will take dominion from the nations of the world and restore it to Israel.

    G.   "When will this come about? 'When saviors will come up on Mount Zion' (Obad 1:21)."

Israel controls its own condition, its conduct governs its own fate. Because Israel sinned, gentiles rule; when Israel by an act of will repents, then Israel will regain dominion over itself. The nations serve as instruments of God's wrath; nothing that they do comes about by their own volition, but only by consequence of Israel's. Israel is justly punished for its own sins, and its present condition demonstrates the working of God's justice. All things are foreseen, but free will is accorded to Israel, and within those two principles is located a clear and reasonable explanation for the enormous anomaly that idolators rule God's people. That rule by idolaters turns out not anomalous but wholly coherent to the principle of the rule of justice.

But if Israel is in control, one must wonder why punishment should take the particular form of subjugation to idolators. The reason is that Israel's condition responds not only to its own actions and intentions, which ought to have subjected Israel to the penalty meted out to Adam for his act of rebellion. Israel enjoys also the protection and intervention of the founders of Israel, the patriarchs. They establish the point of difference between Adam and Israel: God's intervention, his identification of the patriarchs as the means by which he will ultimately make himself known to humanity. Hence the very formation of Israel bears within itself the point of differentiation between Adam and Israel. As to the dominion of the gentiles, entailing also exile from the Land of Israel, that penalty for sin represents a choice made by Abraham. Foreseeing all that would come about through time, God set forth the four constituents of Israelite being: the gentiles, Gehenna (Hell), the sacrifices, the Torah. They formed a balance: if Israel practices the commandments and studies the Torah, they will be spared gentile rule and Gehenna; that is, they will thrive under the dominion of the kingdom of heaven, on the one side, and they will inherit the world to come, on the other. But God knows that Israel will sin. So, to begin with, Abraham is offered the choice of penalties. He chooses the lesser of the two penalties, the dominion of the gentiles, reserving for Israel the greater of the two alternatives, life eternal. The system at each point recapitulates its main principles. Here is how the matter is spelled out.

Pesiqta Rabbati XV [=Pesiqta deRab Kahana V]:II.1

1. A. "Great things have you done, O Lord my God; your wonderful purposes and plans are all for our good; [none can compare with you; I would proclaim them and speak of them, but they are more than I can tell]" (Prov 40:5).

Now begins the process of the justification of subjugation to the nations; whatever happens then happens for the good of Israel:

   B. R. Hinena bar Pappa says two [teachings in respect to the cited verse]: "All those wonders and plans which you made so that our father, Abraham, would accept the subjugation of Israel to the nations were for our good, for our sake, so that we might endure in the world."
   C. Simeon bar Abba in the name of R. Yohanan: "Four things did the Holy One, blessed be He, show to our father, Abraham: the Torah, the sacrifices, Gehenna, and the rule of the kingdoms.
   D. "The Torah: '. . . and a flaming torch passed between these pieces' (Gen 15:17).
   E. "Sacrifices: 'And he said to him, Take for me a heifer divided into three parts' (Gen 15:9).
   F. "Gehenna: 'behold a smoking fire pot.'
   G. "The rule of the kingdoms: 'Lo, dread, a great darkness' (Gen 15:12)."

Here is the principal message: Torah and sacrifice preserve Israel, the subjugation to the nations and Gehenna penalize Israel for failing to maintain Torah-study and sacrifice:

   H. "The Holy One, blessed be He, said to our father, Abraham, 'So long as your descendants are occupied with the former two, they will be saved from the latter two. If they abandon the former two of them, they will be judged by the other two.

    I.   "'So long as they are occupied with study of the Torah and performance of the sacrifices, they will be saved from Gehenna and from the rule of the kingdoms.'"

Israel's failure is foreseen, if not foreordained, and now Abraham is offered a choice for his descendants' future:

    J.   "'But [God says to Abraham] in the future the house of the sanctuary is destined to be destroyed and the sacrifices nullified. What is your preference? Do you want your children to go down into Gehenna or to be subjugated to the four kingdoms?'"

All this conformed to Abraham's wishes:

    K.   R. Hinena bar Pappa said, "Abraham himself chose the subjugation to the four kingdoms.

    L.   "What is the scriptural basis for that view? 'How should one chase a thousand and two put ten thousand to flight, except their rock had given them over' (Deut 32:30). That statement concerning the rock refers only to Abraham, as it is said, 'Look at the rock from which you were hewn' (Isa 51:1).

    M.   "'But the Lord delivered them up' (Deut 32:30) teaches that God then approved what he had chosen."

Once more working out their own narratives in response to Scripture's, the text now presents an account of Abraham's thinking when he made the fateful choice:

  2. A.   R. Berekhiah in the name of R. Levi: "Now Abraham sat and puzzled all that day, saying, 'Which should I choose, Gehenna or subjugation to the kingdoms? Is the one worse than the other?'

       B.   "Said the Holy One, blessed be He, to him, 'Abraham, how long are you going to sit in puzzlement? Choose without delay.' That is in line with this verse: 'On that day the Lord made a covenant with Abram saying' (Gen 15:18)."

       C.   What is the meaning of, saying?

       D.   R. Hinena bar Pappa said, "Abraham chose for himself the subjugation to the four kingdoms."

       E.   We have reached the dispute of R. Yudan and R. Idi and R. Hama bar Haninah said in the name of a certain sage in the name of Rabbi: "The Holy One, blessed be He, [not Abraham] chose the subjugation to the four kingdoms for him, in line with the following verse of Scripture: 'You have caused men to ride over our heads, we have been overcome by fire and water' (Ps 66:12). That is to say, 'you have made ride over our heads various nations, and it is as though we went through fire and through water' (Ps 66:21)."

Since Israel lives out the patterns originally set by the patriarchs, to understand Israel's condition, one has to examine the deeds of Abraham and his selected son and grandson. But those deeds embodied the fundamental truths of the system. Torah and sacrifices preserve Israel from Gehenna and the rule of the kingdoms (the one personal, the other communal, in both instances). Faced with the choice of Gehenna or subjugation, Abraham chose the latter.

God foresaw all that has come upon Israel. The importance of that conviction comes to the surface when readers see the corollary: [1] The kingdom of heaven continues to encompass Israel, even while it is ruled by the gentiles, and [2] the anomaly and injustice of gentile hegemony will ultimately come to an end, by reason of Israel's own act of will.

The prophets called the gentiles the instruments of God's wrath. The sages took the same view. They explained that the gentiles do not act on their own but carry out God's will. What happens to Israel therefore reassures Israel that the holy people continue to live in the kingdom of heaven, and the very fact of the anomaly of pagan rule turns out to guarantee God's rule and Israel's role. Israel has not lost its position in the unfolding of the story of creation of a just world order set forth in the revelation of Sinai. Israel is now writing, and will continue to write, its own chapter of that story. Israel is God's principal agent and protagonist in that story. Not only so, but Israel is not subordinate to the world empires but their equal, standing in its assigned position at the end and climax of that part of the story of creation that the gentile empires are assigned to write.

The exposition then commences with the main point. The dominance of the gentiles, particularly in the form of the standard cluster of the succession of four world empires, guarantees that the just pattern that God has foreordained will impose structure and order upon history. That pattern leads inexorably from one gentile kingdom to the next in order, but finally to the rule of holy Israel, defined as those who know God. Israel will be the fifth and final monarchy, inaugurating God's rule and the end of Israel as a sector of humanity altogether. The sages maintained that world order is not only just and proportionate, but also regular and balanced. Hence they conceived that patterns reproduce themselves, because order governs.

Accordingly, and principally, the four kings marked the beginning and also the end of Israel's history. When the fourth kingdom (Rome) falls, Israel will take over:

Genesis Rabbah XLII:II.2

A.   Said R. Abin, "Just as [Israel's history] began with the encounter with

four kingdoms, so [Israel's history] will conclude with the encounter
with the four kingdoms.

B. "'Chedorlaomer, king of Elam, Tidal, king of Goiim, Amraphel, king
of Shinar, and Arioch, king of Ellasar, four kings against five' (Gen
14:9).

C. "So [Israel's history] will conclude with the encounter with the four
kingdoms: the kingdom of Babylonia, the kingdom of Medea, the
kingdom of Greece, and the kingdom of Edom."

So too the following finds the world empires at the end in the first encounter
of nascent Israel with the nations, Abraham's in the time of Amraphel. So
what happened at the outset will happen at the end. This then is spelled out
at the final comment, which tells Israel how to tell time—that is, what will
signify the advent of the end:

Genesis Rabbah XLII:IV.4

A. Another matter: "And it came to pass in the days of Amraphael, king
of Shinar" (Gen 14:1) refers to Babylonia.

B. "Arioch, king of Ellasar" (Gen 14:1) refers to Greece.

C. "Chedorlaomer, king of Elam" (Gen 14:1) refers to Media.

D. "And Tidal, king of Goiim [nations]" (Gen 14:1) refers to the wicked
government [Rome], which conscripts troops from all the nations of
the world.

E. Said R. Eleazar bar Abina, "If you see that the nations contend with
one another, look for the footsteps of the king-messiah. You may know
that that is the case, for lo, in the time of Abraham, because the kings
struggled with one another, a position of greatness came to Abraham."

The same pattern recurs at Genesis Rabbah LXVI:IX.1:

F. R. Abba bar R. Pappi, R. Joshua of Sikhnin in the name of R. Levi:
"Since our father, Abraham, saw the ram get himself out of one thicket
only to be trapped in another, the Holy One, blessed be He, said to
him, 'So your descendants will be entangled in one kingdom after
another, struggling from Babylonia to Media, from Media to Greece,
from Greece to Edom. But in the end, they will be redeemed by the
horns of a ram: 'And the Lord God will blow the horn . . . the Lord of
Hosts will defend them' (Zech 9:14-15)."

What is at stake now is clear: a systematic explanation for the workings of
history. In a moment one will also notice how the world empires signify
chaos, with Israel's rule under God coming to reestablish world order. The
point is clear throughout.

The world empires were built into the very structure of creation. Here
exegesis links the four kingdoms to the condition of the world at creation:

Genesis Rabbah II:IV.1

A. ["And the earth was unformed and void. And darkness was upon the face of the deep" (Gen 1:2)] R. Simeon b. Laqish interpreted the verses at hand to speak of the empires [of the historical age to come].

B. "'The earth was unformed' refers to Babylonia, 'I beheld the earth and lo, it was unformed' (Jer 4:23).

C. "'And void' refers to Media: 'They hasted [using the letters of the same root as the word for void] to bring Haman' (Esth 6:14).

D. "'Darkness' refers to Greece, which clouded the vision of the Israelites through its decrees, for it said to Israel, 'Write on the horn of an ox [as a public proclamation for all to see] that you have no portion in the God of Israel.'

E. "'. . . upon the face of the deep' refers to the wicked kingdom [of Rome].

F. "Just as the deep surpasses investigation, so the wicked kingdom surpasses investigation.

G. "'And the spirit of God hovers' refers to the spirit of the Messiah, in line with the following verse of Scripture: 'And the spirit of the Lord shall rest upon him' (Isa 11:2)."

Choosing a verse deemed to refer to the specified world empire and finding the correct point of intersection with a verse concerning creation, the exegete accomplishes his goal. It is to show that the chaos of creation finds its match in the chaos of the present age, the epoch of gentile domination. And then the point is made explicit: this age will come to an end, the act of creation at the beginning matched and completed by the advent of the Messiah at the end.

The various prophets foresaw the domination of the four empires and the ultimate rise of holy Israel. Much of the Thirteenth Parashah of Leviticus Rabbah is devoted to that very matter. Set forth is only the exposition of how Moses conveyed future history when he specified animals that Israel may not eat, the camel, rock badger, hare, and pig. Each one of these represents one of the four pagan empires, and the traits of the respective empires are embodied in the chosen animal. Specifically, the animals forbidden at Deuteronomy 14:7, camel, rock badger, hare, and pig, represent Babylonia, Media, Greece, and Rome:

Leviticus Rabbah XIII:V.9ff.

9. A. Moses foresaw what the evil kingdoms would do [to Israel].

B. "The camel, rock badger, and hare" (Deut 14:7). [Compare: "Nevertheless, among those that chew the cud or part the hoof, you shall not eat these: the camel, because it chews the cud but does not part the hoof, is unclean to you. The rock badger, because it chews the cud but does not part the hoof, is unclean to you. And the hare, because it chews the cud but does not part the hoof, is unclean to you, and the pig, because it parts the hoof and is cloven-footed, but does not chew the cud, is unclean to you" (Lev 11:4-8).]

The exposition starts with a simple statement of the proposition:

C. The camel (GML) refers to Babylonia, [in line with the following verse of Scripture: "O daughter of Babylonia, you who are to be devastated! Happy will be he who requites (GML) you, with what you have done to us" (Ps 147:8)].

D. "The rock badger" (Deut 14:7)—this refers to Media.

I. "The pig" (Deut 14:7)—this refers to Edom [Rome].

Now reasons are given for the identification of the four animals with the four empires.

11. A. Another interpretation: "The camel" (Lev 11:4).

B. This refers to Babylonia.

C. "Because it chews the cud (MLH\GRH) [but does not part the hoof]" (Lev 11:4).

D. For it brings forth praises [(MQLS) with its throat] of the Holy One, blessed be He. [The Hebrew words for "chew the cud"—bring up cud—are now understood to mean "give praise." GRH is connected with GRWN, throat, hence, "bring forth (sounds of praise through) the throat."]

N. "The rock badger" (Lev 11:5)—this refers to Media.

O. "For it chews the cud"—for it gives praise to the Holy One, blessed be He: "Thus says Cyrus, king of Persia, 'All the kingdoms of the earth has the Lord, the God of the heaven, given me'" (Ezra 1:2).

P. "The hare"—this refers to Greece.

Q. "For it chews the cud"—for it gives praise to the Holy One, blessed be He.

S. "The pig" (Lev 11:7)—this refers to Edom.

T. "For it does not chew the cud"—for it does not give praise to the Holy One, blessed be He.

U. And it is not enough that it does not give praise, but it blasphemes and swears violently, saying, "Whom do I have in heaven, and with you I want nothing on earth" (Ps 73:25).

A different set of elaborations now serves the same purpose, in each case showing the reason for the identification of beast with empire.

12. A. Another interpretation [of GRH, cud, now with reference to GR, stranger]:

B. "The camel" (Lev 11:4)—this refers to Babylonia.

C.   "For it chews the cud" [now: brings up the stranger]—for it exalts righteous men: "And Daniel was in the gate of the [Babylonian] king" (Dan 2:49).

D.   "The rock badger" (Lev 11:5)—this refers to Media.

E.   "For it brings up the stranger"—for it exalts righteous men: "Mordecai sat at the gate of the king [of Media]" (Esth 2:19).

F.   "The hare" (Lev 11:6)—this refers to Greece.

G.   "For it brings up the stranger"—for it exalts the righteous.

J.   "The pig" (Lev 11:7)—this refers to Rome.

K.   "But it does not bring up the stranger"—for it does not exalt the righteous.

L.   And it is not enough that it does not exalt them, but it kills them.

M.   That is in line with the following verse of Scripture: "I was angry with my people, I profaned my heritage; I gave them into your hand, [you showed them no mercy; on the aged you made your yoke exceedingly heavy]" (Isa 47:6).

N.   This refers to R. Aqiba and his colleagues.

Finally come the climax and the point of the construction: a trait that differentiates one beast from another also points toward the resolution of the tension of Israel's history with the nations—the place of Israel on the list of world empires:

13. A.   Another interpretation [now treating "bring up the cud" (GR) as "bring along in its train" (GRR)]:

B.   "The camel" (Lev 11:4)—this refers to Babylonia.

C.   "Which brings along in its train"—for it brought along another kingdom after it.

D.   "The rock badger" (Lev 11:5)—this refers to Media.

E.   "Which brings along in its train"—for it brought along another kingdom after it.

F.   "The hare" (Lev 11:6)—this refers to Greece.

G.   "Which brings along in its train"—for it brought along another kingdom after it.

H.   "The pig" (Lev 11:7)—this refers to Rome.

I.   "Which does not bring along in its train"—for it did not bring along another kingdom after it.

J.   And why is it then called "pig" (HZYR)? For it restores (MHZRT) the crown to the one who truly should have it [namely, Israel, whose dominion will begin when the rule of Rome ends].

K.   That is in line with the following verse of Scripture: "And saviors will come up on Mount Zion to judge the Mountain of Esau [Rome], and the kingdom will then belong to the Lord" (Obad 1:21).

The key always comes as the climax: Edom/Esau/Rome will give way to Israel; Obadiah 1:21 suffices to make that point explicit. The upshot is, through the elaboration of the list, the sages make their statement in powerful and compelling form.

That is not to suggest that continuous narrative plays no role; far from it. The sages appeal to the form of a tale—first comes this, then that happens, then, finally, the other thing takes place—to convey their message. In the present instance they take up a narrative of the life of Jacob and translate it into the story of what would happen to his children. For, the Rabbinic the sages held that the patriarchs joined God in planning Israel's future history, so far as God, not Israel itself, would play a determinative part in the formation of that history. Here, Israel's history was predetermined by Jacob's conduct at a crucial turning in his life, and everything that happened with the four kingdoms followed from that event.

Leviticus Rabbah XXIX:II.1

J.   R. Berekhiah, R. Helbo, and R. Simeon b. Menassia: "Meir expounded [the following verse:] 'Nonetheless they still sinned and did not believe in his wondrous works' [Ps 78:32]. [This verse] speaks of Jacob, who did not believe and so did not ascend.

K.   "Said to him the Holy One, blessed be He, 'Jacob! If you had believed and ascended, you would never again have gone down. Now that you did not believe and did not ascend, lo, your sons will be held fast among the nations and wander aimlessly among the kingdoms, from one to the next, from Babylonia to Media, from Media to Greece, and from Greece to Edom.'

L.   "He said before him, 'Lord of the ages, is it forever?'

M.   "Said to him the Holy One, blessed be He, 'Then fear not, O Jacob my servant . . . nor be dismayed, O Israel, for lo, I will save you from afar' [Jer 30:10]: from Gallia and Aspamia and nearby lands.

N.   "'And your offspring from the land of their captivity:' 'Jacob shall return from Babylonia.

O.   "'And have quiet' from Media.

P.   "'And ease' from Greece.

Q.   'And none shall make him afraid' on account of Edom."

Narrative enters in especially when the stories of the lives of the patriarchs are asked to account for world history. Here is how the sages show that Jacob experienced the future history of Israel involving the four monarchies:

Genesis Rabbah XLIV:XVII.4

A.   "[And it came to pass, as the sun was going down,] lo, a deep sleep fell on Abram, and lo, a dread and great darkness fell upon him" (Gen 15:12):

B. ". . . lo, a dread" refers to Babylonia, as it is written, "Then was Nebuchadnezzar filled with fury" (Gen 3:19).

C. ". . . and darkness" refers to Media, which darkened the eyes of Israel by making it necessary for the Israelites to fast and conduct public mourning.

D. ". . . great . . ." refers to Greece.

G. ". . . fell upon him" refers to Edom, as it is written, "The earth quakes at the noise of their fall" (Jer 49:21).

The paradigm, independent of history and considerations of temporal order, can work backwards as well as forwards:

H. Some reverse matters:

I. ". . . fell upon him" refers to Babylonia, since it is written, "Fallen, fallen is Babylonia" (Isa 21:9).

J. ". . . great . . ." refers to Media, in line with this verse: "King Ahasuerus did make great" (Esth 3:1).

K. ". . .and darkness" refers to Greece, which darkened the eyes of Israel by its harsh decrees.

L. ". . . lo, a dread" refers to Edom, as it is written, "After this I saw . . . a fourth beast, dreadful and terrible" (Dan 7:7).

The paradigm, moreover, takes command of diverse passages of Scripture and delivers its message in each one. Here is a completely different way of utilizing the one pattern. Isaac prefigured the four kingdoms in asking for venison.

Genesis Rabbah LXV:XIII.3

A. Another matter: "Now then take your weapons, your quiver and your bow and go out to the field":

B. "Weapons" refers to Babylonia, as it is said, "And the weapons he brought to the treasure house of his god" (Gen 2:2).

C. "Your quiver" speaks of Media, as it says, "So they suspended Haman on the gallows" (Esth 7:10). [The play on the words is the same as at No. 2.]

D. "And your bow" addresses Greece: "For I bend Judah for me, I fill the bow with Ephraim and I will story up your sons, O Zion, against your sons, O Javan [Greece]" (Zech 9:13).

E. "and go out to the field" means Edom: "Unto the land of Seir, the field of Edom" (Gen 32:4).

In these and similar compositions the sages link verses to make their point, recasting the narratives of Scripture into demonstrations of propositions framed in symbolic language. The main point should not be missed for the rich and dense elaboration: God foresaw Israel's sin and chose the nations as the instrument to punish them. Hence Israel's present situation validates the main principle of the Oral Torah, the justice of the world order that has dictated the very character of creation.

Readers will ask what then God hopes to accomplish through exercising dominion over Israel by means of the nations. The prophetic tradition governs: the nations are the rod of God's wrath. Idolaters' governance is the medium for reestablishing his rule over Israel through Israel's own conduct. First of all, Israel will be lead through suffering in exile to repentance, at which point God will forgive them. That point the sages learn at Leviticus 26:

> Sifra CCLXIX:II.1, 3
>
> A. "But if they confess their iniquity and the iniquity of their fathers [in their treachery which they committed against me, and also in walking contrary to me, so that I walked contrary to them and brought them into the land of their enemies; if then their uncircumcised heart is humbled and they make amends for their iniquity; then I will remember my covenant with Jacob, and I will remember my covenant also with Isaac and my covenant also with Abraham, and I will remember the land. But the land shall be left by them and enjoy its Sabbaths while it lies desolate without them; and they shall make amends for their iniquity, because they spurned my ordinances, and their soul abhorred my statutes. Yet for all that, when they are in the land of their enemies, I will not spurn them, neither will I abhor them so as to destroy them utterly and break my covenant with them; for I am the Lord their God; but I will for their sake remember the covenant with their forefathers whom I brought forth out of the land of Egypt in the sight of the nations, that I might be their God: I am the Lord. These are the statutes and ordinances and laws which the Lord made between him and the people of Israel on Mount Sinai by Moses]" (Lev 26:40-46):
>
> B. This is how things are as to repentance,
>
> C. for as soon as they confess their sins, I forthwith revert and have mercy on them,
>
> D. as it is said, "But if they confess their iniquity and the iniquity of their fathers in their treachery which they committed against me. . . ."

The second point is that Israel cannot opt out of the story. God will never permit Israel to remove itself from his dominion; willy-nilly they will remain his kingdom:

> 3. A. ". . . and brought them into the land of their enemies":
>   B. This is a good deal for Israel.
>   C. For the Israelites are not to say, "Since we have gone into exile among the gentiles, let us act like them."

D. [God speaks:] "I shall not let them, but I shall call forth prophets against them, who will bring them back to the right way under my wings."

E. And how do we know?

F. "What is in your mind shall never happen, the thought, 'Let us be like the nations, like the tribes of the countries, and worship wood and stone.' 'As I live,' says the Lord God, 'surely with a mighty hand and an outstretched arm and with wrath poured out, I will be king over you. [I will bring you out from the peoples and gather you out of the countries where you are scattered, with a mighty hand and an outstretched arm and with wrath poured out'" (Ezek 20:32-34).

G. Whether you like it or not, with or without your consent, I shall establish my dominion over you."

Israel, subject to the gentiles, then gains the opportunity to repent and reconcile itself with God, and that is the plan that God has devised to overcome the workings of strict justice; exile and subjugation then form acts of mercy on God's part, just as Abraham had foreseen when he wisely chose the rule of the nations over Gehenna.

The final question that requires attention returns us to our starting point, the comparison of Israel and the nations. That point is framed in terms of Israel and Adam, meaning, the sector of humanity within, and the part of humanity outside of, the circle of the Torah. By reason of disobedience Adam sinned and was justly punished by exile from Eden; that represented an act of mercy, he was not wiped out, as Eve had said he and she would be. Because of disobedience Israel sinned and was justly punished by exile from the Land of Israel, counterpart to Eden. But then is Israel not just another Adam—rebellious and permanently punished on that account? There is a distinction, one that makes all the difference. The Torah, carrying with it the possibility of repentance, changes Israel's condition. The Torah embodies God's presence in Israel: wisdom, spirit, power, presence, empowerment, not just possibility.

Israel is like Adam, but Israel is the Other, the Last Adam, the opposite of Adam. The exegete now systematically compares Adam and Israel, the first humanity and the last, and show how the story of Adam matches the story of Israel—but with a difference:

Genesis Rabbah XIX:IX.1–2

2. A. R. Abbahu in the name of R. Yosé bar Haninah: "It is written, 'But they are like man [Adam], they have transgressed the covenant' (Hos 6:7).

B. "'They are like a man,' specifically, like the first man. [We shall now compare the story of the first man in Eden with the story of Israel in its land.]

Now the composer identifies an action in regard to Adam with a counterpart action in regard to Israel, in each case matching verse for verse, beginning with Eden and Adam:

> C. "'In the case of the first man, I brought him into the garden of Eden, I commanded him, he violated my commandment, I judged him to be sent away and driven out, but I mourned for him, saying "How. . ."' [which begins the book of Lamentations, hence stands for a lament, but which, as we just saw, also is written with the consonants that additionally yield, "Where are you"].
>
> D. "'I brought him into the garden of Eden,' as it is written, 'And the Lord God took the man and put him into the garden of Eden' (Gen 2:15).
>
> E. "'I commanded him,' as it is written, 'And the Lord God commanded . . .' (Gen 2:16).
>
> F. "'And he violated my commandment,' as it is written, 'Did you eat from the tree concerning which I commanded you' (Gen 3:11).
>
> G. "'I judged him to be sent away,' as it is written, "And the Lord God sent him from the garden of Eden' (Gen 3:23).
>
> H. "'And I judged him to be driven out.' 'And he drove out the man' (Gen 3:24).
>
> I. "'But I mourned for him, saying, "How. . . ."' 'And he said to him, "Where are you"' (Gen 3:9), and the word for 'where are you' is written, 'How. . . .'"

Now comes the systematic comparison of Adam and Eden with Israel and the Land of Israel:

> J. "'So too in the case of his descendants, [God continues to speak,] I brought them into the Land of Israel, I commanded them, they violated my commandment, I judged them to be sent out and driven away but I mourned for them, saying, "How. . . ."'
>
> K. "'I brought them into the Land of Israel.' 'And I brought you into the land of Carmel' (Jer 2:7).
>
> L. "'I commanded them.' 'And you, command the children of Israel' (Exod 27:20). 'Command the children of Israel' (Lev 24:2).
>
> M. "'They violated my commandment.' 'And all Israel have violated your Torah' (Dan 9:11).
>
> N. "'I judged them to be sent out.' 'Send them away, out of my sight and let them go forth' (Jer 15:1).
>
> O. "'. . . and driven away.' 'From my house I shall drive them' (Hos 9:15).
>
> P. "'But I mourned for them, saying, "How. . . ."' 'How has the city sat solitary, that was full of people' (Lam 1:1)."

Here the story ends where it began, Israel in exile from the land, like Adam in exile from Eden. But the Torah is clear that there is a difference, which is going to be addressed in its proper place: Israel can repent. The Torah teaches how, and the Torah sets forth not only the possibility but the power.

Conclusion

The just world order is comprised by the division of humanity into Israel with the Torah, and the gentiles with their idols. The one is destined to life eternal with God, the other to the grave, there to spend eternity. World order then finds its center and focus in Israel, and whatever happens that counts under heaven's gaze takes place in relationship to Israel. That division yields rich and dense details but only a simple story, easily retold. In a purposeful act of benevolence, the just God created the world in so orderly a way that the principle of justice and equity governs throughout. Fair rules apply equally to all persons and govern all circumstances. God not only created humanity but made himself known to humanity through the Torah. But humanity, possessed of free will, enjoys the choice of accepting and obeying the Torah, therefore living in the kingdom of heaven, or rejecting the Torah and God in favor of idolatry and idols.

Now readers realize the full potentiality contained in the simple doctrines with which they began: that those who accept the Torah are called Israel, and the others, who reject the Torah in favor of idolatry, are called gentiles. The gentiles hate Israel because of the Torah, and they also hate God. But the world as now constituted is such that the gentiles rule, and Israel is subjugated. One then wonders where the justice is in that inversion of right, with God's people handed over to the charge of God's enemies. Israel has sinned, so rebelled against God, and the gentiles then form God's instrument for the punishment of Israel. God's justice governs, the world conforms to orderly rules, embedded in the very structure of creation. Israel's own condition stands as the surest testimony of the world's good and just order. That guarantee is for now and all time to come. Now one must ask what the Halakhah has to say about the same theological topic. It remains to be seen how the law defines norms of behavior in the setting of idolaters and their idols, to match the beliefs set forth in this chapter.

Chapter 2

The Halakhic Theology of Idolatry

An Outline of the Halakhah of Abodah Zarah in the Mishnah, Tosefta, Yerushalmi, and Bavli

This account now turns to the Halakhah that mediates between Israel and the world beyond the boundaries of the people, Israel. The world of the gentiles forms an undifferentiated realm of idolatry, and the definition of the gentile is "an idolater."[3] The Halakhah takes as its task the negotiation between Israelites and the pagan world in which they live. It explains in detail how they are to conduct themselves in accord with the Torah so that at no point and in no way do they give support to idolatry. In its basic exposition of the theme of idolatry, the Halakhah rests squarely on the foundations of Scripture, supplying rules and regulations that carry out the fundamental Scriptural commandments about destroying idols and everything that has to do with idolatry. But the issues of the Halakhah do not simply recapitulate those of Scripture.

The Halakhah formulates the entire topic of idolatry into an essay on Israel's relationships with non-Israelites, who are idolaters by definition. Here too, the Halakhah addresses the condition of individuals, the ordinary life of common folk, rather than concentrating on the situation of all Israel, viewed as a collective entity. While the Aggadah speaks of the community of all Israel, the Halakhah addresses the condition of the private person, a point to which this account will return at the end of chapter 5. We will now see how a theology of the gentiles as idolaters and enemies of God produces concrete laws—on the one hand segregating idolaters, when they practice idolatry, from Israelites, and on the other, accommodating diversity in society when the gentiles are not engaged in the practice of idolatry. But the basic theology of the gentiles as undifferentiated idolaters comes to expression in attitudes of fear and loathing that are supposed to govern relationships of an everyday character, for example, mutual respect. At places the specific laws cross the boundaries of theological difference altogether.

For the Written Torah the community at large forms the focus of the law, and idolatry is not subject to negotiation by the collectivity of holy Israel. In its land Israel is to wipe out idolatry, even as a memory. Scripture is clear that Israel is to obliterate all mention of idols (Exod 23:13), not bow down to idolaters' gods or serve them but overthrow them and break them into pieces (Exod 23:24): "You shall break down their altars and dash in pieces their pillars and hew down their Asherim and burn their graven images with fire" (Deut 7:5). Israelites are commanded along these same lines:

> The graven images of their gods you shall burn with fire; you shall not covet the silver or the gold that is on them or take it for yourselves, lest you be ensnared by it; for it is an abomination to the Lord your God. And you shall not bring an abominable thing into your house and become accused like it (Deut 7:25-26).
>
> You shall surely destroy all the places where the nations whom you shall dispossess served their gods, upon the high mountains and upon the hills and under every green tree; you shall tear down their altars and dash in pieces their pillars and burn their Asherim with fire; you shall hew down the graven images of their gods and destroy their name out of that place (Deut 12:2-3).

Accordingly, so far as the Written Torah supplies the foundations for the treatment of the matter by the Oral Torah, the focus is the total eradication of idolatry. Scripture's Halakhah does not contemplate Israel's coexisting, in the land, with idolaters and their idolatry.

But the Halakhah speaks to a world that is not so simple. The land belongs to Israel, but idolaters live there too—and run things. And Israel no longer forms a coherent collectivity but a realm made up of individuals, each with distinctive and particular interests. The Halakhah of the Oral Torah commences its treatment of the same subject with the opposite premise: idolaters live side by side (whether or not in the Land of Israel) with Israelites, and Israelites have to sort out the complex problems of coexistence with idolatry. And that coexistence involves not whole communities—the People, Israel, and the peoples, whoever they may be. It involves individuals—this Israelite living side by side with that idolater.

The Oral Torah also uses idolatry to contemplate a condition entirely beyond the imagination of Scripture—the hegemony of idolatrous nations and the subjugation of holy Israel. The Oral Torah, fully considered, uses idolatry as the occasion to discuss Israel's place among the nations of the world and of Israel's relationships with idolaters. Furthermore, the Oral Torah's theory of who Israel is finds its context in the contrast with the idolaters. The meeting point between the Oral and Written Torah is the indicative trait of the idolaters—their idolatry; that is all that matters about them. But while the Halakhah of the Oral Torah expounds the local details of everyday relationships with idolaters, the Aggadah of the same Oral Torah vastly expands the range of thought and takes up the more profound issues of idolater dominance in this age, Israel's subjugated position, the power of the idolaters, and the like. Once more, one will observe, the Aggadah deals with the world at large, the Halakhah, the world at home.

The Halakhah of the Oral Torah deals first with commercial relationships; second, with matters pertaining to idols; and finally, with the particular prohibition against wine, part of which has served as a libation to an idol. The whole is regularized and ordered. There are relationships with idolaters that are absolutely prohibited, particularly occasions of idol-worship; the Halakhah recognizes that these are major commercial events. When it comes to commerce with idolaters Israelites may not sell or in any way benefit from certain things, may sell but may not utilize certain others, and may sell and utilize yet others. Here, the complex and systematic mode of thought governing the Oral Torah's treatment of the topic vastly transcends the rather simple conception that animates Scripture's discussion of the same matter.

Unstated premises presupposed by the Halakhah are as follows: [1] what an idolater is not likely to use for the worship of an idol is not prohibited; [2] what may serve not as part of an idol but as an appurtenance thereto is prohibited for Israelite use but permitted for Israelite commerce; [3] what serves idolatry is prohibited for use and for benefit. In reflecting upon relationships with the idolaters, the Oral Torah moreover takes for granted a number of facts. These turn out to yield a single generalization: idolaters are assumed routinely to practice bestiality, murder, and fornication. Further negative stereotypes concerning idolaters occur. The picture of the Halakhah finds its context in the larger theory of idolatry and its ephemeral hegemony that the Aggadah sets forth, as readers will note in the concluding section of this chapter.

In my outline of the Halakhah, I present the Mishnah's passages in **bold face type**, the Tosefta's in regular type, the Yerushalmi's in *italics*, and the Bavli's in SMALL CAPS. This immediately signals the origin of a legal statement. It permits the reader to follow the unfolding of the details of the law from the earliest to the latest documents of the formative age. It shows, furthermore, how much of the law is provided in the opening document, the Mishnah, ca. 200 C.E. The same procedure is followed in chapter 4.

The opening unit of the Halakhah, following the exposition of the Mishnah as amplified by the Tosefta, takes up the conduct of Israelites at pagan fairs, when idolatrous celebrations took place. Israelites are to avoid doing business with pagans in the time of their celebration, so as to avoid the slightest contact with idolatry. This means (M. Abodah Zarah 1:1) that one must avoid the run up to the festivals, the three days in advance.

Commercial Relationships with Idolaters

Festivals and Fairs

M. 1:1 **Before the festivals of idolaters for three days it is forbidden to do business with them. (1) To lend anything to them or to borrow anything from them. (2) To lend money to them or to borrow money from them. (3) To repay them or to be repaid by them.**

T.   1:1 Under what circumstances [M. A.Z. 1:1A]? In the case of recurrent festivals, but in the case of festivals which do not recur, prohibited is only that day alone. And even though they have said, It is forbidden to do business with them [M. A.Z. 1:1A]—under what circumstances? In the case of something which lasts. But in the case of something which does not last, it is permitted. And even in the case of something which lasts, [if] one bought or sold it, lo, this is permitted.

T.   1:2 A person should not do business with an idolater on the day of his festival, nor should one talk frivolously, nor should one ask after his welfare in a situation which is taken into account. But if one happened to come across him in a routine way, he asks after his welfare with all due respect.

T.   1:3 They ask after the welfare of idolaters on their festivals for the sake of peace. Israelite workmen who were working with an idolater—in the case of an Israelite's household, it is permitted. In the case of an idolater's household, it is prohibited. And even though one has finished work on his utensils before his festival, he should not deliver them to him on the day of his festival, because this increases his rejoicing [on his festival].

M. 1:2 **Before their festivals it is prohibited, but after their festivals it is permitted.**

The next issue concerns personal holidays of the pagan, which an Israelite is not to celebrate. But these are singleton occasions, not sets of three successive days.

M. 1:3 **(1) On the day on which [an idolater] shaves off his beard and lock of hair, (2) on the day on which he came up safely from an ocean voyage, (3) on the day on which he got out of prison. And an idolater who made a banquet for his son—it is prohibited for only that day, and in regard to only that individual alone [to enter into business relationships of any sort, as listed at M. 1:1].**

T.   1:4   [If] one town celebrates, and another town does not celebrate, one people celebrates, and another people does not celebrate, one family celebrates, and another family does not celebrate—those who celebrate are subject to the stated prohibitions, and those who do not celebrate are permitted in regard to them. As to Calendae, even though everyone observes the festival, it is permitted only with regard to the actual rite of sacrifice itself. Saturnalia is the day on which they took power. Kratesis is the day of the anniversary of the emperors [cf. M. A.Z. I:3B–C]. The day of each and every emperor—lo, it is tantamount to a public festival.

The text now asks about coming into contact with idols. Here again the Israelite is to avoid contact. Since there is no town without its idols, the rule covers a vast range of space. It is permitted to do business in the location of idolatry, but not in space unaffected by the idol.

M. 1:4 **A city in which there is an idol—[in the area] outside of it—it is permitted [to do business]. [If] an idol was outside of it, [in the area] inside it is permitted. What is the rule as to going to that place? When the road is set aside for going to that place only, it is prohibited. But if one is able to take that same road to some other place, it is permitted. A town in which there is an idol, and there were in it shops which were adorned and shops which were not adorned—those which are adorned are prohibited, but those which are not adorned are permitted.**

The Tosefta, as is its way, greatly amplifies the principles of what the Mishnah embodies in its rules; these principles are expressed in a variety of details, but the basic considerations are uniform. The point remains simple: idolatry is to be avoided, but relationships not tainted by idolatry are permitted.

T.   1:6   [If] there is a fair in the town, into the town it is prohibited [to go], but outside of the town it is permitted. And if it is outside of the town, outside of the town it is forbidden [to go], but into the town it is permitted [M. A.Z. 1:4A–C]. And shops which are decorated under any circumstances, lo, these are forbidden [M. A.Z. 1:4I]. [If] a person is passing in a caravan from one place to another, and enters a town in which a fair is going on, he need not scruple that he may appear to be going to the fair [M. A.Z. I:4E–F].

T.   1:7   A fair which the empire held, or which a province held, or which the
            leaders of a province held, is permitted. Prohibited is only a fair hon-
            oring an idol alone.

T.   1:8   They go to an idolaters' fair and accept healing from them—healing
            involving property, but not healing involving the person. And they do
            (not) purchase from them fields, vineyards, boy-slaves, and girl-slaves,
            because he is as one who rescues these from their power. And one writes
            and deposits [a deed] in an archive. A priest contracts uncleanness [in
            connection with redemption of land] to give testimony and to engage
            in a lawsuit against them abroad. And just as he contracts uncleanness
            in connection with affairs abroad, so he surely contracts uncleanness in
            a graveyard [in the same matter]. And [a priest] contracts uncleanness
            [if it is] to study Torah or to marry a woman.

T.   1:9   Merchants who pushed up the day of a fair or who pushed back the day
            of a fair—it is permitted. Prohibited is only the time of the fair alone.

T.   1:15 Israelites who are going to a fair—it is permitted to do business with
            them. And on [their] return, it is [likewise] permitted. Idolaters who
            are going to their debauchery—it is forbidden to do business with
            them. And on [their] return, it is permitted. For [the fair] is tanta-
            mount to idolatry, which [on their return trip] its worshippers have
            abandoned. And as to an Israelite, whether it is on the way there or on
            the way back, it is prohibited.

T.   1:16 A. One should not travel with a caravan [en route to an idolatrous fair],
            even to go out, even to go before it, even to be with it when it gets dark,
            even if one is fearful because of idolaters, thugs, or an evil spirit, since
            it is said, "You shall not go after other gods" (Deut 6:14).

This part of the account now concludes with a rule contributed by the
Bavli about conduct in the presence of idols. The case is a simple one: one
must bend down in front of an idol to pull a splinter out of one's foot. That
action gives the appearance of bowing down to the idol, even if that is not
the Israelite's intent. He is not to do that. This point is made through a variety of cases.

B.   1:4AA–F/12A IF WHILE SOMEONE IS IN FRONT OF AN IDOL, HE GOT A
          SPLINTER IN HIS FOOT, HE SHOULD NOT BEND OVER TO REMOVE IT,
          BECAUSE HE LOOKS AS THOUGH HE IS BOWING DOWN TO THE IDOL. BUT
          IF IT DOES NOT LOOK THAT WAY, HE IS PERMITTED TO DO SO. IF HIS
          MONEY GOT SCATTERED IN FRONT OF AN IDOL, HE SHOULD NOT BOW
          DOWN TO PICK IT UP, BECAUSE HE LOOKS AS THOUGH HE IS BOWING
          DOWN TO THE IDOL. BUT IF IT DOES NOT LOOK THAT WAY, HE IS PER-
          MITTED TO DO SO. IF A SPRING FLOWS IN FRONT OF AN IDOL, ONE
          SHOULD NOT BEND DOWN TO DRINK, BECAUSE HE LOOKS AS THOUGH
          HE IS BOWING DOWN TO THE IDOL. BUT IF IT DOES NOT LOOK THAT

WAY, HE IS PERMITTED TO DO SO. ONE SHOULD NOT PUT HIS MOUTH
ON THE MOUTH OF HUMAN FIGURES WHICH SERVE AS FOUNTAINS IN
TOWNS IN ORDER TO DRINK WATER, BECAUSE HE MAY APPEAR TO BE KISS-
ING THE IDOL.

So much for prohibited locations and actions and seasons. The premise
of the law is clear: idolaters have a permanent place in the Land of Israel, and
Israelites must negotiate affairs in such a way that they can relate to idolaters
but not idolatry. As to commerce Israelites may not sell idolaters objects that
they are certain to use for idolatry. But if there is a matter of doubt as to the
ultimate purpose of the purchased item, it is permitted to tell it to them. If
there is no doubt, it is forbidden. The account begins with a list that illustrates that point.

Objects Prohibited Even in Commerce

M. 1:5 **What are the things that are forbidden to sell to idolaters? (1) fir**
cones, (2) white figs, (3) and their stalks, (4) frankincense, and (5)
a white cock. And as to everything else, [if] they are left without
specification [as to their proposed use], it is permitted, but [if]
they are specified [for use for idolatry], it is prohibited.

T.   1:21 One sells [the stated substances] to a merchant, but does not sell [them]
to a householder [M. A.Z. 1:5A]. But if the merchant was suspect [of
idolatrous practices], it is prohibited to sell [them] to him. One sells
them pigs and does not scruple that he might offer them up to an idol.
One sells him wine and does not scruple that he might offer it as a libation to an idol. But if he explicitly stated to him [that his intent was to
make use of what he was buying for idolatry], it is prohibited to sell
him even water, even salt [M. A.Z. 1:5F].

T   2:1   A. They purchase a beast from them for a trial and return it to them
that entire day. And just as they purchase from them a beast for a trial
and return it to them that entire day so they purchase from them (a
beast) slave-boys and slave-girls for a trial and return them to them that
entire day. So long as you have the right to return [what is purchased]
to an Israelite, you have the right to return [the same thing] to an idolater. [If] you have not got the right to return [what is purchased] to an
Israelite, you have not got the right to return [the same thing] to an
idolater. An Israelite sells his beast to an idolater on the stipulation that
the latter slaughter it, with an Israelite supervising him while the idolater slaughters the beast [so as to make sure it is not turned into a sacrifice to an idol]. They purchase from [idolaters] cattle for an offering,
and need not scruple on the count of [the idolater's having practiced]
bestiality or suffered bestiality, or having set aside the beast for idolatrous worship, or having actually worshipped [the beast].

Local custom prevails when it comes to selling beasts—small cattle, goats, sheep, and the like. They may or may not be made into offerings, depending on the place. But large cattle are surely going to be used as offerings and may not be sold to idolaters by Israelites.

> **M. 1:6 In a place in which they are accustomed to sell small cattle to idolaters, they sell them. In a place in which they are accustomed not to sell [small cattle] to them, they do not sell them. And in every locale they do not sell them large cattle, calves, or foals, whether whole or lame.**
>
> T. 2:2 And just as they do not sell them a large domesticated beast, so they do not sell them a large wild beast [M. A.Z. 1:6B]. And also in a situation in which they do not sell them a small domesticated beast, they do not sell them a small wild beast.
>
> Y. 1:6 III.2 *[If] one transgressed [the law in a locale in which it is prohibited to sell such beasts to idolaters] and sold [such a beast to an idolater], do they impose a fine upon him [so depriving the Israelite of the use of the proceeds]? Just as the sages impose such a penalty on the Israelite in the case of the violation of a law [e.g., deliberately blemishing a firstling so that the priest has no claim to it], so they impose a penalty on him for the violation of a custom [operative in a given locale].*

Idolaters are not to be provided with wild animals to be used in cruel ways, for inflicting the death penalty for example. One may not assist them in building constructions that serve their cult or administration. But one may help build public or private bathhouses. However, at the point at which the idol is installed, the Israelite worker desists.

> **M. 1:7 They do not sell them (1) bears or (2) lions, or (3) anything which is a public danger. They do not build with them (1) a basilica, (2) scaffold, (3) stadium, or (4) judges' tribunal. But they build with them (5) public bathhouses or (6) private ones. [Once] they reach the vaulting on which they set up an idol, it is forbidden [to help build any longer].**
>
> T. 2:3 And just as they do not sell [the listed animals] to them, they also do not exchange them with them, either bad ones for good ones, or good ones for bad ones; either lame ones for healthy ones, or healthy ones for lame ones.

Obviously one may not make ornaments for an idol or produce anything that may be devoted to idolatry. That applies in particular when it is still in the ground.

> **M. 1:8 And they do not make ornaments for an idol: (1) necklaces, (2) earrings, or (3) finger rings. They do not sell them produce as yet unplucked. But one may sell it once it has been harvested.**

T. 2:4 They do not sell them either a sword or the paraphernalia for a sword. And they do not polish a sword for them. And they do not sell them stocks, neck-chains, ropes, or iron chains, scrolls, phylacteries, or *mezuzot*. All the same are the idolater and the Samaritan. They sell them fodder which has been cut down, grain which has been harvested, and trees which have been picked.

There is no attending the amphitheaters. One must avoid participating in the bloody rites that take place in them or even paying attention to it.

T. 2:7 He who goes up into idolaters' amphitheaters, if he was going about on account of the service of the state's requirements, lo, this is permitted. If one takes account [of what is happening therein], lo, this is forbidden. He who sits in an amphitheater [e.g., where gladiators are fighting], lo, this one is guilty of bloodshed. They may go to stadiums because [an Israelite] will cry out in order to save the life of the loser, and to the performance in a camp on account of the task of preserving order in the province. But if one takes account of what is happening [in the entertainment], lo, this is forbidden.

In theory one may not rent out a house to an idolater, who uses it as a shelter also for his idol. The Tosefta goes over this same ground and elaborates.

M. 1:9 Even in the situation concerning which they have ruled [that they may] rent, it is not for use as a residence that they ruled that it is permitted, because he brings an idol into it, as it is said, "You shall not bring an abomination into your house" (Deut 7:26). And in no place may one rent him a bathhouse, since it would be called by his [the Israelite's] name [and its use on the Sabbath will be attributed to the Israelite].

T. 2:8 They do not rent to them houses, fields, or vineyards. And they do not provide for them fields on the basis of sharecropping [a variable or fixed proportion of the crop, respectively] or of contracting to raise beasts. All the same are an idolater and a Samaritan.

T. 2:9 Here and there an Israelite should not rent out his house to an idolater, because it is certain that the latter will bring an idol into it [M. A.Z. 1:9A–C]. But they may rent out to them stables, storehouses, and inns, even though it is certain that the idolater will bring into it an idol.

The Halakhah takes it for granted that just as the idolater is likely to practice his offense against God whenever he can, so he is assumed to be beyond all limits of humanity. He will practice bestiality on all manner of beasts and to engage in unrestrained sexual relations. He will murder an Israelite if he has the chance. Israelites should not help idolaters in childbirth. The enemies of God stand entirely outside the range of decency.

M. 2:1 **They do not leave cattle in idolaters' inns, because they are suspect in regard to bestiality. And a woman should not be alone with them, because they are suspect in regard to fornication. And a man should not be alone with them, because they are suspect in regard to bloodshed. An Israelite girl should not serve as a midwife to an idolater woman, because she serves to bring forth a child for the service of idolatry. But an idolater woman may serve as a midwife to an Israelite girl. An Israelite girl should not give suck to the child of an idolater woman. But an idolater woman may give suck to the child of an Israelite girl, when it is by permission.**

Samaritans are not classified as idolaters and are deemed civilized by the Torah.

T. 3:1 They leave cattle in Samaritans' inns, even male [cattle] with women, and female [cattle] with men, and female [cattle] with women. And they hand over cattle to their shepherds, and they hand over a child to him to teach him reading and to teach him a craft, and to be alone with him. An Israelite girl serves as a midwife and gives suck to the child of a Samaritan woman. And a Samaritan woman serves as midwife and gives suck to an Israelite child.

T. 3:2 They do not leave cattle in idolaters' inns [M. A.Z. 2:1A], even male cattle with men, and female cattle with women, because a male may bring a male [beast] over him, and a female may do the same with a female beast, and it goes without saying, males with women, and females with men. And they do not hand over cattle to their shepherds. And they do not hand a child over to him to teach him reading, to teach him a craft, or to be alone with him.

T. 3:3 An Israelite girl should not give suck to the child of an idolater woman [M. A.Z. 2:1J], because she raises a child for the service of idolatry [cf. M. A.Z. 2:1H]. But an idolater woman may give suck to the child of an Israelite girl, when it is by permission [M. A.Z. 2:1K]. An Israelite girl should not serve as a midwife to an idolater woman, because she serves to bring forth a child for the service of idolatry [M. A.Z. 2:1G–H].

Idolatrous persons may be employed to repair one's property but not as physicians. They are, once again, assumed to be as ready to kill an Israelite as heal him.

M. 2:2 **They accept from them healing for property, but not healing for the person.**

T. 3:4 They accept from them healing as to matters of property, but not healing as to matters of the person [M. A.Z. 2:2A–B]. An idolater woman should not be called upon to cut out the foetus in the womb of an Israelite girl. And she should not give her a cup of bitters to drink, for they are suspect as to the taking of life. And an Israelite should not be alone with an idolater either in a bathhouse or in a urinal. [When] an Israelite goes along with an idolater, he puts him at his right hand, and he does not put him at his left hand.

T. 3:5 An Israelite who is getting a haircut from an idolater watches in the mirror [cf. M. A.Z. 2:2C–E]. [If it is] from a Samaritan, he does not watch in the mirror. They permitted the house of Rabban Gamaliel to look at themselves in the mirror, for they are close to the government.

T. 3:6 An Israelite who is giving a haircut to an idolater, when he has reached the forelock, removes his hands [from the hair and does not cut it off]. They purchase from an idolater scrolls, phylacteries, and *mezuzot*, so long as they are written properly.

Slaves once purchased by an Israelite are converted to Judaism and instructed in the faith. Then they cannot be resold to idolaters. If an Israelite sells his slave to an idolater, the slave automatically goes free and the Israelite is required to supply a writ of emancipation. Once an Israelite, the slave is afforded every protection against idolatry.

T. 3:16 He who sells his slave to idolaters—[the slave] has gone forth free. And he requires a writ of emancipation from his first master. Whether he sold him to him or gave him to him as a gift, he has gone forth free. And if not, he has not gone forth free, lest he has gone forth to a domain which is not a domain. He borrows money from an idolater on the strength of him. If the idolater did what the law requires [making acquisition], he has gone forth free. And if not, he has not gone forth free. [If] he took him in compensation for his debt, or if he fell to him under the law of the usurper, he has gone forth free. [If] one has inherited slaves from idolaters, before they have actually entered his domain, he is permitted to sell them to idolaters. Once they have actually entered his domain, he is prohibited from selling them to idolaters. And so you say in the case of wine which has served for a libation, which one has inherited: before it has come into one's domain, money received for it is permitted. Once it has come into one's domain, money received for it is prohibited.

T. 3:17 An Israelite and an idolater who made a purchase in partnership and went and made another purchase—he may not say to him, "You take the things which are in such-and-such a place in lieu of the first purchase, and I shall take the things which are in such-and-such a place in lieu of the second purchase." But he says to him, "You take the things which are in such-and-such a place, and I shall take the things which are in such-and-such a place." In lieu of the first purchase, you take the things which are in such-and-such a place, and I shall take the things which are in such-and-such a place in lieu of the second purchase."

T. 3:18 He who sells his slave abroad—he has gone forth free. And he needs a writ of emancipation from his second master.

T. 3:19 He who sells his slave to an idolater fair—the money received for him is prohibited, and one must take it to the Salt Sea. And they force his master to redeem him, even at a hundred times the price received for him, and then he puts him out to freedom. You turn out to rule: He who does business at an idolater fair—in the case of a beast, it is to be hamstrung. In the case of clothing and utensils, they are left to rot. In the case of money and metal utensils, they are to be taken off to the Salt Sea. As to produce, that which is usually poured out is to be poured out. That which is usually burned is to be burned. That which is usually buried is to be buried.

Just as one may not sell to an idolater objects used for idolatrous worship, so one may not purchase from him what surely has served for idolatry, for example, wine or wine-derivatives, certain kinds of earthenware, and hides pierced at the heart. The assumption is that the wine serves as a libation, readily offered with the flick of a finger, and so throughout.

M. **2:3 These things belonging to idolaters are prohibited, and the prohibition affecting them extends to deriving any benefit from them at all: (1) wine, (2) vinegar of idolaters which to begin with was wine, (3) Hadrianic earthenware, and (4) hides pierced at the heart. With those who are going to an idolatrous pilgrimage—it is prohibited to do business. With those that are coming back it is permitted.**

T. 4:7 What are hides pierced at the heart [M. A.Z. 2:3B]? Any which is perforated at the heart [of the beast], and made into a kind of peep-hole. But if it is straight, it is permitted [M. A.Z. 2:3C].

T. 4:8 A. Pickled and stewed vegetables of idolaters, into which it is customary to put wine and vinegar, and Hadrianic earthenware [cf. M. A.Z. 2:3B, 2:6D]—the prohibition affecting them is a prohibition extending to deriving any benefit from them whatsoever. Sodden olives which are sold at the doors of bathhouses are prohibited for eating, but permitted so far as deriving benefit.

The Yerushalmi's contribution is to classify types of wine, rendering the law more nuanced.

Y. *2:3 I.2Gff. There are three types of wine [so far as the prohibition of idolaters' wine on the count of libation to idolatry is concerned]: [There is wine] that [an Israelite] assuredly saw an idolater offer up as a libation to an idol. This sort of wine imparts uncleanness of a severe sort, like a dead creeping thing. [There is] ordinary wine [of an idolater]. It is prohibited [for Israelite use or benefit]. But it does not impart uncleanness. [If an Israelite] deposited [wine] with [an idolater], sealed by a single seal, it is prohibited for drinking, but permitted for [other sorts of] gain [e.g., sale].*

The law differentiates prohibiting an object for use from prohibiting it for commerce. Israelites may do business in objects they may not themselves use, and the distinction explains why libation wine is absolutely forbidden for use or sale, while wine originating with Israelites that idolaters have possessed may be sold but not used.

Objects Prohibited For Use but Permitted in Commerce

M. 2:4 **Skins of idolaters and their jars, with Israelite wine collected in them—the prohibition affecting them does not extend to deriving benefit from them. Grape pits and grape skins belonging to idolaters if they are moist, they are forbidden. If they are dry, they are permitted. Fish brine and Bithynian cheese belonging to idolaters—the prohibition of them does not extend to deriving benefit from them.**

T. 4:9 A water tank on wheels and a leather-bottle belonging to idolaters, with Israelite wine collected in them—[the wine] is prohibited for drinking, but available for other benefit [cf. M. A.Z. 2:4 A, C].

T. 4:10 Skins belonging to idolaters which are scraped are permitted. Those which are sealed or covered with pitch are prohibited. [If] an idolater works it and pitches it, while an Israelite supervises him, one may collect wine or oil in it without scruple. Jars belonging to idolaters—new ones are permitted. Old ones which are old and rubbed are prohibited. And one in which an idolater collected water—[if] an Israelite filled out, an Israelite is permitted also to put wine or oil into it. And if an idolater collected wine in it, an Israelite fills it with water for three whole days, seventy-two hours. [Then] he may collect wine in it without scruple. And in one in which an idolater collected Israelite wine, pickling brine, or brine an Israelite is permitted to collect wine.

Y. 2:4 II:3 *[If] an idolater has collected water in [jars], an Israelite [who wishes to make use of the same jars] puts water into them and then goes and puts wine into them and need not scruple. [If] an idolater collected brine or fish-brine in them, an Israelite may then put wine into those same jars. [If] an idolater collected wine in them, an Israelite may put into them brine or fish-brine and then go and put wine into them, and he need not scruple.*

The law now supplies a systematic catalogue of classes of objects that may not be used but that may be traded, and it further lists idolater products that Israelites may consume, under specified circumstances.

M. 2:6 **And what are things of idolaters which are prohibited, but the prohibition of which does not extend to deriving benefit from them? (1) milk drawn by an idolater without an Israelite's watching him; (2) their bread; and (3) their oil—(4) stewed and pickled [vegetables] into which it is customary to put wine and vinegar; (5)**

minced fish; (6) **brine without kilbit-fish floating in it; (7) hileq fish, (8) drops of *asafoetida*, and (9) *sal-conditum*—lo, these are prohibited, but the prohibition affecting them does not extend to deriving benefit from them.**

M. 2:7 **These are things which [to begin with] are permitted for [Israelite] consumption. (1) milk which an idolater drew, with an Israelite watching him; (2) honey; (3) grape clusters, (even though they drip with moisture, they are not subject to the rule of imparting susceptibility to uncleanness as liquid); (4) pickled vegetables into which it is not customary to put wine or vinegar; (5) unminced fish; (6) brine containing fish; (7) a [whole] leaf of asafoetida, and (8) pickled olive cakes. Locusts which come from [the shopkeeper's] basket are forbidden. Those which come from the stock [of his shop] are permitted. And so is the rule for heave-offering.**

As is its way, the Tosefta supplies a mass of detail to articulate the distinctions made by the Mishnah and illustrated by the Mishnah's few cases.

T. 4:11 They purchase from idolaters grain, pulse, dried figs, garlic, and onions, under all circumstances, and they do not scruple on account of uncleanness. As to red berry of sumac, under all circumstances it is deemed unclean. As to cedar, under all circumstances it is deemed clean. A hunter is believed to testify, "This bird is unclean," "This bird is clean." An 'am ha'ares is believed to testify, "These pickled vegetables did I pickle in a state of cleanness, and I did not sprinkle liquids [capable of imparting susceptibility to uncleanness] upon them." But he is not believed to testify, "These fish I caught in a state of cleanness, and I did not shake the net over them." Their caper-fruit, leeks, liverwort, boiled water and parched corn [prepared by idolaters] are permitted. An egg roasted by them is prohibited. A loaf of bread which an idolater baked, not in the presence of an Israelite, and cheese which an idolater curdled, not in the presence of an Israelite, are prohibited. A loaf of bread which an Israelite baked, even though the idolater kneaded the dough, and cheese which an Israelite curdled, even though an idolater works it—lo, this is permitted. An Israelite may sit at the other side of his corral, and an idolater may milk the cows and bring the milk to him, and one does not scruple. What is unminced fish [M. A.Z. 2:7E]? Any in which the backbone and head are discernible. What is brine containing fish [M. A.Z. 2:7F]? Any in which one or two kilbit-fish are floating. A piece of meat on which there is a recognizable sign, whether it is on the whole of it or only part of it, and even if it is on only one out of a hundred—lo, this is permitted. Brine made by an expert, lo, this is permitted.

T. 4:12 Boiled wine and aromatic water—lo, these are prohibited because they begin as wine. Aromatic water in its natural condition—lo, this is permitted. Apple-wine which comes from storage, the storehouse, or a ship—lo, this is permitted. But if it is sold over the counter in the market, lo, this is prohibited, because it may be adulterated [with idolater wine or vinegar]. Locusts and pieces of meat which come from storage or from the storehouse or from a ship—lo, these are permitted. But if they are sold in a basket in front of a store, lo, they are prohibited, because they sprinkle them with wine so as to improve their appearance [M. A.Z. 2:7F–H].

Idols

From the effects of idolatry, the exposition of the law shifts to the source: the idol itself. Here the Rabbinic sages walk a fine line. They cannot concede that the idol is God. But they also cannot ignore the attitude toward the idol of the idolater, who (in their view) regards the idol as a god. The first point is that an idol is defined by the idolater's attitude toward the object: if such a thing can be worshipped, it is classified as an idol, pure and simple.

General Principles

M. 3:1 Images are prohibited that have in its hand a staff, bird, or sphere.

Broken idols are null and discarded, unless the shard resembles an object of worship.

M. 3:2 He who finds the shards of images—lo, these are permitted. [If] one found [a fragment] shaped like a hand or a foot, lo, these are prohibited, because objects similar to them are worshipped.

M. 3:3 He who finds utensils upon which is the figure of the sun, moon, or dragon, should bring them to the Salt Sea. One breaks them into pieces and throws the powder to the wind or drops them into the sea. Also: they may be made into manure, as it is said, "And there will cleave nothing of a devoted thing to your hand" (Deut 13:18).

Now the Tosefta, as is its way, introduces refinements and complications.

T. 5:2 A. A ring on which there is an idol—when it projects, it is prohibited for benefit. But if it does not project [outward from the ring], it is permitted for benefit. And one way or the other, it is prohibited to make a seal with it. And one on which there is no idol is permitted for benefit and permitted for use as a seal. A ring on which there is a seal is permitted for use as a seal. A ring, the seal of which is incised, is prohibited for use as a seal, because with it an image which projects is made. But it is permitted to put it on one's hand. And one, the seal of which projects, is permitted for use as a seal, because the seal which it

makes is embedded [in the clay and does not project]. And it is forbidden to put it on one's hand. A ring on which there is a figure is
permitted for use as a seal. The reptile-shaped gem which is made in
the figure of a dragon is prohibited, and one on which a dragon is suspended—[if] one takes it off and throws it out, as to the rest [of the
object], lo, this is permitted.

Matters are not so simply resolved, when the law takes into account the
range of things subjected to idolatrous worship. After all, the pagans worship
hills and valleys (so the Rabbinic legislators maintain). What is to be done
with them requires attention.

> **M. 3:5 Idolaters who worship hills and valleys—these [hills or valleys] are
> permitted, but what is on them is forbidden [for Israelite use], as
> it is said, "You shall not covet the silver or gold that is upon them
> nor take it." On what account is an asherah prohibited? Because it
> has been subject to manual labor, and whatever has been subject to
> manual labor is prohibited.**

The law attends to unavoidable contact with a pagan temple. Here the
law does not require tearing down the shared wall, but prohibits rebuilding
it if it falls down on its own.

> **M. 3:6 He [the wall of] whose house was adjacent to [and also served as
> the wall of the temple of] an idol, and [whose house] fell down—
> it is forbidden to rebuild it. What should he then do? He pulls back
> within four cubits inside his own property and then rebuilds his
> house. [If there was a wall belonging] both to him and to [the tem-
> ple of an] idol, it is judged to be divided half and half. The stones,
> wood, and mortar deriving from it impart uncleanness in the sta-
> tus of a dead creeping thing, for it is said, "You will utterly detest
> it" (Deut 7:26).**
>
> T. 6:2 He who designates his house for an idol—the whole of it imparts
> uncleanness upon entry [to one who comes in]. And he who stands in
> it, it is as if he is standing in a temple of idolatry. If the public way cuts
> through it, however, unclean is only that path alone. He who sets up
> his house near a temple—the whole of it imparts uncleanness upon
> entry. [If someone else] set up [a temple] near his house, the whole of
> it does not impart uncleanness upon entry. But that wall [which is
> nearest to the idol] is deemed to be divided half and half [M. A.Z.
> 3:6E]. [If the house] fell down, however, it is permitted to rebuild it [if]
> one has rebuilt it, it has returned to its original condition. [If other peo-
> ple] rebuilt it, not the whole of it imparts uncleanness upon entry, but
> only that wall alone. It is deemed to be divided half and half. He who
> sells his house to an idol—the proceeds received for it are forbidden,
> and one has to bring them to the Salt Sea. But idolaters who forced

someone and took over his house and set up an idol in it—the proceeds received for it are permitted. And one may write a deed in that regard and deposit it in the archives.

The power of the Rabbinic law is to classify data in the manner of natural history and to derive from the classification the rule governing each taxon. What is made for idolatry is forbidden. What is not made for idolatry but adapted for that purpose is permitted when the adaptation is removed, with variations.

The Asherah

M. 3:7 **There are three sorts of houses [so far as use as a shrine for idolatry is concerned]: (1) a house which was built to begin with for the purposes of idolatry—lo, this is prohibited. (2) [If] one stuccoed and decorated it for idolatry and renovated it, one removes the renovations. (3) [If] one brought an idol into it and took it out—lo, this is permitted. There are three sorts of stones: (1) a stone which one hewed to begin with for a pedestal—lo, this is forbidden. (2) [If] he set up an idol on [an existing] stone and then took it off, lo, this is permitted. There are three kinds of asherahs: (1) A tree which one planted to begin with for idolatry—lo, this is prohibited. (2) [If] he chopped it and trimmed it for idolatry, and it sprouted afresh, he may remove that which sprouted afresh. (3) [If] he set up an idol under it and then annulled it, lo, this is permitted.**

T. 6:3 He who pokes his head and the greater part of his body into a temple containing an idol is unclean. A clay utensil, the contained airspace of which one has poked into a temple containing an idol, is unclean. Benches and chairs, the greater part of which one has poked into a temple containing an idol, are unclean.

The next rule treats the object of idolatry as equivalent to a corpse. Numbers 19 sets forth the rule that a corpse is a primary source of uncleanness; what passes under its shadow is affected by it; if a roof is over the corpse, the corpse-uncleanness is diffused thereby to whatever is under the same roof. Now the reader sees the same rule applied to the asherah. If one passed underneath the shadow of a tree that is venerated, he is unclean.

M. 3:8 **One should not sit in [an asherah's] shade, but if he sat in its shade, he is clean. And he should not pass underneath it, but if he passed underneath it, he is unclean. If it was overshadowing public domain, taking away property from public use, and one passed beneath it, he is clean. And they sow seeds underneath it in the rainy season, but not in the dry season. But as to lettuce, neither in the dry season nor in the rainy season [may one plant it there].**

T. 6:8 Idolaters who worship hills and valleys [M. A.Z. 3:5A]—even though they [hills and valleys] are permitted, those who worship them are put to death by stoning. A humanity who is worshipped—even though he is permitted, those who worship him are put to death through stoning. And what is an asherah [M. A.Z. 3:7N]? It is any tree which idolaters worship and guard, and the produce of which they do not eat. They sow seeds underneath it in the rainy season, but not in the dry season. But as to lettuce, neither in the dry season nor in the rainy season [may one plant it there] [M. A.Z. 3:8C–E]. He who comes under it is as if he came into a temple of idolatry. But if the public way passed through it, lo, this is permitted [cf. M. A.Z. 3:8C].

M. 3:9 **[If] one has taken pieces of wood from [an asherah], they are prohibited for benefit. [If] he lit a fire in the oven with them, if it is a new oven, it is to be overturned. If it is an old oven, it must be allowed to cool down. [If] he baked a loaf of bread in [the oven heated by the wood of an asherah], it is prohibited for benefit. [If] the loaf of bread was mixed up with other loaves of bread, all of them are prohibited as to benefit. [If] one took a piece of wood for a shuttle, it is forbidden for benefit. [If] he wove a garment with the shuttle, the garment is forbidden for benefit. [If] it was mixed up with other garments, and other garments with still others, all of them are forbidden for benefit.**

M. 3:8 **How does one desecrate [an asherah]? [If] one trimmed it or pruned it, took from it a branch or twig, even a leaf—lo, this constitutes desecration. [If] one has trimmed it for the good of [the tree], it remains forbidden. [If he trimmed it] not for the good of the tree, it is permitted.**

T. 6:9 A. An Israelite who trimmed an asherah, whether it was for the good of the tree, or whether it was for his own good—it is prohibited. An idolater who trimmed an asherah—if it was for the good of the tree, the tree is prohibited, but he is permitted. If it was for his own good, one way or the other, it is prohibited [cf. M. A.Z. 3:10].

From the tree the law moves on to a small statue and offerings made to it— a Zeus. At issue is the status of that which is left by the statue. The sages do not automatically assign debris to the statue and hence to idolatry.

The Merkolis

M. 4:1 **Three stones, one beside the other, beside a Merkolis (Mercury) statue,—those which appear to belong to it are forbidden, and those which do not appear to belong to it are permitted.**

Y. 4:1 I:1 *[If an Israelite] put on the second stone [thus not completing the idol, and also slaughtered a beast before the incomplete idol, and the beast was the dam of an offspring that had been slaughtered on that day, or the offspring of a dam that had been slaughtered on that day, so that there are two transgressions in view, one, building an idol, the other, slaughtering a dam and its offspring on the same day], and they had warned [the Israelite] concerning violation of the law against slaughtering the dam and its offspring on the same day, [the Israelite] is given a flogging [on the count of violating the prohibition against slaughtering the dam and its offspring on the same day], but on the count of idolatry he is not stoned to death.]*

Characteristic offerings to the Zeus-statue are not money, clothing, or utensils but bunches of grapes, garlands of corn, and the like. The Rabbinic law takes account of the facts of the cult of idols.

M. 4:2 [If] one found on its head coins, clothing, or utensils, lo, these are permitted. [If one found] bunches of grapes, garlands of corn, jugs of wine or oil, or fine flour or anything the like of which is offered on the altar—it is forbidden.

The Tosefta once more amplifies the law, reaching into Scripture for data as well.

T. 6:10 One should not climb up to the top of a pedestal, even to disfigure it, even to defile it, as it is said, "Nothing of what is dedicated shall cleave to your hand" (Deut 13:18).

T. 6:11 One should not say to his fellow, "Wait for me by the idol of so and so," or, "I'll wait for you by the idol of such-and-such," as it is said, "You will not make mention of the name of any other god" (Exod 23:13).

T. 6:12 An idol and everything on it—lo, this is forbidden. [If] one found on it jugs of wine, oil, or fine flour, or anything the like of which is offered on the altar [M. A.Z. 4:2C], it is forbidden. [If he found on it] utensils which are used for it and for its body, they are forbidden. [If they are] not [used] for its body, they are permitted. Also as to utensils which are used for them and for its body, [if] priests of idolatry stole and sold them—lo, they are permitted.

T. 6:13 A. One verse of Scripture says, "You shall not covet the silver or the gold that is on them or take it for yourself" (Deut 7:25). And one verse of Scripture says, "And you have seen their detestable things, their idols of wood and stone, of silver and gold, which were among them" (Deut 29:17). How is it possible to carry out both of these verses? On them—whether its body is clothed in them or not clothed in them, they are forbidden. Among them—those, the body of which is clothed in them, are forbidden, and those, the body of which is not clothed in them, are permitted. And also clothing in which the body [of the idol] is clothed [if] they have sold them, lo, these are permitted. A Merkolis and whatever is on it is forbidden. [If] one found on it jugs of wine, oil, or fine flour, or anything, the like of which is offered on the altar, it is forbidden. [If one found on it] coins or utensils, they are permitted.

T. 6:14 Stones which dropped away from a Merkolis, if they appeared to belong with it, they are forbidden, and if not, they are permitted [M. A.Z. 4:1C]. An Israelite who brought stones from a Merkolis—lo, they are forbidden, for they have been forbidden by the idol. An idolater who brought stones from a Merkolis—lo, they are permitted, for they are in the status of an idol where worshippers have abandoned it. And a Merkolis which was ripped up from its place is permitted for benefit [for Israelites].

Once more the issue of nullification emerges. Now the issue is the use of public facilities that are adorned with idols or owned by temples. An Israelite may use a bathhouse devoted to an idol if that use is not to the advantage of the idol or the temple.

Nullifying an Idol

M. 4:3 An idol which had a garden or a bathhouse—they derive benefit from them [when it is] not to the advantage [of the temple], but they do not derive benefit from them [when it is] to the advantage [of the temple]. If it belonged both to the idol and to outsiders, they derive benefit from them whether or not it is to the advantage [of the temple].

T. 6:1 A cow which one fattened using vetches belonging to an idol—[or if such a cow] went down to pasture in a garden which one has manured with a manure belonging to an idol— [the field] must be left fallow. A garden which one ploughed with [a plough made of] pieces of wood of an asherah—[the field] must be left fallow. Kelilan-wool which one stamped with wood belonging to an idol—one must burn it. Others say, "One assigns to it the more stringent ruling until its appearance will return to what it was." [If] there were bagpipes belonging to an idol, one is prohibited from making a lamentation with them. If they were rented from the state, even though they were made for the use of an idol, it is permitted to make a lamentation using them. Ships belonging to an idol—it is prohibited to rent [space] in them. But if they were rented from the state, even though they were made for the use of an idol, it is permitted to rent them. Charity collectors for a temple of idolatry—it is prohibited to give anything to them. But if they were paid by the state, even though they are working for the welfare of an idol, it is permitted to give a contribution to them [cf. M. A.Z. 4:3].

T. 6:4 All places which are called by names complimentary to idolatry does one rename with euphemisms insulting to idolatry. A place which they call, "The face of god," do they call, "The face of the dog." "A spring for all" ('YN KL) do they call "A spring of a thorn" ('YN QOS) "Good fortune (GDGYA)" do they call "A mound (GLYA)." He whose coins were scattered in the direction of an idol should not bend over before it to pick them up, because it looks as if he is bowing down to an idol. But he turns his back on the idol and collects the coins [with his behind toward the idol]. And in a place in which he is not seen, it is all right [to do it the other way].

T. 6:5 A spring which flows out of an idol—one should not bend down before it and drink, because he appears to bow down before an idol. But he turns his back and drinks. And in a place in which he is not seen, it is all right.

T. 6:6 Figures which spout out water in towns—one should not place his mouth on the mouth of the figurine and drink, because it appears that he is kissing the idol. But he collects the water in his hand and drinks it.

Y. 4:3 I:1 *As to bagpipes belonging to an idol, it is forbidden to sell them [to make a lamentation with them]. If they were rented from the state, even though they were made for use of an idol, it is permitted to make lamentation using them. Shops belonging to an idol's [temple] it is prohibited to rent space in them. But if they provided a rental for the state, even though they were built for the use of an idol's [temple], it is permitted to rent them. Charity collectors for a temple of idolatry—it is prohibited to give anything to them. But if they provided funds to the state, even though they are working for the welfare of an idol—it is permitted to give a contribution to them [as at M. A.Z. 4:3D].*

An object resembling an idol is not necessarily an idol. If it belongs to an idolater, it is forthwith an idol when it is fully manufactured. If it is made for an Israelite, it is classified as an idol only when it has been worshipped. Only an idolater has the power to nullify an idol; an Israelite's attitude does not affect the idol's status. Since he does not believe in the divinity of the idol, he cannot nullify it by an act of will.

M. 4:4 **An idol belonging to an idolater is prohibited forthwith [when it is made]. And one belonging to an Israelite is prohibited only after it will have been worshipped. An idolater has the power to nullify an idol belonging either to himself or his fellow idolater. But an Israelite does not have the power to nullify an idol belonging to an idolater. He who nullifies an idol has nullified its appurtenances. [If] he nullified [only] its appurtenances, its appurtenances are permitted, but the idol itself [remains] prohibited.**

T. 5:3 He who purchases metal filings from idolaters and found an idol therein takes it and tosses it away, and the rest—lo, this is permitted. An Israelite who found an idol before it has come into his domain may tell an idolater to nullify it. For an idolater has the power to nullify an idol, whether it belongs to him or to his fellow [M. A.Z. 4:4C], whether it is an idol which has been worshipped or whether it is one which has not been worshipped, whether it is inadvertent or deliberate, whether it is under constraint or willingly. But an Israelite who made an idol—it is prohibited, even though he has not worshipped it [vs. M. A.Z. 4–4B] Therefore he does not have the power to nullify it.

T. 5:4   A. An idolater who made an idol—it is permitted until it has been worshipped [vs. M. A.Z. 4:4A]. Therefore he has the power to nullify it.

T. 5:5   An idolater who sold an idol to people who worship it—it is prohibited. If he sold it to people who do not worship it, it is permitted. One may lend money on the strength of it [as a pledge]. [If] a wreck fell on it, if a river swept it away, or thugs grabbed it—as in the case of the war of Joshua—if the owner is going to go looking for it, it is forbidden. If not, it is permitted.

T. 5:6   The pedestals which idolaters set up during the persecution [by Hadrian]—even though the time of persecution is over—lo, these are forbidden. Is it possible that an idol which an idolater nullified—is it possible that it should be deemed prohibited? Scripture says, "The graven images of their gods you shall burn with fire" (Deut 7:25). That which he treats as a god is prohibited. And that which he does not treat as a god is permitted. Is it then possible that an idol which an idolater nullified should be deemed permitted? Scripture says, "The graven images of their gods. . . . Whether he treats it as a god or does not treat it as a god, it is forbidden."

T. 5:7   How does one nullify [an idol]? An idolater nullifies an idol belonging to himself or to an Israelite. But an Israelite does not nullify an idol belonging to an idolater [cf. M. A.Z. 4:4C–D].

T. 5:9   At what point is it called "set aside [for idolatrous purposes]"? Once some concrete deed has been done to it [for that purpose].

Now the Tosefta's formulation identifies the governing principle that animates the diverse cases: there is no such thing as an act of consecration for idolatry.

T. 5:10 What is one which has been worshipped? Any one which people worship—whether inadvertently or deliberately. What is one which has been set aside? Any which has been set aside for idolatry. But if one has said, "This ox is for idolatry," "This house is for idolatry," he has said nothing whatsoever. For there is no such thing as an act of consecration for idolatry.

The valid act of nullification of an idol involves damage done to the object, not merely disrespect shown to it, a distinction that registers in the following:

M. 4:5 How does one nullify it? [If] he has cut off the tip of its ear, the tip of its nose, the tip of its finger, [if] he battered it, even though he

did not break off [any part of] it, he has nullified it. [If] he spit in its face, urinated in front of it, scraped it, threw shit at it, lo, this does not constitute an act of nullification.

T. 5:8 A pedestal, the greater part of which was damaged—lo, this is permitted. One the whole of which was damaged is prohibited until one will restore it. That belonging to him is permitted, and that belonging to his fellow is prohibited. Before it has been sanctified, it is prohibited. After it has been sanctified, it is permitted.

An abandoned idol is classified by the circumstances in which it was abandoned. If the act was coerced, then the attitude of the idolater was not to nullify the idol, but if it was done willingly, then the idol is nullified.

M. 4:6 An idol, the worshippers of which have abandoned it in time of peace, is permitted. [If they abandoned it] in time of war, it is forbidden. Idol pedestals set up for kings—lo, these are permitted, since they set [images up on them only] at the time kings go by.

Libation Wine

The final chapters of the exposition of the subject of idolatry in the Halakhic corpus are devoted to a single topic, wine. The concern of the Rabbinic sages is simply explained. In their view the pagan would routinely flick from any wine they got into their hands a drop as a libation-offering. That action rendered the remainder of the wine the residue of an offering to an idol and forbidden to Israelites. But if the idolater was under Israelite supervision and instructed not to make a libation-offering, then the picture changes. Not only so, but the idolater would make a libation-offering only if his hands were in direct contact with the wine, not covered by gloves. And if the wine is boiled, it is no longer suitable for a libation. (Wine called "kosher" in the contemporary law of Judaism is wine that has not been subjected to the possibility of use for a libation, for example, wine that has been boiled.). The opening rule of the Mishnah explains its distinction and spells out the operative consideration.

M. 4:8 They purchase from idolaters [the contents of] a wine press which has already been trodden out, even though [the idolater] takes [the grapes] in hand and puts them on the heap ["apple"], for it is not made into wine used for libations until it drips down into the vat. [And if wine has] dripped into the vat, what is in the cistern is prohibited, while the rest is permitted.

T. 7:1 At first they ruled, "They do not gather grapes with an idolater. And they do not press grapes with an Israelite who prepares his wine in a state of uncleanness" [cf. M. A.Z. 4:9C–D]. Truly they gather grapes

with an idolater. All the same are new and old ones: they assist him
until he passes out of sight. Once he has passed out of sight, he may
turn the wine into libation wine [but Israelites are not responsible for
the fact].

T.   7:3   An Israelite who works with an idolater at the winepress—lo, this one
brings up the "bread" [that is, the mass of wine-pulp] to the "apple"
[the heap to be pressed], and brings down the wine from the "apple."
Even though the wine flows over his hands, it is permitted. For it is not
their custom to make a libation under such circumstances [M. A.Z.
4:8A–C]. An idolater who works with an Israelite at the winepress—lo,
this one brings up the "bread" to the "apple," and brings down the
"bread" from the "apple." Even though the wine flows over his hands,
it is permitted. For it is not their custom to make a libation under such
circumstances.

The Yerushalmi contributes a refinement of the basic principle, once more
explaining itself.

Y.   4:8 I:2   *A winepress that an idolater stopped up [filling in the cracks]—[if he*
stopped up the vat from] the inside, [the wine] is forbidden, [and if he
stopped up the vat] from the outside, it is permitted. [The basis for this dis-
tinction is that] it is not possible that there was not there a single moist drop
[of wine in one of the cracks], which the idolater will touch and offer as a
libation, thus rendering into libation wine whatever thereafter flows into
the cistern.

If the idolater has control of the wine-cistern, he is assumed to make a libation-offering from it. If not, he is not assumed to have ruined the wine for
Israelite use and commerce.

M. 4:10   An idolater who is found standing beside a cistern of wine—if he
had a lien on the vat, it is prohibited. [If] he had no lien on it, it
is permitted. [If] he fell into the vat and climbed out, or (2) [if
idolaters] measured it with a reed—or (3) [if] he flicked out a hor-
net with a reed, or [if] (4) he patted down the froth on the mouth
of a jar—in regard to each of these—there was a case, let it be sold.
[If] (5) he took a jar and threw it in a fit of temper into the vat—
this was a case, and they declared it valid.

T.   7:4   He who weighs out grapes on a scale—even though the wine flows over
his hands, it is permitted, for it is not their custom to make a libation
[under such circumstances]. He who presses wine into a jar, even
though the wine flows over his hands—it is permitted. For it is not
their custom to make a libation under such circumstances. [If an idol-
ater] fell into the cistern and even a single drop of wine of any amount
touched him, it is forbidden [M. A.Z. 4:10D]. [If] he went down to
draw the grape-skins and the grape pits out of the cistern—this was a

case, and they asked sages. And they ruled, "Let the whole of it be sold to idolaters."

T. 7:5 An idolater who was bringing up grapes in baskets and barrels at the winepress, even though one has beaten them in the winepress, and the wine has spurted onto the grapes—it is permitted. For it is not their custom to make a libation under such circumstances. He who bought pressed grapes from an idolater, and found under it little holes [containing wine]—it is prohibited.

The following rule refers to "a condition of cleanness." This refers to the preservation of food and utensils from sources of uncleanness that affect the conduct of the Temple cult in Jerusalem, specified at Leviticus 11–15. Some Israelites would observe those same taboos in connection with eating their food at home, in the Holy Land but not in the Temple. Since the rules of Scripture applied in the main to priests eating their share of the Temple offerings, the governing consideration was for Israelites to act as if they were in the Temple and to pretend to be priests eating priestly rations or even Holy Things. This matter is distinct from the concern for avoiding idolatry. The issue in the following exposition concerns Israelites working for idolaters and the conditions under which the status of the wine is protected for Israelite use. The key point is that the law assumes the idolater will not ruin his wine for the Israelite market.

M. 4:11 He who in a condition of cleanness prepares the wine belonging to an idolater, and leaves it in his domain, in a house which is open to the public domain, in a town in which there are both idolaters and Israelites—[the wine] is permitted. [If it is] in a town in which all the residents are idolaters, [the wine] is prohibited, unless he sets up a guard. And the guard need not sit there and watch [the room all the time]. Even though he comes in and goes out, [the wine] is permitted.

T. 7:7 An Israelite who put wine into the domain of an idolater—if there is a lock or a seal on [the jug of wine], it is permitted. And if not, it is forbidden [cf. M. A.Z. 4:12A–B]. [If] one borrowed money on the strength of it from an idolater, even though there is on it a lock or a seal, it is forbidden [cf. M. A.Z. 4:12C–D]. But if the storehouse was open to the public domain, it is permitted. In a town, all the residents of which are idolaters, it is forbidden, unless one sits down and guards it [cf. M. A.Z. 4:11].

T. 7:9 An Israelite who prepared the wine of an idolater in a condition of cleanness, and put it in two courtyards or in two towns, even though [the Israelite] comes out and goes in from this courtyard to that courtyard, or from this town to that town—it is permitted. For it is in the assumption of being guarded [cf. M. A.Z. 4:11F–G]. But if it is taken for granted that [the Israelite] spends the night in some one place, it is forbidden [since the idolater may then make a libation of that which he assumes the Israelite will not see].

M. 4:12 He who prepares the wine of an idolater in a condition of cleanness and leaves it in his domain, and the latter wrote for [the Israelite a receipt, saying], "I received its price from you"—it is permitted. But if an Israelite wants then to remove the wine, and [the idolater] would not let him do so unless he paid the price of the wine—this was a case in Bet Shean, and sages declared [the wine] forbidden.

T. 7:8 An Israelite who prepared the wine of an idolater in a condition of cleanness, and the latter wrote for him a quittance, saying, "I received its price from you" [M. A.Z. 4:12A–B] . . . [if the idolater will not let him remove the wine unless he paid the price of the wine—this was a case, and they came and asked R. Simeon b. Eleazar, who ruled, "Whatever was in the domain of an idolater is subject to the same law" [M. A.Z. 4:11H].

The exposition now turns to subsidiary issues. The status of the salary paid to an Israelite worker for preparing libation wine is addressed. The answer is clear: the salary is classified as payment for participating in idolatry and is forbidden. But that rule is subjected to a narrow interpretation: the action must specifically benefit the wine used for a libation. What happens outside of this specific situation is another matter.

M. 5:1 An [idolater] who hires an [Israelite] worker to work with him in the preparation of libation wine—[the Israelite's] salary is forbidden. [If] he hired him to do some other kind of work, even though he said to him, "Move a jar of libation wine from one place to another," his salary is permitted. He who hires an ass to bring libation wine on it—its fee is forbidden. [If] he hired it to ride on it, even though the idolater [also] put a flagon [of libation wine] on it, its fee is permitted.

T. 7:10 A market into which an Israelite and an idolater bring wine, even though the jars are open, and the idolater is sitting nearby—it is permitted. Because it is assumed to be guarded. He who hires a worker to work with him for half a day in that [wine] which was subject to a prohibition, and half a day in that [wine] which was subject to permission, and one put all [the wine which had been prepared] in a single town—lo, these [both] are forbidden. [If] these are kept by themselves and those are kept by themselves, the first ones are forbidden, and the second ones are permitted. [An idolater] who hires a worker to do work with him toward evening, and said to him, "Bring this flagon to that place," even though an Israelite is not permitted to do so—his wages are permitted. A person may say to his ass drivers and his workers, "Go and get yourselves some food with this denar," "Go and get yourselves some wine with this denar" and he does not scruple because of tithes, violation of the rules governing the seventh year, or the prohibition of wine used for libations. But if he had said to them, "Go and eat a loaf of bread, and you pay for it," lo, this one then must take account of the matter of tithes, produce of the seventh year, and use of libation-wine."

T. 8:1 He who pours out wine from one utensil to another [M. A.Z. 5:7H] [if he places] the spout against the lips of the jar and below—lo, this is prohibited. The vat, ladle, and siphon of idolaters—sages prohibit. And on what account are these prohibited and those permitted? These are made for holding liquid, and those are not made for holding liquid. As to those of wood and of stone, one has to dry them off [M. A.Z. 5:1 A–E]. If they were of pitch, he has to scale them.

Mixtures of libation wine with valid wine are subjected to a standard pattern. If the libation wine can be separated from the valid wine—e.g., a mixture of what remains separate—the libation wine is rinsed off and the remainder is valid. If the libation wine was absorbed by the valid wine and cannot be removed, then the entire vat is null. If the libation wine was mixed with other produce than grapes, figs, or dates, then if it has imparted its flavor to the figs or dates, the figs or dates are forbidden. If not, they are permitted.

M. 5:2 **Libation wine which fell on grapes—one may rinse them off, and they are permitted. But if [the grapes] were split, they are prohibited. [If] it fell on figs or dates, if there is sufficient [libation wine absorbed] to impart a flavor [to them], they are forbidden. This is the governing principle: anything which bestows benefit through imparting a flavor is forbidden, and anything which does not bestow benefit through imparting a flavor is permitted—for example, vinegar [from libation wine] which falls on crushed beans.**

M. 5:3 **An idolater who with an Israelite was moving jars of wine from place to place—if [the wine] was assumed to be watched, it is permitted. If [the Israelite] informed him that he was going away [the wine is prohibited if he was gone] for a time sufficient to bore a hole [in a jug of wine] and stop it up and [for the clay] to dry.**

Once more the Rabbinic sages assume people will not ruin the property of another if they think they are supervised. But if the idolater has the opportunity to make a libation-offering unobserved by the Israelite, then he is assumed to do just that.

M. 5:4 **He who leaves his wine on a wagon or in a boat and went along by a shortcut, entered into a town and bathed—it is permitted. But if he informed [others] that he was going away, [the wine is prohibited if he was gone] for a time sufficient to bore a hole and sop it up and for the clay to dry. He who leaves an idolater in a store, even**

though he is going out and coming in all the time—it is permitted. But if he informed him that he was going away, [the wine is prohibited if he was gone] for a time sufficient to bore a hole and stop it up and for the clay to dry.

T. 7:12 He who leaves his wine in a store and went into a town, even though he remained there for a considerable time, lo, this [wine] is permitted. But if he informed him or locked the store, it is forbidden.

T. 7:13 He who leaves his wine on a boat and entered town, even though he remained there for a considerable time, it is permitted. But if he informed him that he was going away, or if the boat cast anchor, lo, this is forbidden [cf. M. A.Z. 5:4A–C].

M. 5:5 [If an Israelite] was eating with [an idolater] at the same time, and he put a flagon [of wine] on the table and a flagon on a side table, and he left it and went out—what is on the table is forbidden. But what is on the side table is permitted. And if he had said to him, "You mix and drink [wine]," even that which is on the side table is forbidden. Jars which are open are forbidden. And those which are sealed [are forbidden if he was gone] for a time sufficient to bore a hole and stop it up and for the clay to dry.

T. 7:14 He who sends a jug of wine with a Samaritan, or one of juice, vinegar, brine, oil, or honey, with an idolater—if he recognizes his seal, which stopped it up, it is permitted. And if not, it is forbidden. Wine with an idolater which is sealed is forbidden on the count of libation-wine. But as to juice, brine, oil, and honey, if he saw an idolater who offered them up as a libation, they are forbidden. If not, they are permitted.

T. 7:15 An Israelite who is suspect—they drink from his wine-cellar, but they do not drink from his flask. If he was suspect of [opening the jars and] sealing them, even wine from his wine-cellar is prohibited.

M. 5:6 A band of idolater [raiders] which entered a town in peacetime— open jars are forbidden, closed ones, permitted. [If it was] wartime, these and those are permitted. because there is no time for making a libation.

What the workers do who are paid in libation wine is defined. Before they take possession of the wine, they are permitted to reject payment in that form. But if the libation wine has already entered their domain, they cannot resell the wine and collect their wages from the proceeds. This same distinction recurs.

M. 5:7 Israelite craftsmen, to whom an idolater sent a jar of libation wine as their salary, are permitted to say to him, "Give us its value." But if it has already entered their possession, it is prohibited. He who sells his wine to an idolater [and] agreed on a price before he had measured it out—proceeds paid for it are permitted. [If] he had measured it out before he had fixed its price, proceeds paid for it

are prohibited. [If] he took the funnel and measured it out into the flask of the idolater and then went and measured wine into the flask of an Israelite, if there remained [in the funnel] a drop of wine [from what had been poured into the idolater's flask, then what is in the Israelite's flask] is forbidden. He who pours [wine] from one utensil to another—that from which is emptied [the wine] is permitted. But that into which he emptied [the wine] is forbidden.

T. 7:16 An idolater who owed [money] to an Israelite, even though he sold libation-wine and brought him the proceeds, [or sold] an idol and brought him the proceeds, it is permitted [cf. M. A.Z. 5:7A]. But if not [that is, the idolater did not sell the wine or idol, but delivered the wine or idol to him directly], it is forbidden. But if he said to him, "Wait until I sell my libation-wine [or my] idol and I'll bring you the proceeds," it is forbidden.

T. 7:17 He who makes an agreement to sell wine to an idolater, and agreed on the price and measured out the wine—even though he is going to dry out the siphons and the measures, it is permitted [cf. M. A.Z. 5:7C–D]. And a storekeeper, one way or the other, is permitted, for each drop as it comes becomes an obligation upon [the idolater] [M. A.Z. 5:7C–D]. An idolater who sent a flagon to an Israelite, and a drop of wine is in it—lo, this one fills up the flagon and takes from him the value of the whole of it and does not scruple [about libation-wine which may be in it].

There is no minimum volume of libation-wine that will invalidate that with which it is mixed. Any volume at all suffices to impart the status of idolatrous offerings to other wine. That rule, at M. Abodah Zarah 5:8, is then expanded to list other substances any small measure of which suffices to impart a prohibition to that with which they are mixed.

M. 5:8 Libation wine is forbidden and imparts a prohibition [to wine with which it is mixed] in any measure at all. [If it is] wine [poured] into wine, or [libation] water [poured] into water, in any quantity whatever [it is forbidden]. [If it is] wine [poured] into water or water [poured] into wine, [it is forbidden] if it imparts flavor. This is the governing principle: [If it is] one species [poured] into its own species [B], [it is forbidden] in any measure at all. [If it is] not [poured] into its own species [C], it is forbidden if it imparts flavor.

M. 5:9 These are forbidden and impose a prohibition in any measure at all: (1) libation wine, (2) an idol, (3) hides with a hole at the heart, (4) an ox which is to be stoned, (5) a heifer, the neck of which is to be broken, (6) birds belonging to a *mesora'*, (7) the hair cut off a Nazir (Num 6:18), (8) the [unredeemed] firstborn of an ass (Exod 13:13), (9) meat in milk, (10) the goat which is to be sent forth, (11) unconsecrated beasts which have been slaughtered in the

Temple courtyard—lo, these are forbidden and impose a prohibition in any measure at all.

M. 5:10 Libation wine that fell into a vat—the whole of [the vat] is forbidden for benefit.

M. 5:11 A stone wine press which an idolater covered with pitch—one scours it, and it is clean. And one of wood—let him scale off the pitch. And one of earthenware—even though one has scaled off the pitch, lo, this is forbidden.

M. 5:12 He who purchases utensils [for use with food] from an idolater—that which is usually immersed one must immerse. That which is usually scalded one must scald. That which is usually heated to a white-hot flame one must heat to a white-hot flame. A spit or gridiron one must heat to a white-hot flame. A knife one must polish, and it is clean.

T.   8:2 He who purchases utensils from idolaters [M. A.Z. 5:12A]—in the case of things which one knows have not been used, one immerses them and they are clean. In the case of things which one knows have been used, in the instance of cups and flasks, one rinses them in cold water [M. A.Z. 5:12B]. [If they were] pitchers, water-kettles, frying pans, or kettles, one rinses them in boiling water [M. A.Z. 5:12C]. In the case of knives, spits, and grid-irons, one heats them to a white heat, and they are clean [M. A.Z. 5:12D]. In the case of all of them which have been used before they have been polished, if one has scalded, immersed, or heated them to white heat, (and) lo, this is permitted.

T.   8:3 He whose wine-vats and olive-presses were unclean and who wants to clean them—the boards and the two posts supporting the beams of the press and the troughs does he dry, and they are clean. The cylinders of twigs and of hemp does he dry. As to those of bast and of reeds, he leaves them unused.

Analysis: The Problematics of the Topic, Abodah Zarah

The details that form the medium of the law coalesce into a few overarching principles. The Rabbinic sages do more than record facts. They adduce facts in evidence of propositions that they wish to register. They bring to the facts questions of their own. So in the law of Judaism is contained a topic to be spelled out, and there are questions that govern the exposition of the topic. That is what is meant by "the problematics of the topic." Describing the law then does not suffice. This account must now analyze its main features, to gain perspective on the whole.

While the Written Torah concerns itself with the disposition of idolatry—destroying idols, tearing down altars, and the like—the Oral Torah in the Halakhah considers the relationship of the Israelite to the idolater, who is assumed to practice idolatry. The Halakhah asks about the way in which the Israelite can interact with the idol-worshipping idolater in such a way as to be uncorrupted by his idolatry. So the treatment of the Halakhah of Abodah Zarah not only shifts the focus but vastly broadens the treatment of it, providing a handbook for the conduct of foreign relations between Israel and the idolaters. (In this regard Bavli-tractate Abodah Zarah commences with a massive and compelling essay on how Israel and the idolaters relate and why God has rejected the idolaters in favor of Israel, the Torah supplying the center of the discussion.) The relationship between the two components of the Torah may be simply stated: the Written Torah provides instruction on destroying idolatry, in the premise that Israel has the opportunity to do so. The Halakhah of the Oral Torah explains how to coexist with idolatry, recognizing that Israel has no choice but to do so.

The question arises how exactly the Israelite is supposed to live in a world dominated by idolatry, and how Israel is subjugated to pagan nations to conduct its life with God. The question is not one that concerns the morale of holy Israel, let alone its theological apologetics. Rather, at issue is the conduct of everyday life—a fine instance of what is meant when it is claimed that the Halakhah takes up issues of the interiority of Israel's life, the inner structure and architectonics of its everyday life. In the present case, the problematics find their definition in differentiating what is absolutely forbidden for all purposes, what is forbidden for Israelite use but permitted for Israelite trade, and what is wholly permitted for both trade and utilization. The tractate focuses upon commercial transactions; personal relationships are not at the center of the exposition and do not precipitate the more protracted exegeses of the topic.

The tractate signals its problematics when it opens with rules on how to deal with idolaters before and after festivals. The issue bears heavy consequence, and the presentation of the Halakhah accords the position of prominence to what must be deemed the most fundamental question the Halakhah must address. That concerns whether Israelites participate in the principal trading occasions of the life of commerce, which are permeated with idolatrous celebration.

Since the festival defined a principal occasion for holding a market, and since it was celebrated with idolatrous rites, the mixture of festival and fair formed a considerable problem for the Israelite merchant. Sages, with their focus upon the householder, by definition an enlandised component of the social order, identified the principal unit of (agricultural) production with the main building block of Israelite society, and they gave nothing to the Israelite traders. Indeed, they so legislated as to close off a major channel of commerce. In connection with idolater festivals, which were celebrated with fairs, Israelites—meaning, traders, commercial players of all kinds—could not enter into business relationships with idolater counterparts (let alone themselves participate). Cutting off all contractual ties, lending or borrowing in any form, meant the Israelite traders in no way could participate in a principal medium of trade. That principle is announced at the outset, and the Tosefta amplifies and supplies many details to instantiate the main point. The Mishnah's prohibition of all commercial relationships is simply repeated by the Tosefta's, "A person should not do business with an idolater on the day of his festival."

But the sages differentiate between actual commercial relationships on the occasion of festivals and fairs, on the one hand, and transactions of a normal, humane character, on the other. They do not require Israelites to act out Scripture's commandments utterly to destroy idolatry; they permit them to maintain normal social amenities with their neighbors, within some broad limits. The effect is to reshape Scripture's implacable and extreme rulings into a construction more fitting for an Israel that cannot complete the task of destroying idolatry but is not free to desist from trying.

The Halakhah encompasses, also, relationships other than commercial ones. The basic theory of idolaters, all of them assumed to be idolaters, is, first, idolaters always and everywhere and under any circumstance are going to perform an act of worship for one or another of their gods. Second, idolaters are represented as thoroughly depraved (not being regenerated by the Torah), so they will murder, fornicate, or steal any chance they get; they routinely commit bestiality, incest, and various other forbidden acts of sexual congress. Within that datum, the Halakhah will be worked out, and the problematics then precipitates thought on how Israel is to protect itself in a world populated by utterly immoral persons, wholly outside of the framework of the Torah and its government. Basically, the Halakhah embodies the same principle of compromise where possible but rigid conformity to the principles of the Torah under all circumstances, at whatever cost, that governed commercial transactions. Just as Israel must give up all possibility of normal trading relationships with idolaters, depriving itself of the most lucrative transactions, those involving fairs, so Israel must avoid more than routine courtesies and necessary exchanges with idolaters.

That prohibition involves the principle that one must avoid entering into situations of danger, e.g., allowing for opportunities for idolaters to carry out their natural instincts of murder, bestiality, and the like. Cattle are not to be left in their inns, a woman may not be left alone with idolaters, nor a man, the former by reason of probable fornication, the latter, murder, on the part of the idolater. Their physicians are not to be trusted, though when it comes to using them for beasts, that is all right. One also must avoid appearing to conduct oneself as if he were an idolater, even if he is not actually doing so, thus if while someone is in front of an idol, he got a splinter in his foot, he should not bend over to remove it, because he looks as though he is bowing down to the idol. But if it does not look that way, he is permitted to do so. But there are objects that are assumed to be destined for idolatrous worship, and these under all circumstances are forbidden for Israelite trade. Israelites simply may not sell to idolaters anything that idolaters are likely to use, or that they explicitly say they are intending to use, for idolatry. That includes wine and the like. Whatever idolaters have used for idolatry may not be utilized afterward by Israelites, and that extends to what is left over from an offering, e.g., of meat or wine. Israelites also may not sell to idolaters anything they are going to use in an immoral way, e.g., wild animals for the arena, materials for the construction of places in which idolater immorality or injustice will occur, ornaments for an idol, and the like.

Israelites may, however, derive benefit from, that is, conduct trade in, what has not been directly used for idolatrous purposes. The appurtenances of wine, e.g., skins or tanks, may be traded, but not used for their own needs by Israelites. In the case of jars that have served for water, Israelites may use the jars and put wine into them; idolaters are not assumed to offer water to their idols, so too, brine or fish-brine. Idolater milk, bread, oil, and the like, may be traded by Israelites. When it comes to milk Israelites have supervised, or honey, and the like, Israelites may purchase and eat such commodities. What idolaters never use for idolatry is acceptable.

When the Halakhah comes to treat idols themselves, there are found no surprises and few problems that require much subtle analysis. Idols are to be destroyed and disposed of—no surprises there. The Scripture has provided the bulk of the Halakhah, and the Oral Torah in the Mishnah and its successor-documents contribute only a recapitulation of the main points, with some attention to interstitial problems of merely exegetical interest. When it comes to the asherah, the Merkolis, and the nullification of an idol, the Halakhah presents no surprises. When it comes to libation wine, the issue is equally unremarkable. But the details here show the same concern that readers noticed in connection with trade.

These details pertain to how the Israelite is to live side by side with the idolater in the land. Here sages find space for the householder-farmer to conduct his enterprise, that is, idolater workers may be employed and idolater produce may be utilized. The contrast with the blanket prohibition against participating in trade fairs proves striking; here sages find grounds for making possible a kind of joint venture that, when it comes to the trade fair, they implacably prohibit. Thus they recognize that the idolaters do not deem as wine suitable for libation the grapes in various stages of preparation. Idolater grapes may be purchased, even those that have been trodden. Idolater workers may participate to a certain point as well. Israelite workers may accept employment with idolaters in the winepress. The basic point is not particular to wine-making; the Halakhah recognizes that faithful Israelites may work with other Israelites, meaning, those who do not keep the Halakhah as sages define it, subject to limitations that where there is clear violation of the law, the Israelite may not participate in that part of the venture. The Halakhah generally treats the idolater as likely to perform his rites whenever he can, but also as responsive to Israelite instructions wherever it is to the idolater's advantage or Israelite supervision is firm.

Interpretation: Religious Principles of Abodah Zarah

The Halakhah takes as its religious problem making the distinction between Israelites and idolaters concrete. It demonstrates where and how the distinction makes a huge difference in the practice of everyday affairs. What is at stake is that Israel stands for life, the idolaters, like their idols, for death. An asherah tree, like a corpse, conveys uncleanness to those who pass underneath it, as are noted at M. 3:8: "And he should not pass underneath it, but if he passed underneath it, he is unclean." That is comparable to the law set forth at Numbers 19:1ff.: the uncleanness conveyed by the corpse to whatever is located underneath the same tent as the corpse.

Before proceeding, let us consider a clear statement of why idolatry defines the boundary between Israel and everybody else. The reason is that idolatry—rebellious arrogance against God—encompasses the entire Torah. The religious duty to avoid idolatry is primary; if one violates the religious duties, he breaks the yoke of commandments, and if he violates that single religious duty, he violates the entire Torah. Violating the prohibition against idolatry is equivalent to transgressing all Ten Commandments.

The Halakhah treats idolaters as undifferentiated, but as individuals. The Aggadah treats idolaters as "the nations" and takes no interest in individuals or in transactions between private persons. In the theology of the Oral Torah, the category idolaters or the nations, without elaborate differentiation, encompasses all who are non-Israelites, or those who do not belong to Israel and therefore do not know and serve God. That category takes on meaning only as complementary and opposite to its generative counterpart, having no standing—self-defining characteristics—on its own.

That is, since Israel encompasses the sector of humanity that knows and serves God by reason of God's self-manifestation in the Torah, the idolaters are comprised by everybody else: those placed by their own intention and active decision beyond the limits of God's revelation. Guided by the Torah Israel worships God; without its illumination idolaters worship idols. At the outset, therefore, the main point registers: by "idolaters" sages understand God's enemies, and by "Israel" sages understand those who know God as God has made himself known, which is through the Torah. In no way does the account deal with secular categories, but with theological ones.

The Halakhah then serves as the means for the translation of theological conviction into social policy. Idolaters are assumed to be ready to murder any Israelite they can get their hands on, rape any Israelite women, commit bestiality with any Israelite cow. The Oral Torah cites few cases to indicate that that conviction responds to ordinary, everyday events; the hostility to idolaters flows from a theory of idolatry, not the facts of everyday social intercourse, which sages recognize is full of neighborly cordiality. Then why the law takes for granted that idolaters routinely commit the mortal sins of not merely idolatry but bestiality, fornication, and murder remains to be explained. That assumption is because the Halakhah takes as its task the realization of the theological principle that those who hate Israel hate God, those who hate God hate Israel, and God will ultimately vanquish Israel's enemies as his own—just as God too was redeemed from Egypt. So the theory of idolatry, involving alienation from God, accounts for the wicked conduct imputed to idolaters, without regard to whether, in fact, that is how idolaters conduct themselves. That matter of logic is stated in so many words as readers saw in chapter 1, Sifré to Numbers LXXXIV:IV.

When God blesses idolater nations, they do not acknowledge him but blaspheme, but when he blesses Israel, they glorify him and bless him; these judgments elaborate the basic principle that the idolaters do not know God, and Israel does. But what emerges here is that even when the idolaters ought to recognize God's hand in their affairs, even when God blesses them, they still deny him, turning ignorance into willfulness. What is striking is the exact balance of three idolaters as against three Israelites, all of the status of world-rulers, the common cluster—Pharaoh, Sennacherib, and Nebuchadnezzar—versus the standard cluster—David, Solomon, and Daniel:

Pesiqta deRab Kahana XXVIII:I.1

    A. "On the eighth day you shall have a solemn assembly. [You shall do no laborious work, but you shall offer a burnt-offering, an offering by fire, a pleasing odor to the Lord. . . . These you shall offer to the Lord at your appointed feasts in addition to your votive-offerings and your freewill-offerings, for your burnt-offerings and for your cereal-offerings and for your drink-offerings and for your peace-offerings]" (Num 29:35-39):

B. But you have increased the nation, "O Lord, you have increased the nation; [you are glorified; you have enlarged all the borders of the land]" (Isa 17:25).

The proposition having been stated, the composer proceeds to amass evidence for the two contrasting propositions, first idolater rulers:

C. You gave security to the wicked Pharaoh. Did he then call you "Lord?" Was it not with blasphemies and curses that he said, "Who is the Lord, that I should listen to his voice!" (Exod 5:2).

D. You gave security to the wicked Sennacherib. Did he then call you "Lord"? Was it not with blasphemies and curses that he said, "Who is there among all the gods of the lands" (2 Kgs 18:35).

E. You gave security to the wicked Nebuchadnezzar. Did he then call you "Lord"? Was it not with blasphemies and curses that he said, "And who is God to save you from my power" (Dan 3:15).

Now, nicely balanced, come Israelite counterparts:

F. ". . . you have increased the nation; you are glorified":

G. You gave security to David and so he blessed you: "David blessed the Lord before all the congregation" (1 Chr 29:10).

H. You gave security to his son, Solomon, and so he blessed you: "Blessed is the Lord who has given rest to his people Israel" (1 Kgs 8:56).

I. You gave security to Daniel and so he blessed you: "Daniel answered and said, 'Blessed be the name of God' (Dan 2:20)."

Here is another set of opposites—three enemies, three saints, a fair match. In each case, the Israelite responded to God's favor with blessings, and the idolater with blasphemy. In this way the idolaters show the price they pay for not knowing God but serving no gods instead. A single cause accounts for diverse phenomena; the same factor that explains Israel has also to account for the opposite, that is, the idolaters; what Israel has, idolaters lack, and that common point has made all the difference. Idolatry is what angers God and turns him against the idolaters, stated in so many words at b. A.Z. 1:1 I.23/4b:

That time at which God gets angry comes when the kings put their crowns on their heads and prostrate themselves to the sun. Forthwith the Holy One, blessed be He, grows angry.

That is why it is absolutely forbidden to conduct any sort of commerce with idolaters in connection with occasions of idolatrous worship, e.g., festivals and the like.

Sages must devote a considerable account to the challenge to God's justice represented by the power and prosperity of idolaters and Israel's subordination and penury. For if the story of the moral order tells about justice that encompasses all creation, the chapter of idolaters' rule vastly disrupts the account. Gentile rule forms the point of tension, the source of conflict, attracting attention and demanding explanation. The critical problematic inherent in the category, Israel, is that its anticategory, the idolaters, dominate. So what rationality of a world ordered through justice accounts for the world ruled by idolaters. And that explains why the systemic problematic focuses upon the question, how justice can be thought to order the world if the idolaters rule. That formulation furthermore establishes the public counterpart to the private perplexity: that the wicked prosper and the righteous suffer. The two challenges to the conviction of the rule of moral rationality—idolaters' hegemony, and the prosperity of wicked persons—match.

Here the Halakhah makes an important point. The Halakhah presupposes not idolaters' hegemony but only their power; and it further takes for granted that Israelites may make choices, may specifically refrain from trading in what idolaters value in the service of their gods, and may hold back from idolaters what idolaters require for that service. In this regard the Halakhah parts company from the Aggadah, the picture gained by looking inward not corresponding to the outward-facing perspective. Focused upon interiorities that prove real and tangible, not matters of theological theory at all, the Halakhah of Abodah Zarah legislates for a world in which Israelites, while subordinate in some ways, control their own conduct and govern their own destiny. Israelites may live in a world governed by idolaters, but they form intentions and carry them out. They may decide what to sell and what not to sell, whom to hire for what particular act of labor and to whom not to sell their own labor, and, above all, Israelite traders may determine to give up opportunities denied them by the circumstance of idolatry.

The Halakhah therefore makes a formidable statement of Israel's freedom to make choices, its opportunity within the context of everyday life to preserve a territory free of idolatrous contamination, much as Israel in entering the land was to create a territory free of the worship of idols and their presence. In the setting of world order Israel may find itself subject to the will of others, but in the House of Israel, Israelites can and should establish a realm for God's rule and presence, free of idolatry. To establish a domain for God, Israelites must practice self-abnegation, refrain from actions of con-siderable weight and consequence—much of the Torah concerns itself with what people are not supposed to do—and God's rule comes to realization in acts of restraint.

Accordingly, the religious problem of the Halakhah focuses on the inner world of Israel in command of itself. The religious problem of the Aggadah, by contrast, rationalizes as best it can idolaters' hegemony, which the Halakhah takes for granted that idolaters simply do not exercise. The Halakhah sees that world within Israel's dominion for which Israel bears responsibility; there sages legislate. The Aggadah forms a perspective upon the world subject to idolater rule; that is, the world beyond the limits of Israel's own power. The Halakhah speaks of Israel at the heart of matters, the Aggadah, of Israel within humanity.

To see the contrast between the Halakhah and the Aggadah on idolaters, a brief reprise the Aggadic account of the matter serves. Who, speaking cat-egorically not historically, indeed these "non-Israelites," called idolaters ("the nations," "the peoples," and the like) remains to be explained. The answer is dictated by the definition of who exactly a "non-Israelite" is. Then the answer concerning the signified is always relative to its signifier, Israel. Within humanity-other-than-Israel, differentiation articulates itself along gross, political lines, always in relationship to Israel. If humanity is differen-tiated politically, then, it is a differentiation imposed by what has happened between a differentiated portion of humanity and Israel. It is, then, that seg-ment of humanity that under given circumstances has interacted with Israel: [1] Israel arising at the end and climax of the class of world empires, Babylonia, Media, Greece, Rome; or [2] Israel against Egypt; or [3] Israel against Canaan. That is the point at which Babylonia, Media, Greece, Rome, Egypt, or Canaan take a place in the narrative, become actors for the moment, but never givens, never enduring native categories. Then, when politics do not impose their structure of power-relationships, then humanity is divided between Israel and everyone else.

In the story of the moral plan for creation, the nations find their pro-portionate position in relationship to Israel. If the nations acquire impor-tance by reason of their dealings with Israel, the monarchies that enjoy prominence benefit because they ruled Israel:

Mekhilta attributed to R. Ishmael XX:II.5–7

5. A.   ". . . the mind of Pharaoh and his servants was changed toward the peo-ple":

    B.   This indicates that when the Israelites went out of Egypt, the monar-chy of the Egyptians came to an end,

    C.   as it is said, "Who are our servants?"

6. A. "[and they said, 'What is this that we have done, that we have let Israel go] from serving us?'"

    B. "Who are our servants?" They said, "Now all the nations of the world will be chiming in against us like a bell, saying, 'Now these, who were in their domain, they let go to leave them, how!'

    C. "Now how are we going to send to Aram Naharaim and Aram Soba officers and taskmasters to bring us slave-boys and slave-girls?"

    D. This indicates that Pharaoh ruled from one end of the world to the other, having governors from one end of the world to the other.

    E. This was for the sake of the honor of Israel.

    F. Of Pharaoh it is said, "The king sent and loosed him, even the ruler of peoples, and set him free" (Ps 105:20).

The narrative now recapitulates the matter, moving through the sequence, Assyria, then the recurring cluster of Babylonia, Media, Greece, and Rome, the last four standing for the world empires to that time, the first six centuries C.E., so far as sages' memories reconstructed history:

7. A. And so you find that every nation and language that subjugated Israel ruled from one end of the world to the other, for the sake of the honor of Israel.

    B. What does Scripture say in connection with Assyria? "And my hand has found as a nest the riches of the peoples, and as one gathers lost eggs have I gathered all the earth, and there was none that moved the wing or opened the mouth or chirped" (Isa 10:14).

    C. What does Scripture say of Babylonia? "And it shall come to pass that the nation and kingdom that will not serve this same Nebuchadnezzar, king of Babylonia" (Jer 27:8).

    D. What does Scripture say of Media? "Then king Darius wrote to all the peoples" (Dan 6:26).

    E. What does Scripture say of Greece? "The beast had also four heads and dominion was given to it" (Dan 7:6).

    F. What does Scripture say of the fourth kingdom [Rome]? "And shall devour the whole earth and shall tread it down and break it in pieces" (Dan 7:23).

    G. So you learn that every nation and language that subjugated Israel ruled from one end of the world to the other, for the sake of the honor of Israel.

A nation is distinguished by its interaction with Israel, and that interaction brings about the magnification of the name of that nation. It would be difficult to express with greater power the proposition that Israel then forms the center and heart of humanity, and the idolaters circle in their orbits around it. Little in the Halakhic repertoire recapitulates these convictions, which the Halakhah in no way acknowledges. For the Halakhah matters are very different.

What difference there is between the idolater and the Israelite, individually and collectively (there being no distinction between the private person and the public, social and political entity) has to be specified. A picture in cartographic form of the theological anthropology of the Oral Torah would portray a many-colored Israel at the center of the circle, with the perimeter comprised by all-white idolaters, since, in the Halakhah, idolaters like their idols are a source of uncleanness of the same virulence as corpse-uncleanness. The perimeter would be an undifferentiated white, the color of death. The law of uncleanness bears its theological counterpart in the lore of death and resurrection, a single theology animating both. Idolater-idolaters and Israelite worshippers of the one and only God part company at death. For the moment Israelites die but rise from the grave, idolaters die and remain there. The roads intersect at the grave, each component of humanity taking its own path beyond. Israelites—meaning, those possessed of right conviction—will rise from the grave, stand in judgment, but then enter upon eternal life, to which no one else will enjoy access. So, in substance, humanity viewed as a whole is divided between those who get a share in the world to come—Israel—and those who will not.

Clearly, the moral ordering of the world encompasses all humanity. But God does not neglect the idolaters or fail to exercise dominion over them. For even now, idolaters are subject to a number of commandments or religious obligations. God cares for idolaters as for Israel. He wants idolaters as much as Israel to enter the kingdom of heaven, and he assigns to idolaters opportunities to evince their acceptance of his rule. One of these commandments is not to curse God's name:

> b. San. 7:5 I.2/56a
>> A.B. "Any man who curses his God shall bear his sin" (Lev 24:15)":
>> C. It would have been clear had the text simply said, "A man."
>> D. Why does it specify, "Any"?
>> E. It serves to encompass idolaters, who are admonished not to curse the Name, just as Israelites are so admonished.

Not cursing God, even while worshipping idols, seems a minimal expectation.

But, in fact there are seven such religious obligations that apply to the children of Noah. It is not surprising—indeed, it is predictable—that the definition of the matter should find its place in the Halakhah of Abodah Zarah, where the Tosefta situates it:

> Tosefta-tractate Abodah Zarah 8:4–6
> T. 8:4 A. Concerning seven religious requirements were the children of Noah admonished:

B. Setting up courts of justice, idolatry, blasphemy [cursing the Name of God], fornication, bloodshed, and thievery.

The text now proceeds to show how each of these religious obligations is represented as applying to idolaters as much as to Israelites:

C. Concerning setting up courts of justice—how so [how does Scripture or reason validate the claim that idolaters are to set up courts of justice]?

D. Just as Israelites are commanded to call into session in their towns courts of justice.

E. Concerning idolatry and blasphemy—how so? . . .

F. Concerning fornication—how so?

G. "On account of any form of prohibited sexual relationship on account of which an Israelite court inflicts the death-penalty, the children of Noah are subject to warning," the words of R. Meir.

H. And sages say, "There are many prohibited relationships, on account of which an Israelite court does not inflict the death-penalty and the children of Noah are [not] warned. In regard to these forbidden relationships the nations are judged in accord with the laws governing the nations.

1. "And you have only the prohibitions of sexual relations with a betrothed maiden alone."

The systemization of Scripture's evidence for the stated proposition continues:

T. 8:5   A. For bloodshed—how so?

B. An idolater [who kills] an idolater and an idolater who kills an Israelite are liable. An Israelite [who kills] an idolater is exempt.

C. Concerning thievery?

D. [If] one has stolen, or robbed, and so too in the case of finding a beautiful captive [woman], and in similar cases:

E. an idolater in regard to an idolater, or an idolater in regard to an Israelite—it is prohibited. And an Israelite in regard to an idolater—it is permitted.

T. 8:6   A. Concerning a limb cut from a living beast—how so?

B. A dangling limb on a beast, [which] is not [so connected] as to bring about healing,

C. is forbidden for use by the children of Noah, and, it goes without saying, for Israelites.

D. But if there is [in the connecting flesh] sufficient [blood supply] to bring about healing,

E. it is permitted to Israelites, and, it goes without saying, to the children of Noah.

As in the case of Israelites, so the death penalty applies to a Noahide, so:

b. San. 7:5 I.4–5/57a

> On account of violating three religious duties are children of Noah put
> to death: on account of adultery, murder, and blasphemy.
> R. Huna, R. Judah, and all the disciples of Rab say, "On account of
> seven commandments a son of Noah is put to death. The All-Merciful
> revealed that fact of one of them, and the same rule applies to all of
> them.

But just as Israelites, educated in the Torah, are assumed to exhibit certain
uniform virtues, e.g., forbearance, so idolaters, lacking that same education,
are assumed to conform to a different model.

Idolaters, by reason of their condition outside of the Torah, are characterized by certain traits natural to their situation, and these are worldly. In
addition, the sages' theology of idolaters shapes the normative law in how to
relate to them. If an Israelite by nature imparted in the Torah is forbearing
and forgiving, the idolater by nature is ferocious. That explains why in the
Halakhah as much as in the Aggadah idolaters are always suspect of the cardinal sins—bestiality, fornication, and bloodshed—as well as constant idolatry. That view of matters is embodied in normative law.

In chapters 1 and 2, we have seen that the law of the Mishnah corresponds to the lore of scriptural exegesis; the theory of the idolaters governs
in both. Beyond the Torah there is not only no salvation from death, there
is not even the possibility of a common decency. The Torah makes all the difference. The upshot may be stated very simply. Israel and the idolaters form
the two divisions of humanity. The one division, called Israel, will die but
rise from the grave to eternal life with God. When the other division, called
idolaters, dies, it perishes; that is the end. Moses said it very well: choose life.
The idolaters sustain comparison and contrast with Israel, the point of ultimate division being death for the one, eternal life for the other.

That leaves open the question, how Israel, sinful as is the nature of
humanity, is to restore and maintain its relationship with God. That carries
us from the outside of the Rabbinic system of law and theology to its interior: the matter of repentance and atonement.

Chapter 3

The Aggadic Theology of Sin, Repentance, and Atonement

Defining Sin

Judaism deals with both the outside world and the inner life of Israel, the holy people. We have now seen how lore and law negotiate the world of the borders and beyond, so defining Israel in relationship with the gentiles in terms of Israel's relationship to God. That raises the question: What of that relationship when Israel sins? From relationships with outsiders, the narrative now turns to the interior dynamics of Rabbinic theology: the relationship with God of the Israelite and of corporate Israel, which forms a moral entity subject to God's judgment unique in humanity. Each person individually is subject to divine rule. Israel collectively, not solely Israelites individually, is judged as well. Concerning the matter of sin, repentance, and atonement, the Aggadic exposition produces a cogent narrative. The Halakhic counterpart does the same. But the two tales scarcely intersect. The one—the Aggadah—explains the human condition, reaching back to the narrative of the fall from Eden, and the other, the Halakhah, devotes itself to atoning for sin through the blood-rite of the Temple on the Day of Atonement. Only at the very end—as readers will see in the conclusion of chapter 4—do the two narratives come together in a sublime account of God's requirement for authentic repentance and true atonement.

Sin explains the condition of Israel. The governing theory of Israel, that had Israel kept the Torah from the beginning, holy Israel would never have had any history at all but would have lived in a perfect world at rest and balance and order, is now invoked. There would have been nothing to write down, no history, had Israel kept the Torah. None can imagine a more explicit statement of how the world order is disrupted by sin, and, specifically, sinful attitudes, than the following:

Bavli-tractate Nedarim 3:1 I.14ff./22a–b

I.18 A. Said R. Ada b. R. Hanina, "If the Israelites had not sinned, to them would have been given only the Five Books of the Torah and the book of Joshua alone, which involves the division of the Land of Israel.

B. "How come? 'For much wisdom proceeds from much anger' (Qoh. 1:18)."

Adam ought to have stayed in Eden. With the Torah in hand, Israel, the new Adam, ought to have remained in the land, beyond the reach of time and change, exempt from the events of interesting times. Sin ruined everything, for Adam, for Israel, bringing about the history recorded in Scripture—not a very complicated theodicy.

That the theology of the Aggadah spins out a simple but encompassing logic makes the character of its treatment of sin entirely predictable. First, the system must account for imperfection in the world order of justice; sin supplies the reason. Second, it must explain how God remains omnipotent even in the face of imperfection. The cause of sin, humanity's free will corresponding to God's, tells why. Third, it must allow for systemic remission. Sin is so defined as to accommodate the possibility of regeneration and restoration. And, finally, sin must be presented to fit into the story of the creation of the perfect world.

Defined in the model of the first sin, the one committed by Adam and Eve, representing all humanity, in Eden, sin is an act of rebellion against God. Rebellion takes two forms. As a gesture of omission sin embodies the failure to carry out one's obligation to God set forth in the Torah. As one of commission, it constitutes an act of defiance. In both cases sin comes about by reason of humanity's intentionality to reject the will of God, set forth in the Torah. However accomplished, whether through omission or commission, an act becomes sinful because of motivation—the attitude that accompanies the act. That is why humanity is responsible for sin, answerable to God in particular, who may be said to take the matter personally, just as it is meant. The consequence of sin is death for the individual, exile and estrangement for holy Israel, and disruption for the world. That is why sin accounts for much of the flaw of creation.

Since sin represents an act of rebellion against God, God has a heavy stake in the matter. It follows that sin in public is worse than sin in private, since in public one's sin profanes God's name:

Bavli-tractate Qiddushin 1:10 I.10/40a

A. Said R. Abbahu in the name of R. Hanina, "It is better for someone to transgress in private but not profane the name of heaven in public: 'As for you, house of Israel, thus says the Lord God: Go, serve every one his idols, and hereafter also, if you will not obey me; but my holy name you shall not profane' (Ezek 20:39)."

B. Said R. Ilai the Elder, "If someone sees that his impulse to sin is overpowering him, he should go somewhere where nobody knows him and put on ordinary clothing and cloak himself in ordinary clothing and do what he wants, but let him not profane the name of heaven by a public scandal."

Sin therefore defines one important point at which God and humanity meet and world order is affected. The just arrangement of matters that God has brought about in creation can be upset by humanity's intervention, for humanity alone has the will and freedom to stand against God's plan and intention for creation.

It follows that the consequences of the correspondence of God and humanity account for all else. If the one power in all of creation that can and does stand against the will of God is humanity's will or intentionality, then humanity bears responsibility for the flawed condition of creation. God's justice comes to its fullest expression in the very imperfection of existence, a circularity that marks a well-crafted, severely logical system. But free will also forms the source of remission; God's mercy intervenes when humanity's will warrants. Specifically, God restores the perfection of creation by providing atonement through repentance. That presents no anomaly but conforms to the encompassing theory of matters. Repentance represents another act of human will that, like the transaction that yields *zekhut*, is countered with a commensurate act of God's will. The entire story of the world, start to finish, therefore records the cosmic confrontation of God's will and humanity's freedom to form and carry out an intention contrary to God's will. The universe is not animate but animated by the encounter of God and, in his image, after his likeness, humanity—the story, the only story, that the Oral Torah recapitulates from, and tells in completion of, the Written Torah.

The moral order encompasses exactly commensurate penalties for sin, the logic of a perfectly precise recompense forming the foundation of the theory of world order set forth by the Aggadah. But knowing the just penalty tells us little about the larger theory of how sin disrupts the perfection of the world created by the one, just God. Since sin is deemed not personal alone but social and even cosmic, explaining sin carries us to the very center of matters. What is at stake in sin is succinctly stated: it accounts for the deplorable condition of the world, defined by the situation of Israel. But sin is not a permanent feature of world order. It is an orderly progression, as God to begin with had planned, from chaos, which gave way to creation, to the Torah, which after the Flood through Israel restored order to the world, and onward to the age of perfection and stasis. To understand that doctrine, this account must first examine the place of sin in the unfolding of creation. The history of the world is divided into these three periods, indicated by Israel's relationship with God:

> Bavli-tractate Abodah Zarah 1:1 II.5/9a
>
> A. The Tannaite authority of the household of Elijah [stated], "The world will last for six thousand years: two thousand years of chaos, two thousand years of Torah, two thousand years of the time of the Messiah. But because of the abundance of our sins, what has passed [of the foreordained time] has passed."

The "two thousand years of chaos" mark the period prior to the giving of the Torah at Sinai, as God recognized the result of creating humanity in his image and the consequence of the contest between humanity's will and God's. Then come the two thousand years of Torah, which is intended to educate humanity's will and endow humanity with the knowledge to want what God wants. Then comes the time of the Messiah. Now the persistence of sin has lengthened the time of the Torah and postponed the advent of the Messiah. It follows that, to understand how the sages account for the situation of the world in this age, revealing God's justice out of the elements of chaos in the here and now, readers must pay close attention to the character of the sages' doctrine of sin.

What has already been said about sin as an act of rebellion bears the implication that an act may or may not be sinful, depending upon the attitude of the actor, a view that our inquiry into intentionality has adumbrated. In fact only a few actions are treated as in themselves sinful. Chief among them are, specifically, murder, fornication, and idolatry. Under all circumstances a man must refrain from committing such actions, even at the cost of his own life. These represent absolute sins:

> Genesis Rabbah XXXI:VI.1
>
> A. Another matter: "For the earth is filled with violence" (Gen 6:13):
> B. Said R. Levi, "The word for violence refers to idolatry, fornication, and murder.
> C. "Idolatry: 'For the earth is filled with violence' (Gen 6:13).
> D. "Fornication: 'The violence done to me and to my flesh be upon Babylonia' (Jer 51:35). [And the word for 'flesh' refers to incest, as at Lev 18:6].

E.   "Murder: 'For the violence against the children of Judah, because they have shed innocent blood' (Joel 4:19).

F.   "Further, the word for 'violence' stands for its ordinary meaning as well."

Since these were the deeds of the generation of the Flood that so outraged God as to bring about mass destruction, they form a class of sin by themselves. The children of Noah, not only the children of Israel, must avoid these sins at all costs. But there is a sin that Israel may commit that exceeds even the cardinal sins. Even those three are forgivable, but rejection of the Torah is not:

Yerushalmi-tractate Hagigah 1:7/I:3

A.   R. Huna, R. Jeremiah in the name of R. Samuel bar R. Isaac: "We find that the Holy One, blessed be He, forgave Israel for idolatry, fornication, and murder. [But] for their rejection of the Torah he never forgave them."

B.   What is the scriptural basis for that view?

C.   It is not written, "Because they practiced idolatry, fornication, and murder," but rather, "And the Lord said, 'Because they have forsaken my Torah.'"

D.   Said R. Hiyya bar Ba, "'If they were to forsake me, I should forgive them, for they may yet keep my Torah. For if they should forsake me but keep my Torah, the leaven that is in [the Torah] will bring them closer to me.'"

E.   R. Huna said, "Study Torah [even if it is] not for its own sake, for, out of [doing so] not for its own sake, you will come [to study it] for its own sake."

Still, that the classification of an action, even of the most severe character, depends upon the intentionality or attitude of the actor governs even here.

An Israelite's rejection of the Torah is forthwith set into the context of will or intentionality. God does not object to insincerity when it comes to study of the Torah, because the Torah purifies. It itself contains the power to reshape the will of humanity (as framed succinctly by the sages elsewhere, "The commandments were given only to purify the heart of humanity," "God craves the heart," and similar formulations). The very jarring intrusion at D in the above passage, developing C but making its own point, underscores that conviction. God can forgive Israel for forsaking him, because if they hold on to the Torah, they will find their way back. The Torah will reshape Israel's heart. And then, amplifying that point but moving still further from the main proposition, comes Huna's sentiment, E, that studying the Torah does not require proper intentionality, because the Torah in due course will effect the proper intentionality. Two critical points emerge. First, intentionality plays a central role in the discussion of principal sins. Second, sin ordinarily does not form an absolute but only a relative category. An action that is sinful under one set of circumstances, when the intent is wicked, is not sinful but even subject to forgiveness under another set of circumstances.

That the variable of sin is humanity's intentionality in carrying out the action, not the intrinsic quality of most sinful actions (though not all), emerges in a striking formulation of matters. Here one finds a position that is remarkable, yet coherent with the principal stresses of the theology of the Aggadah. Sages maintain that it is better sincerely to sin than hypocritically to perform a religious duty; to "sin boldly," the sages would respond, "No, rather, sin sincerely!" It would be difficult to state in more extreme language the view that all things are relative to attitude or intentionality than to recommend sincere sin over hypocritical virtue:

Bavli-tractate Horayot 3:1–2 I.11/10b
11. A. Said R. Nahman bar Isaac, "A transgression committed for its own sake, in a sincere spirit, is greater in value than a religious duty carried out not for its own sake, but in a spirit of insincerity.
B. "For it is said, 'May Yael, wife of Hever the Kenite, be blessed above women, above women in the tent may she be blessed' (Judg 5:24).
C. "Now who are these women in the tent? They are none other than Sarah, Rebecca, Rachel, and Leah." [The murder she committed gained more merit than the matriarchs great deeds.]

The saying shocks and is immediately challenged:

D. But is this really true, that a transgression committed for its own sake, in a sincere spirit, is greater in value than a religious duty carried out not for its own sake, but in a spirit of insincerity. And did not R. Judah say Rab said, "A person should always be occupied in study of the Torah and in practice of the commandments, even if this is not for its own sake [but in a spirit of insincerity], for out of doing these things not for their own sake, a proper spirit of doing them for their own sake will emerge"?
E. Say: it is equivalent to doing them not for their own sake.

Now the account reverts to the view that insincere Torah-study and practice of the commandments still have the power to transform a man:

12. A. Said R. Judah said Rab, "A person should always be occupied in study of the Torah and in practice of the commandments, even if this is not for its own sake [but in a spirit of insincerity], for out of doing these things not for their own sake, a proper spirit of doing them for their own sake will emerge."

Now comes a concrete case of blatant insincerity's producing a reward; the Messiah himself is the offspring of an act of hypocrisy on the part of Balak, the king of Moab, the ancestor of Ruth, from whom the scion of David, the Messiah, descends:

> B. For as a reward for the forty-two offerings that were presented by the wicked Balak to force Balaam to curse Israel, he was deemed worthy that Ruth should descend from him.
>
> C. For said R. Yosé b. R. Hanina, "Ruth was the granddaughter of Eglon, the grandson of Balak, king of Moab."

The upshot is, as readers already realize, intentionality or virtue is everything; sin is rarely absolute but ordinarily conditioned upon the attitude of the actor; and sincerity in sin exceeds in merit hypocrisy in virtue.

The Rabbinic sages find the origins of sin in the attitude of arrogance, the beginnings of virtue in that of humility. Arrogance leads to rebellion against God, humility, to submission to him. Israel, therefore, is in command of its own fate. Redemption depends upon righteousness, just as the present age comes about by reason of arrogance:

b. Shab. 20:1 III.10–12/139a

> A. It has been taught on Tannaite authority:
>
> B. R. Yosé b. Elisha says, "If you see a generation on which great troubles break, go and examine the judges of Israel, for any punishment that comes into the world comes only on account of the judges of Israel, as it is said, 'Hear this, please you heads of the house of Jacob and rulers of the house of Israel, who abhor judgment and pervert all equity. They build up Zion with blood and Jerusalem with iniquity. The heads thereof judge for reward, and the priests thereof teach for hire, and the prophets thereof divine for money, yet will they lean upon the Lord?' (Mic 3:9-11). They are wicked, yet they put their trust in him who by speaking brought the world into being. Therefore the Holy One, blessed be He, will bring upon them three punishments for three transgressions for which they bear responsibility, as it is said, 'Therefore shall Zion for your sake be ploughed as a field, and Jerusalem shall become heaps, and the mountain of the house as the high places of a forest' (Mic 3:12).
>
> C. "And the Holy One, blessed be He, will bring his Presence to rest on Israel only when the wicked judges and rulers will come to an end in Israel, as it is said, 'And I will turn my hand upon you and thoroughly purge away your dross and will take away all your tin, and I will restore your judges as at the first and your counselors as at the beginning' (Isa 1:25-26)."

Sages contrast righteousness and arrogance, the one effecting redemption, the other forming an obstacle to it:

> III.11 A. Said Ulla, "Jerusalem will be redeemed only through righteousness, as it is written, 'Zion shall be redeemed with judgment and her converts with righteousness' (Isa 1:27)."
>
> B. Said R. Pappa, "If the arrogant end [in Israel], the Magi will end [in Iran], if the judges end [in Israel], the rulers of thousands will come to an end [in Iran]. If the arrogant end [in Israel], the Magi will end [in Iran], as it is written, 'And I will purely purge away your haughty ones and take away all your sin' (Isa 1:25). If judges end [in Israel], the rulers of thousands will come to an end [in Iran], as it is written, 'The Lord has taken away your judgments, he has cast out your enemy' (Zeph 3:15)."

The theology therefore finds in arrogance the secret of Israel's subjugation, and in humility, of its redemption.

Given the sages' focus upon intentionality, it is not surprising that the matched traits of arrogance and humility should take priority in their systematic thinking about the imperfections of the world order. Arrogance perfectly embodies the bad attitude, and reason leads to the expectation that the arrogant will be cut down to size. If the arrogant person repents, however, then he abandons the bad attitude and adopts the good one, of humility, the condition of repentance. God is the model of humility, as is Moses. The resurrection of the dead involves the exaltation of the humble—dust itself. Scripture and parable serve to convey these points, but the system at its core insists upon them. But God favors the humble and accepts humility as equivalent to offerings in the Temple, responding to prayers of the humble.

Explaining Sin: Origin and Meaning

Why do people rebel against God? The answer is arrogance, which must be explained. Specifically, they become arrogant when they are prosperous; then they trust in themselves and take for granted that their own power has secured abundance. They forget that it is God who, by his act of will, has given them what they have gotten. Prosperity and success bear their own threatening consequence in the change of humanity's attitude that they may well bring about. So arrogance comes from an excess of good fortune, but it is the absence of humility that accounts for the wrong attitude:

> Sifré to Deuteronomy CCCXVIII:I.1ff.
>
> 1. A. ["So Jeshurun grew fat and kicked—you grew fat and gross and coarse—he forsook the God who made him and spurned the rock of his support. They incensed him with alien things, vexed him with

abominations. They sacrificed to demons, no-gods, gods they had never known, new ones, who came but lately, who stirred not your fathers' fears. You neglected the rock that begot you, forgot the God who brought you forth" (Deut 32:15-18).]

B.   "So Jeshurun grew fat and kicked":
C.   Out of satiety people rebel.

Now comes a standard trilogy of probative cases, the archetypal sinners: the generation of the Flood, the generation of the dispersion from the tower of Babel, and the generation of Sodom and Gomorrah. They will exhibit the same trait in common, and therefore prove the point at hand. In each case, people misunderstood their own prosperity and arrogantly claimed to control their own destiny. First comes the generation of the flood:

2.   A.   So you find in connection with the people of the generation of the flood, that they rebelled against the Holy One, blessed be He, only from an abundance of food, drink, prosperity.
     B.   What is said in their regard?
     C.   "Their houses are safe, without fear" (Job 21:9).
     D.   And so for the rest of the matter, as stated in connection with Deuteronomy.

Next is the generation of the dispersion from the tower of Babel:

3.   A.   So you find in connection with the people of the generation of the tower, that they rebelled against the Holy One, blessed be He, only from prosperity.
     B.   What is said in their regard?
     C.   "And the whole earth was of one language" (Gen 11:1).

Finally the narrative must come to Sodom:

4.   A.   So you find in connection with the people of Sodom, that they rebelled against the Holy One, blessed be He, only from abundance of food.
     B.   What is said in their regard?
     C.   "As for the earth, it produces bread" (Job 28:5).
     D.   And so for the rest.
     E.   And thus Scripture says, "As I live, says the Lord God, Sodom, your sister, has not done . . ." (Ezek 16:48f.).

Next the account moves from the idolaters to Israel, showing that the Israelites, too, rebel by reason of prosperity:

6.   A.   So you find in connection with the people of the wilderness, that they rebelled only out of an abundance of food.
     B.   For it is said, "And the people sat down to eat and drink and rose up to make merry" (Exod 32:6).

C. What then is stated in their regard? "They have turned aside quickly out of the way . . ." (Exod 32:8).

Then from Israel in general discussion reaches Israel in the land itself:

7. A. Said the Holy One, blessed be He, to Moses, "Say to Israel, 'When you enter the land, you are going to rebel only out of abundance of food, drink, and prosperity.'"
   B. For it is said, "For when I shall have brought them into the land which I swore to their fathers, flowing with milk and honey, and they shall have eaten their fill and gotten fat and turned to other gods and served them . . . " (Deut 31:20).
   C. Said Moses to Israel, "When you enter the land, you are going to rebel only out of abundance of food, drink, and prosperity."
   D. For it is said, "lest when you have eaten and are satisfied . . . and when your herds and flocks multiply . . . when your heart is lifted up and you forget the Lord your God" (Deut 8:12ff.).

Then comes Job, who presents no intractable challenge; his complaint is readily addressed:

8. A. So you find concerning the sons and daughters of Job, that punishment came upon them only out of eating and drinking.
   B. For it is said, "While he was yet speaking, another came and said, 'Your sons and your daughters were eating and drinking wine in their eldest brother's house and behold, there came a great wind'" (Job 12:18-19).

Then the story turns to the ten tribes, who end the list of those who have suffered severe penalties for their arrogance, therefore embodying Israel in exile by reason of sin:

9. A. So you find in the case of the ten tribes, that they went into exile only out of an abundance of eating, drinking, and prosperity.
   B. For it is said, "That lie on beds of ivory, that drink wine in bowls . . . therefore now shall they go captive at the head of them who go captive" (Amos 6:4, 6, 7).

Israel when the Messiah comes is the last case in the sequence from the beginning of the story of humanity to the end:

10. A. So you find in connection [even] with the days of the Messiah, that [the Israelites] are going to rebel only out of an abundance of eating and drinking.
    B. For it is said, "So Jeshurun grew fat and kicked—you grew fat and gross and coarse—he forsook the God who made him and spurned the rock of his support."

Given the high stakes in obedience to God's will—both nature and history respond to Israel's conduct, with dire results—why in the world, one asks, would anyone rebel anyhow. The answer is, people forget the precariousness of their existence, and, in times of prosperity, they rebel. The rest follows.

Here is the crux of the matter: humanity by nature is sinful, and only by encounter with the Torah knows how to do good. That explains why the idolaters, with idolatry in place of the Torah, in the end cannot overcome their condition but perish, while Israel, with Torah as the source of life, will stand in judgment and enter eternal life. The key to humanity's regeneration lies in that fact, that Israel, while part of humanity and by nature sinful, possesses the Torah. That is how and where Israel may overcome its natural condition. Herein lies the source of hope. Idolaters enjoy this world but have no hope of regeneration in the world to come. Here three distinct components of the theology of the Aggadah, [1] theological anthropology, [2] the doctrine of sin, and [3] eschatology intersect to make a single coherent statement accounting for the destiny of the whole of humanity.

The Consequences of Sin

The heaviest cost exacted by sin is neither individual nor communal but cosmic. Sin separated God from humanity. Humanity's arrogance, his exercise of his will to confront the will of God, brings about sin and ultimately exiled Israel from the Land of Israel. That same act of attitude estranges God from Israel. If sin cuts the individual off from God and diminishes him in the world, then the sin of all Israel produces the same result. The costs of sin to Israel have proved catastrophic. Just as Israel was given every advantage by reason of accepting the Torah, so by rejecting the Torah, death, exile, and suffering ensued. When Israel accepted the Torah, death, exile, and suffering and illness no longer ruled them. When they sinned, they incurred all of them. That is because God himself went into exile from the Temple, the city, the land. Matters begin with the penalty of alienation from God, marked by the advent of death:

Leviticus Rabbah XVIII:III.2ff.
2. A. "Yet the harvest will flee away (ND)" (Isa 17:11).
    B. You have brought on yourselves the harvest of the foreign governments, the harvest of violating prohibitions, the harvest of the angel of death.
    C. For R. Yohanan in the name of R. Eliezer, son of R. Yosé the Galilean, said, "When the Israelites stood before Mount Sinai and said, 'All that the Lord has said we shall do and we shall hear' [Exod 24:7]. At that very moment the Holy One, blessed be He, called the angel of death

and said to him, 'Even though I have made you world ruler over all of my creatures, you have no business with this nation. Why? For they are my children.' That is in line with the following verse of Scripture: 'You are the children of the Lord your God' (Deut 14:1)."

D. And it says, "And it happened that when you heard the voice out of the midst of the darkness" (Deut 5:20).

E. Now was there darkness above? And is it not written, "And the light dwells with Him" (Dan 2:22)?

F. That (D) refers to the angel who is called, "Darkness."

At Sinai, for the brief moment from the mass declaration, "We shall do and we shall obey," death died. But when Israel rebelled as Moses tarried on the mountain, sin took over, and the process of alienation from God got under way. Later on, readers will learn when and how death again will die, marking the end of time and change that commenced with Adam's sin. But the main point is clear. Death, exile, suffering, and illness do not belong to the order of nature; they have come about by reason of sin. Israel was exempt from them all when they accepted the Torah. But when they sinned, they returned to the natural condition of unredeemed humanity. A basic rationality then explains the human condition: people bring about their own fate. They possess the power to dictate their own destiny—by giving up the power to dictate to God.

But there is more to the costs of sin, the cosmic charge. Since God now finds himself alienated, he has abandoned not only Israel but the Temple, the city, the land—the world altogether. The estrangement of God from Israel is set forth in concrete terms, as a series of departures. This is set forth in a set of remarkably powerful statements, narratives of profound theological consequence. In one version, God's presence departed in ten stages, as God abandoned the people of Israel and they were estranged from him, and the Sanhedrin was banished in ten stages as well.

Bavli-tractate Rosh Hashanah 4:4A–E I.6/31A–B

[A] Said R. Judah bar Idi said R. Yohanan, "The divine presence [*Shekhinah*] made ten journeys [in leaving the land and people of Israel prior to the destruction of the first Temple]. [That is, "The Divine Presence left Israel by ten stages."] [This we know from] Scripture. And corresponding to these [stages], the Sanhedrin was exiled [successively to ten places of banishment]. [This we know from] tradition."

[B] The divine presence [*Shekhinah*] made ten journeys [in leaving the people, Israel, prior to the destruction of the first Temple]. [This we know from] Scripture: [It went]

(1) from the ark-cover to the cherub;

(2) and from the cherub to the threshold [of the Holy of Holies];

(3) and from the threshold to the [Temple] court;

(4) and from the court to the altar;

(5) and from the altar to [Temple] roof;

(6) and from the roof to the wall;

(7) and from the wall to the city;

(8) and from the city to the mountain;

(9) and from the mountain to the wilderness;

(10) and from the wilderness it ascended and dwelled in its place [in heaven]—as it is said: "I will return again to my place, [until they acknowledge their guilt and seek my face]" (Hos 5:15).

We are now given the facts of Scripture to sustain the point at hand:

[C] From the ark-cover to the cherub;

(2) and from the cherub to the threshold [of the Holy of Holies]—as it is written [proving that the original location of the divine presence was above the ark-cover]: " There I will meet with you, and [from above the ark-cover, from between the two cherubim that are upon the ark of the testimony], I will speak with you" (Exod 25:22). And [showing that, later, the divine presence had moved to the cherub] it is written: "He rode on a cherub and flew" (2 Sam 22:11). And [proving that the divine presence then moved to the threshold] it is written: "Now the glory of the God of Israel had gone up from the cherubim on which it rested to the threshold of the house" (Ezek 9:3).

(3) And from the threshold to the [Temple] court—as it is written: "And the house was filled with the cloud, and the court was full of the brightness of the glory of the Lord" (Ezek 10:4).

(4) And from the court to the altar—as it is written: "I saw the Lord standing beside the altar" (Amos 9:1).

(5) And from the altar to [Temple] roof—as it is written: "It is better to live in a corner of the roof [than in a house shared with a contentious woman]" (Prov 21:9).

(6) And from the roof to wall—as it is written ["He showed me]: behold, the Lord was standing beside a wall built with a plumb line" (Amos 7:1).

(7) And from the wall to the city—as it is written: "The voice of the Lord cries to the city" (Mic 6:9).

(8) And from the city to the mountain—as it is written: "And the glory of the Lord went up from the midst of the city and stood upon the mountain which is on the east side of the city" (Ezek 11:23).

(9) And from the mountain to the wilderness—as it is written: "It is better to live in a land of wilderness [than with a contentious and fretful woman]" (Prov 21:19).

(10)   And from the wilderness it ascended and dwelled in its place [in heaven]—as it is said: "I will return again to my place, [until they acknowledge their guilt and seek my face]" (Hos 5:15).

The systematic proof, deriving from Scripture, shows how God moved by stages from the inner sanctum of the Temple; but the climax comes at C.10, pointing toward the next stage in the unfolding of the theology of the Aggadah that concerns sin and atonement: the possibility of reconciliation and how this will take place. The language that is supplied contains the key.

The next phase in the statement before us expands on that point: God hopes for the repentance of Israel, meaning its freely given act of acceptance of God's will by a statement of a change in attitude—specifically, regret for its act of arrogance. This is articulated in what follows:

[D] Said R. Yohanan, "For sixth months, the divine presence waited on Israel [the people] in the wilderness, hoping lest they might repent. When they did not repent, it said, 'May their souls expire.' [We know this] as it says: 'But the eyes of the wicked will fail, all means of escape will elude them, and their [only] hope will be for their souls to expire' (Job 11:2)."

God's progressive estrangement in heaven finds its counterpart in the sequence of exiles that Israel's political institution suffered, embodying therein the exile of all Israel from the land:

[E] "And corresponding to these [stages through which the divine presence left Israel], the Sanhedrin was exiled [successively to ten places of banishment; this we know from] tradition." [The Sanhedrin was banished] (1) from the Chamber of Hewn Stone [in the inner court of the Temple] to the market; and (2) from the market into Jerusalem [proper], and (3) from Jerusalem to Yabneh, [31b] and (4) from Yabneh to Usha, and (5) from Usha [back] to Yabneh, and (6) from Yabneh [back] to Usha, (7) and from Usha to Shefar, and (8) from Shefar to Beth Shearim, and (9) from Beth Shearim to Sepphoris, and (10) from Sepphoris to Tiberias.

[F] And Tiberias is the lowest of them all [below sea-level at the Sea of Galilee, symbolic of the complete abasement of the Sanhedrin's authority]. [We know of the lowered physical location and reduced status of the Sanhedrin] as it is said: "And deep from the earth you shall speak" (Isa 29:4).

A different reading of the matter uses more general terms to account for the exile of the Sanhedrin, that is to say, the end of Israel's political existence:

[G] [Proposing a different description of the banishment of the Sanhedrin] R. Eleazar says, "There were [only] six [places of] banishment, as it

says: 'For (1) he has brought low the inhabitants of the height, the lofty
city. (2) He lays it low, (3) lays it low (4) to the ground, (5) he casts it
(6) to the dust' (Isa 26:5)."

[H]   Said R. Yohanan, "And from there are destined to be redeemed, as it
says: 'Shake yourself from the dust; arise!' (Isa 52:2)"

In the interim, God has abandoned the holy place to accept Israel's fate.

But there is another side: Israel in this account forms the medium for
bringing God back into the world. That stands to reason, for it is through
Israel that God relates to all humanity, and only to Israel that God has given
the Torah; indeed, Israel is defined as those who have accepted the Torah.
Hence if God abandons Israel, it is not to take up a location in some other
place of humanity, but to give up humanity. This then finds its localization
in movement through the heavens, rather than through the Temple.

God's progress out of the created world is therefore set forth with seven
movements, corresponding to the fixed stars (the visible planets) of the seven
firmaments, out of, and back into, the world; the implication is that the present condition of Israel also comes about by reason of sin and will be reme-
died through attainment of *zekhut*:

Pesiqta deRab Kahana I:i.3, 6

3.   A.   R. Tanhum, son-in-law of R. Eleazar b. Abina, in the name of R.
Simeon b. Yosni: "What is written is not, 'I have come into the garden,'
but rather, 'I have come back to my garden.' That is, 'to my canopy.'

      B.   "That is to say, to the place in which the principal [presence of God]
had been located to begin with.

      C.   "The principal locale of God's presence had been among the lower crea-
tures, in line with this verse: 'And they heard the sound of the Lord
God walking about' (Gen 3:8)."

6.   A.   [Reverting to 3.C,] the principal locale of God's presence had been
among the lower creatures, but when the first humanity sinned, it went
up to the first firmament.

      B.   The generation of Enosh came along and sinned, and it went up from
the first to the second.

      C.   The generation of the flood [came along and sinned], and it went up
from the second to the third.

      D.   The generation of the dispersion [came along] and sinned, and it went
up from the third to the fourth.

      E.   The Egyptians in the time of Abraham our father [came along] and
sinned, and it went up from the fourth to the fifth.

      F.   The Sodomites [came along], and sinned, . . . from the fifth to the
sixth.

      G.   The Egyptians in the time of Moses . . . from the sixth to the seventh.

Now God returns to the world through the founders of Israel:

> H. And, corresponding to them, seven righteous men came along and brought it back down to earth:
> I. Abraham our father came along and acquired merit, and brought it down from the seventh to the sixth.
> J. Isaac came along and acquired merit and brought it down from the sixth to the fifth.
> K. Jacob came along and acquired merit and brought it down from the fifth to the fourth.
> L. Levi came along and acquired merit and brought it down from the fourth to the third.
> M. Kehath came along and acquired merit and brought it down from the third to the second.
> N. Amram came along and acquired merit and brought it down from the second to the first.
> O. Moses came along and acquired merit and brought it down to earth.
> P. Therefore it is said, "On the day that Moses completed the setting up of the Tabernacle, he anointed and consecrated it"(Num 7:1).

God yearns for Israel, but Israel is estranged; why that is the case demands explanation. The required explanation appeals to Israel's sin. The same explanation, in more explicit language, emerges in the account of how God departed from the world. The estrangement took place by reason of the sins of one generation after another. Then the merit of successive generations of Israel brought God back to the world.

Both the question and the answer derive from the sustaining system. The two accounts—God leaves the world by reason of humanity's sin, is brought back through Israel's saints; God leaves the world by reason of Israel's sin but can be restored to the world by Israel's act of repentance—match. They conform to the theory of Israel as the counterpart to humanity, the other Adam, the land as counterpart to Eden, and, now readers see, the exile of Israel as counterpart to the fall of humanity. The first set—God abandons the Temple—without the second story would leave an imbalance; only when the one story is told in the setting of the other does the theology make its complete statement.

If the sages' theology builds upon the foundation of God's justice in creating a perfect world and accounts for the imperfections of the world by appeal to the conflict of humanity's will and God's plan, then people must find the logical remedy for the impasse at which, in the present age, Israel and the world find themselves. Their explanation for flaws and transience in creation, sin brought about by the free exercise of humanity's will, contains within itself the systemic remission—that required, logical remedy for the human condition and creation's as well. It is an act of will to bring about reconciliation between God and Israel, God and the world. And that act of will on humanity's part will evoke an equal and commensurate act of will on God's part. When humanity repents, God forgives, and Israel and the world will attain that perfection that prevailed at Eden. And that is why death will die. Next readers come to the account of restoring world order. Here the restorationist theology of eschatology unfolds, completing and perfecting the sages' theology set forth in the documents of the Aggadah.

Repentance and Atonement

The logic of repentance is simple and familiar, appealing to the balance and proportion of all things. If sin is what introduces rebellion and change, and the will of humanity is what constitutes the variable in disrupting creation, then the theology of the Aggadah makes provision for restoration through the free exercise of humanity's will. That restoration requires an attitude of remorse, a resolve not to repeat the act of rebellion, and a good-faith effort at reparation—in all, transformation from rebellion against to obedience to God's will. So with repentance readers come once more to an exact application of the principle of measure for measure, here, will for will, each comparable to, corresponding with, the other. World order, disrupted by an act of will, regains perfection through an act of will that complements and corresponds to the initial, rebellious one. That is realized in an act of willful repentance (Hebrew: *teshubah*).

Repentance, a statement of regret and remorse for the sin one has committed and hence an act of will effects the required transformation of humanity and inaugurates reconciliation with God. Through a matched act of will, now in conformity with God's design for creation, repentance therefore restores the balance upset by humanity's act of will. So the act of repentance, and with it atonement, takes its place within the theology of perfection, disruption, and restoration, that all together organizes—shows the order of—the world of creation.

Apology does not suffice; an atoning act also is required. That is why repentance is closely related to the categories, atonement and Day of Atonement, and integral to them. The one in the cult, the other in the passage of time, respond to the change of will with an act of confirmation, on God's part, that the change is accepted, recognized, and deemed effective. That act is necessary because, through the act of repentance, a person who has sinned leaves the status of sinner, but must also atone for the sin and gain forgiveness, so that such a person is no longer deemed a sinner. Self-evidently, within a system built on the dialectics of competing wills, God's and humanity's, repentance comes first in the path to reconciliation. The act of will involves a statement of regret or remorse, resolve never to repeat the act, and, finally, the test of this change of heart or will (where feasible). Specifically, it is a trial of entering a situation in which the original sin is possible but is not repeated. Then the statement of remorse and voluntary change of will is confirmed by an act of omission or commission, as the case requires.

Followed by atonement, therefore, repentance commences the work of closing off the effects of sin: history, time, change, inequity. It marks the beginning of the labor of restoring creation to Eden: the perfect world as God wants it and creates it. Since the Hebrew word, *teshubah*, is built out of the root for return, the concept is generally understood to mean returning to God from a situation of estrangement. The turning is not only from sin but toward God, for sin serves as an indicator of a deeper pathology, which is, utter estrangement from God—humanity's will alienated from God's.

Teshubah then involves not humiliation but reaffirmation of the self in God's image, after God's likeness. It follows that repentance forms a theological category encompassing moral issues of action and attitude, wrong action, arrogant attitude, in particular. Repentance forms a step in the path to God that starts with the estrangement represented by sin: doing what I want, instead of what God wants, thus rebellion and arrogance. Sin precipitates punishment, whether personal for individuals or historical for nations. Punishment brings about repentance for sin, which, in turn, leads to atonement and, it follows, reconciliation with God. That sequence of stages in the moral regeneration of sinful humanity, individual or collective, defines the context in which repentance finds its natural home.

True, the penitent one corrects damage actually carried out to his fellow man. But apart from reparations, the act of repentance involves only the attitude, specifically substituting feelings of regret and remorse for the arrogant intention that lead to the commission of the sin. If the person declares regret and undertakes not to repeat the action, the process of repentance gets underway. When the occasion to repeat the sinful act arises and the penitent refrains from doing it again, the process comes to a conclusion. So it is through the will and attitude of the sinner that the act of repentance is realized; the entire process is carried on beyond the framework of religious actions, rites, or rituals. The power of repentance overcomes sins of the most heinous and otherwise unforgivable character. The following is explicit that no sin overwhelms the transformative power of repentance:

Bavli Gittin 5:6 I.26/57b

- A.   A Tannaite statement:
- B.   Naaman was a resident proselyte.
- C.   Nebuzaradan was a righteous proselyte.
- D.   Grandsons of Haman studied Torah in Bene Beraq.
- E.   Grandsons of Sisera taught children in Jerusalem.
- F.   Grandsons of Sennacherib taught Torah in public.
- G.   And who were they? Shemaiah and Abtalion.

Shemaiah and Abtalion are represented as the masters of Hillel and Shammai, who founded the houses (schools of thought) dominant in many areas of the Halakhah set forth in the Mishnah and related writings. The act of repentance transforms the heirs of the destroyers of Israel and the Temple into the framers of the redemptive Torah. A more extreme statement of the power of any attitude or action defies imagining—even the fact of our own day that a distant cousin of Adolph Hitler has converted to Judaism and serves in the reserves of the Israel Defense Army.

That to such a remarkable extent God responds to humanity's will, which time and again has defined the dynamics of complementarity characteristic of the Aggadah's theology, accounts for the possibility of repentance. As much as mercy completes the principle of justice, so repentance forms the complement to sin; without mercy, represented here by the possibility of repentance, justice as God defines it cannot endure. Were humanity to regret sin and see things in God's way without a corresponding response from God, God would execute justice but not mercy, and, from the sages' perspective, the world would fall out of balance. To them, therefore, it is urgent that God have his own distinctive message to the sinner, separate from the voices of Wisdom, Prophecy, and even the Pentateuch (the Torah narrowly defined), of the Written Torah:

Yerushalmi-tractate Makkot 2:6 I:4/10a

- A.   Said R. Phineas: "'Good and upright [is the Lord; therefore he instructs sinners in the way]' (Ps 25:8).
- B.   "Why is he good? Because he is upright.
- C.   "And why is he upright? Because he is good.
- D.   "'Therefore he instructs sinners in the way—that is, he teaches them the way to repentance.'"

Now the narrator interrogates the great compendia of God's will, Wisdom, Prophecy, then turns to God himself, and asks how to treat the sinner:

- E.   They asked wisdom, "As to a sinner, what is his punishment?"
- F.   She said to them, "Evil pursues the evil" (Prov 13:21).
- G.   They asked prophecy, "As to a sinner, what is his punishment?"

H. She said to them, "The soul that sins shall die" (Ezek 18:20).

I. They asked the Holy One, blessed be He, "As to a sinner, what is his punishment?"

J. He said to them, "Let the sinner repent, and his sin will be forgiven for him."

K. This is in line with the following verse of Scripture: "Therefore he instructs sinners in the way" (Ps 25:8).

L. "He shows the sinners the way to repentance."

The response of Wisdom presents no surprise; it is the familiar principle of measure for measure, and prophecy concurs, but God has something more to say. Accordingly, the proposition concerns the distinctive mercy of God, above even the Torah. The data for the composition, E–L in the above passage, respond to the question that is addressed to the components of the Torah— that is, what Prophecy says about the punishment of the sinner. But the question is prior, and the question forms part of the systemic plan: to demonstrate the uniquely merciful character of God, the way in which God is God.

But, the power of repentance is disproportionate, out of all balance with sin in a way in which the penalty for sin never exceeds the gravity of the sin. One may say that, while, when it comes to sin, God effects exact justice, when it comes to repentance, God accords mercy out of all proportion to the arrogance of the act of rebellion. God responds with grace, and "righteousness of deeds" does not come into consideration. That is because the act of will that is represented by repentance vastly outweighs the act of will that brings about sin. That is because one may commit many sins, but a single act of repentance encompasses them all and restores the balance that those sins all together have upset. So repentance makes sense, in its remarkable power, only in the context of God's mercy. It follows that any account of repentance and atonement must commence with a clear statement of God's mercy, the logical precondition for the act of repentance.

Repentance never stands alone but shares traits of two other actions and works with them to elicit God's mercy and avert harsh decrees from heaven. Integral to the process of repentance, these are acts of prayer and of charity, both of them, like repentance, expressions of attitude and will. The act of prayer is a statement of dependence upon heaven, a submission of humanity's will before God's mercy. The act of charity embodies that attitude of will that humanity seeks to evoke from God. In a like manner repentance belongs with charity and prayer; these three actions nullify the evil decree:

Yerushalmi-tractate Taanit 2:1/III:5

A. Said R. Eleazar, "Three acts nullify the harsh decree, and these are they: prayer, charity, and repentance."

Now the facts of Scripture are adduced to validate that statement:

B. And all three of them are to be derived from a single verse of Scripture:

C. "If my people who are called by my name humble themselves, [pray and seek my face, and turn from their wicked ways, then I will hear from heaven and will forgive their sin and heal their land]" (2 Chron 7:14).

D. "Pray"—this refers to prayer.

E. "And seek my face"—this refers to charity,

F. as you say, "As for me, I shall behold thy face in righteousness; [when I awake, I shall be satisfied with beholding thy form"] (Ps 17:15).

G. "And turn from their wicked ways"—this refers to repentance.

H. Now if they do these things, what is written concerning them there?

I. "Then I will hear from heaven and will forgive their sin and heal their land."

To shape one's own future, one can take action to overcome the effects of past sin. Through prayer, acts of charity, and repentance, one may so express a change of attitude as to persuade heaven to respond and change its attitude as well. The message is concrete, having to do with declaring a fast in response to the withholding of rain by heaven.

Just as repentance, prayer, and charity form a natural cluster, so repentance and atonement form another. That is because repentance cannot be fully understood outside of the context of atonement; repentance forms a stage in the quest for atonement for, and complements the process that results in, the forgiveness of sin. While the relationship of repentance and atonement is integral, atonement receives an exposition in its own terms as well. Here we will see how repentance relates to atonement, and, presently, we will take up atonement on its own as the goal of the entire transaction.

Repentance is the precondition of atonement; there is no atonement without the statement of remorse and appropriate, confirming action. If one rebels against God's rule and does not repent, no atonement is possible. But if he does repent, then the Day of Atonement effects atonement for him, so:

Bavli-tractate Shebuot 1:1ff. XVI.2/13A

D. Rabbi says, "For all of the transgressions that are listed in the Torah, whether one has repented or not repented, the Day of Atonement attains atonement, except for one who breaks the yoke [of the kingdom of heaven from himself, meaning, denies God] and one who treats the Torah impudently, and the one who violates the physical mark of the covenant. In these cases if one has repented, the Day of Atonement attains atonement, and if not, the Day of Atonement does not attain atonement."

Now come the facts to validate the proposition:

> E. What is the scriptural basis for the position of Rabbi?
>
> F. It is in line with that which has been taught on Tannaite authority:
>
> G. "Because he has despised the word of the Lord": This refers to one who is without shame in interpreting the Torah.
>
> H. "And broken his commandment": This refers to one who removes the mark fleshly arks of the covenant.
>
> I. "That soul shall utterly be cut of "Be cut off"—before the Day of Atonement. "Utterly"—after the day of atonement.
>
> J. Might one suppose that that is the case even if he has repented?
>
> K. Scripture says, "his iniquity shall be upon him" (Num 15:31)—I say that the Day of Atonement does not effect atonement only when his iniquity is still upon him.

The contrary view invokes the same facts but interprets them differently:

> L. And Rabbis?
>
> M. "That soul shall utterly be cut of "Be cut off"—in this world. "Utterly"—in the world to come.
>
> N. "his iniquity shall be upon him" (Num 15:31)—if he repented and died, death wipes away the sin.

What is reconciled is the atoning power of the Day of Atonement with the intransigence of the sinner. How people explain the limits of the one in the face of the other demands attention. The answer lies in the power of repentance or of failure to repent, which explains when the Day of Atonement atones or fails. When faced with the possible conflict between the power of the Day of Atonement and the enormity of sins against heaven itself, the resolution lies in invoking the matter of intentionality, expressed through the act of repentance or the failure to perform that act.

While repentance is required, in a system of hierarchical classification such as this one, the other components of the process, prayer in this case, have to be situated in relationship to one another. Whether or not repentance accomplishes the whole of atonement is subject to some uncertainty, since prayer retains a critical role in the process:

Leviticus Rabbah X:V.1

> 1. A. Judah b. Rabbi and R. Joshua b. Levi:
>
>   B. Judah b. Rabbi said, "Repentance achieves [only] part, while prayer achieves the complete [atonement]."
>
>   C. R. Joshua b. Levi said, "Repentance achieves the whole [of atonement], while prayer achieves only part [of atonement]."

The two views now must be sustained by fact, and the facts of Scripture serve. But both parties are clear that repentance forms a stage in the path to atonement, with or without the necessity of prayer.

D. In the view of R. Judah b. Rabbi, who has said that repentance achieves [only] part [of the needed atonement], from whom do you derive proof?

E. It is from Cain, against whom a harsh decree was issued, as it is written, "A fugitive and a wanderer will you be on the earth" (Gen 4:12). But when Cain repented, part of the harsh decree was removed from him.

F. That is in line with the following verse of Scripture: "Then Cain went away from the presence of the Lord and dwelt in the land of the wanderer [Nod], east of Eden" (Gen 4:16). "In the land of a fugitive and a wanderer" is not written here, but rather, only "in the land of the wanderer." [The matter of being a fugitive is thus annulled.]

M. When he had left [God], the first humanity met him, saying to him, What happened at your trial?

N. He said to him, "I repented and copped a plea."

Here Cain illustrates the total power of repentance, meaning confession and a statement of remorse:

O. When the first humanity heard this, he began to slap his own face, saying, "So that's how strong repentance is, and I never knew!"

P. At that moment, the first man pronounced [this Psalm], "A Psalm, the song for the Sabbath day" (Ps 92:1) [which says, "It is a good thing to make a confession to the Lord" (Ps 92:2)].

Q. Said R. Levi, "It was the first humanity who made up that psalm."

Now contrary facts are adduced for the opposed position:

2. A. In the view of Judah b. Rabbi, who said that prayer accomplishes the whole of the necessary atonement? From whence do you derive proof? It is from Hezekiah.

B. The allotted time for Hezekiah's rule was only fourteen years. That is in line with the following verse of Scripture: "And it happened in the fourteenth year of King Hezekiah [Sennacherib, king of Assyria came up against all the fortified cities of Judah and took them]" (Isa 36:1).

C. But when Hezekiah prayed, fifteen more years were added to his rule.

D. That is in line with the following verse of Scripture: "Behold, I will add fifteen years to your life" (Isa 38:5).

Another exemplary case is introduced:

3. A. In the view of R. Joshua b. Levi, who has said that repentance effects the whole of the required atonement, from whom do you derive evidence? From the inhabitants of Anathoth:

    B. "Therefore thus says the Lord concerning the men of Anathoth, who seek your life and say, Do not prophecy. . . . Behold, I will punish them; the young men shall die by the sword; [their sons and their daughters shall die by famine; and none of them shall be left. For I will bring evil upon the men of Anathoth, the year of their punishment]' (Jer 11:21-23)."

    C. But because they repented, they enjoyed the merit of being listed in the honorable genealogies: "The men of Anathoth were one hundred twenty-eight" (Ezra 2:23; Neh 7:27).

The account reverts to the position that prayer accomplishes only part of atonement:

7. A. In the view of R. Joshua b. Levi, who has said that prayer only accomplishes part of the required atonement, from whom do you derive proof?

    B. It is from Aaron, against whom a decree was issued.

    C. That is in line with the following verse: "Moreover the Lord was very angry with Aaron, to have destroyed him." (Deut 9:20).

    D. R. Joshua of Sikhnin said in the name of R. Levi, "The meaning of the word 'destruction' used here is only the utter extinction of all offspring, sons and daughters alike.

    E. "That is in line with the following usage: 'And I destroyed his fruit from above and his roots from beneath' (Amos 2:9)."

    F. Yet when Moses prayed on behalf of Aaron, only two of his sons died [Nadab and Abihu], while the other two survived.

    G. "Take Aaron and his sons with him" (Lev 8:2).

This protracted exercise shows how the sages sifted facts of Scripture to test hypothesis. But the complex interplay of repentance and atonement takes the form of not only narratives, exegesis of Scripture, and apodictic statements, but also—and especially—normative law. In the statement of law, the focus is on atonement, of the process of which repentance is a component. But there are other components as well. One is an offering at the Temple, a sin-offering in particular, which is accepted as atonement for an inadvertent act. One cannot deliberately sin and trade off with an animal sacrifice; God wants the heart, and an act of rebellion not followed by a change of heart is indelible. But if a sinful act is not deliberate, then a sin-offering suffices, along with an unconditional guilt-offering.

Other Media of Atonement: Death, the Day of Atonement

Two other media of atonement for sin are death, on the one side, and the advent of the Day of Atonement, which accomplishes atonement: "For on this day atonement shall be made for you to cleanse you of all your sins" (Lev 16:30). Death marks the final atonement for sin, which bears its implication for the condition of humanity at the resurrection. Because one has atoned through sin (accompanied at the hour of death by a statement of repentance, "May my death be atonement for all my sins," in the liturgy in due course), when he is raised from the dead, his atonement for all his sins is complete. The judgment after resurrection becomes for most a formality. That is why "all Israel has a portion in the world to come," with the exception of a few whose sins are not atoned for by death, and that is by their own word.

The Day of Atonement provides atonement, as the Written Torah makes explicit, for the sins of the year for which one has repented, and that accounts for the elaborate rites of confession that fill the day. In chapter 4 readers will meet the Halakhic formulation of this matter, which is at Mishnah-tractate Yoma 8:8–9 and its secondary exposition.

By atonement, the sages understand an act or event (death or the Day of Atonement in particular) that removes the effects of sin by bringing about God's forgiveness. The forms of the Hebrew based on the root KPR do not exhaust the category, for any action that produces the result of removing the effect of a sin will fit into that category, whether or not labeled an act of *kapparah*. The Written Torah speaks of atoning offerings in the Temple. Atonement in this age, without the Temple and its offerings, is accomplished through charity, so:

> b. B.B. 1:5 IV.23/9a
>
> And said R. Eleazar, "When the Temple stood, someone would pay off his sheqel-offering and achieve atonement. Now that the Temple is not standing, if people give to charity, well and good, but if not, the idolaters will come and take it by force. And even so, that is still regarded for them as an act of righteousness: 'I will make your exactors righteousness' (Isa 60:17)."

Atonement without Sacrifice

The principal categorical component is the atonement brought about by the advent of the Day of Atonement. So, for instance, on that day the high priest, representing all Israel, brings about atonement through the rites of the Day of Atonement, beginning with the confession. Scripture presents diverse

facts on a given sin, the penalty thereof, and the media of remission of the
penalty, and reason and exegesis then make possible the classification of
those facts into a coherent whole:

Tosefta-tractate Kippurim 4:6–8
T. Kip. 4:6

    A.   R. Ishmael says, "There are four kinds of atonement.

    B.   "[If] one has violated a positive commandment but repented, he hardly
        moves from his place before they forgive him,

    C.   "since it is said, 'Return, backsliding children. I will heal your back-
        sliding' (Jer 3:22).

4:7 A.   "[If] he has violated a negative commandment but repented, repen-
        tance suspends the punishment, and the Day of Atonement effects
        atonement,

    B.   "since it is said, 'For that day will effect atonement for you' (Lev 16:30).

4:8 A.   "[If] he has violated [a rule for which the punishment is] extirpation or
        death at the hands of an earthly court, but repented, repentance and
        the Day of Atonement suspend [the punishment], and suffering on the
        other days of the year will wipe away [the sin],

    B.   "since it says, 'Then will I visit their transgression with a rod' (Ps
        89:32).

    C.   "But he through whom the name of heaven is profaned deliberately but
        who repented—repentance does not have power to suspend [the pun-
        ishment], nor the Day of Atonement to atone,

    D.   "but repentance and the Day of Atonement atone for a third, suffering
        atones for a third, and death wipes away the sin, with suffering,

    E.   "and on such a matter it is said, 'Surely this iniquity shall not be purged
        from you until you die' (Isa 22:14)."

The four kinds of atonement are worked out in their own systematic and logical terms, but the verses of Scripture then contribute to the validation of the
classification-scheme. There is a grid established by positive and negative commandments, intersecting with the matter of repentance. Then there is the grid
established by the kind of penalty—extirpation or the earthly court's death
sentence; here repentance and the Day of Atonement form the intersecting
grid. Finally, there is the matter of the profanation of the divine name, in
which case repentance and the Day of Atonement come into play along with
suffering and death. So the point of differentiation is established by appeal to
the type of sin, on the one side, and the pertinent penalties, on the second,
and the effects of media of atonement—repentance, death, Day of
Atonement, suffering. The entire complex exhibits the traits of mind that readers have met many times: systematic classification by indicative traits, an interest in balance, order, complementarity, and commensurate proportionality.

But here readers come to an unanticipated fact, which is a moment in humanity's relationship to God to which humanity's intentionality is null. God's mercy so exceeds humanity's just deserts that one's intention as to atonement may or may not affect the actuality of atonement. In the case of one's violation of a positive commandment, even if one did not repent and so conform to the correct intentionality, the Day of Atonement—on its own, by divine decree, as an act of supererogatory mercy utterly unrelated to considerations of justice—accomplishes the atonement. But as to negative commandments that one has deliberately violated, the Day of Atonement atones only if the sinner repents:

Yerushalmi-tractate Yoma 8:7 I:1
A. As to violation of a positive commandment, [the Day of Atonement effects atonement] even if the person did not repent.
B. As to violation of a negative commandment—
C. R. Samuel in the name of R. Zeira: " [The Day of Atonement effects atonement] only if the person repented [of violating the negative commandment]."

If one denies the power of the burnt-offering to effect atonement, nonetheless, his attitude is null, and the offering effects atonement *ex opere operato*:

I:2 A. He who states, "The burnt-offering does not effect atonement, the burnt-offering does not effect atonement for me,"—
B. the burnt-offering effects atonement for him.

But if he declared that he did not want the burnt-offering to effect atonement for him in particular, then the offering is null:

C. [If he said,] "I do not want [the burnt-offering] to effect atonement for me," it does not effect atonement for him against his will.

The same pattern is repeated for other media of atonement, beginning with the Day of Atonement:

D. [If he said,] "The Day of Atonement does not effect atonement," the Day of Atonement effects atonement.
E. [If he said,] "I do not want it to effect atonement for me," it effects atonement for him against his will.
F. [Y. Shebu. 1:6 adds:] As to an offering, whether he said, "I do not believe that this offering effects atonement," or, "that it effects atonement for me," or if he said, "I know it does effect atonement, but I do not want it to effect atonement for me," in all of these cases, it does not effect atonement against his will.

The analysis of these positions shows what is at stake, which is the power of the Day of Atonement to accomplish atonement without regard to the intentionality of those affected by it:

> G. Said R. Haninah b. R. Hillel, "Is it not logical that the rule should be just the opposite? [In the case of an offering, whatever the humanity said, he did indeed bring an offering. But as to the Day of Atonement, if he said that he did not want it to effect atonement for him, it should not effect atonement for him.]"
>
> H. Does someone say to a king, "You are not a king?" [Surely not. So whatever the humanity says, the Day of Atonement does effect atonement.]

Why the burnt-offering does not prove effective if one rejects its affects upon his situation is now spelled out:

> I:3 A. The burnt-offering effects atonement for the murmurings of one's heart.
>
> B. What is the scriptural basis for that statement?
>
> C. "What is in your mind shall never happen" (Ezek 20:32).
>
> D. Said R. Levi, "The burnt-offering effects atonement for what is in your mind, and so Job states, 'And when the days of the feast had run their course, Job would send and sanctify them, and he would rise early in the morning and offer burnt-offerings according to the number of them all'; for Job said, "It may be that my sons have sinned, and cursed God in their hearts." Thus Job did continually' (Job 1:5). This indicates that the burnt-offering effects atonement for the murmurings of the heart."

A further qualification now affects what has already been said, namely, the power of the Day of Atonement to work *ex opere operato*.

> I:4 A. Rabbi says, "For all transgressions which are listed in the Torah the Day of Atonement effects atonement, except for the one who totally breaks the yoke [of heaven] off of him, who removes the signs of the covenant, or who behaves presumptuously against the Torah.
>
> B. "For if such a person does repent, then atonement is effected for him, but if not, it is not effected for him."
>
> C. R. Zebida said R. Yosé raised the question: "Does Rabbi truly maintain that [except for the specified cases] the Day of Atonement [otherwise] effects atonement without [the sinner's] repenting?"
>
> D. R. Asian, R. Jonah, R. Ba, R. Hiyya in the name of R. Yohanan: "Rabbi concurs that the Day of Atonement does not effect atonement without an act of repentance. But one's death washes away sin without an act of repentance."

E.   And so it has been taught: The day of one's death is tantamount to an act of repentance.

F.   Who taught that statement? It was Rabbi.

G.   Is this in line with that which we have learned there:

H.   Death and the Day of Atonement effect atonement [only] with an act of repentance?

I.   That teaching is not in accord with the position of Rabbi.

Facts do not affect outcomes, but what one wills—intentionality—does.

However, the Day of Atonement has its own autonomous power, unaffected by an individual's intentionality. An argument *a fortiori* suggests the opposite. When that view is challenged, the mode of argument is to appeal to a metaphor, in this case, the king. If one tells the king he is not king, he is still king. There are facts that stand in the face of the argument *a fortiori*. But when it comes to suspending the effects of the Day of Atonement, the condition of one's heart makes a difference, since the Day of Atonement serves only with repentance. So intentionality in general is null, but intentionality specifically with reference to the Day of Atonement is effective. Rabbi imposes a special rule having to do with someone outside of the framework of the faith, who rejects the covenant and the Torah. Such a person is untouched by the Day of Atonement and its power, unless he repents and gives effect to that Day. The logic is that one who rejects the entire system gains no benefit, *ex opere operato*, from the system. He is bound by the logic of his own position. So too, death is a universal solvent for the stain of sin.

Sages do recognize limits to the power of repentance and atonement. They recognize that, in the world order, atonement does not always accomplish its goals. With genuinely evil persons repentance on its own may not suffice to accomplish atonement. Specifically, they recognize that genuinely wicked people may repent but not for long, or their repentance in the end proves incommensurate to the affront against God that they have committed. The process of repentance and atonement therefore works only in a limited way. In this doctrine they are able in yet another way to account for the prosperity of the wicked.

The Fathers according to R. Nathan XXXIX:V.1

A.   The repentance of genuinely wicked people suspends [their punishment], but the decree against them has been sealed.

B.   The prosperity of the wicked in the end will go sour.

C.   Dominion buries those that hold it.

D.   Repentance suspends [punishment] and the Day of Atonement achieves atonement.

E.   Repentance suspends [punishment] until the day of death, and the day of death atones, along with repentance.

The wicked enjoy this world, getting their reward now, but they do not gain the life eternal of the world to come. The righteous suffer now, atoning for their sins through suffering, but they will have a still more abundant life in the world to come:

> The Fathers according to R. Nathan XXXIX:VII.1
>
> A. They [immediately, in this world] pay off the reward owing to the wicked [for such good as they may do], while they credit to the righteous [the reward that is coming to them, but do not pay it off, rather paying them off in the world to come].
>
> B. They pay off the reward owing to the wicked [in this world] as though they were people who had carried out the Torah ungrudgingly, in whom no fault had ever been found.
>
> C. They credit to the righteous [the reward that is coming to them, but do not pay it off, rather paying them off in the world to come], as though they were people lacking all good traits.
>
> D. They thus give a little bit to each party, with the bulk of the remainder laid up for them.

In these ways, the complementary doctrines of repentance and atonement are given nuance, fitting together with comparable doctrines to account for the condition of individuals in the here and now.

But that repentance does not serve for certain extreme cases of sin alerts us to the possibility that repentance may not cover certain types of sin. In theory there ought to be no atonement for gossip and involuntary manslaughter, but the Torah has provided means of atonement, in a statement that readers have already noted in another connection:

> Song of Songs Rabbah XLVIII:v.5
>
> 5. A. R. Simon in the name of R. Jonathan of Bet Gubrin: "For two matters there was no atonement, but the Torah has provided atonement for them, and these are they:
>
> B. "Gossip and involuntary manslaughter."

In theory, there should be no atonement, but the Torah provided in the cult for even those who disrupt the community of Israel through slander and gossip. The community must be protected from those who disturb its just order, but even those who do so can atone for their sin in a process commencing with repentance.

So much for the individual Israelite; but what about the community of Israel viewed as a whole? That all Israel may and should engage in acts of repentance and atonement hardly requires articulation; it is taken for granted in every discussion of the Day of Atonement, which speaks of the community as much as of the private person. So from the individual sinner, the Israelite, readers take up that other category of world order, the whole of holy Israel. If God's mercy for the individual sinner vastly outweighs the guilt of the sinner, then all the more so does God treat Israel with abundant mercy. God forgives Israel's sins that vastly exceed those of the idolaters.

How Idolaters Atone

As readers saw in chapters 1 and 2, any discussion involving the community of Israel draws in its wake Israel's antonym, the idolaters, that is, the other component of humanity viewed as a whole. Now here, surely, the nations of the world lay claim to a place in the process of reconciliation. But their condition is defined not by particular acts of rebellion against God, e.g., gossip or transgression of other laws of the Torah, but rather by the condition of idolatry, an act of rebellion that transcends all details. And to overcome their condition, the idolaters have to give up idolatry and accept the Torah, the statement of God's will. Short of doing so, no repentance is possible, no atonement even relevant. That basic definition of the idolaters explains why, in being accorded the opportunity for repentance, Israel gains a role in shaping the destiny of the cosmos; in being denied that opportunity (except so far as they give up their idols and become Israel), the nations remain bystanders to the drama of creation.

Naturally, therefore, the nations raise the question of why Israel should be forgiven by the Day of Atonement, when they do not enjoy the same advantage. The nations of the world indict Israel for committing the same sins that the nations practice, but the Day of Atonement effects atonement for Israel:

Leviticus Rabbah XXI:IV.1

    A.   Rabbis interpret [the intersecting] verse ["The Lord is my light and my salvation; whom shall I fear? The Lord is the stronghold of my life; of whom shall I be afraid?]" (Ps 27:1)] to speak of the New Year and Day of Atonement:

    B.   "'My light' [Ps 27:1] is on the New Year.

    C.   "'And my salvation' [Ps 27:1] is on the Day of Atonement.

    D.   "'Whom shall I fear' [Ps 27:1]: 'The Lord is my strength and my song' [Exod 15:2].

    E.   "'When evildoers come near me' [Ps 27:2] refers to the princes [of heaven] who represent the nations of the world.

As a matter of fact, Israel in ordinary life is neither better than, nor different from the nations. In committing the cardinal, absolute sins of murder, fornication, and idolatry, Israel rebels against God. But Israel repents and atones through the act of repentance and the Day of Atonement, so these effect atonement for Israel, while the idolaters are excluded. Why this is so is explained.

> F. "'To eat my flesh' [Ps 27:2]: For the princes representing the nations of the world come and draw an indictment against Israel before the Holy One, blessed be He, saying before him, 'Lord of the world, these [nations] practice idolatry and those [Jews] practice idolatry. These practice fornication and those practice fornication. These shed blood and those shed blood. Why then do these [nations of the world] go down to Gehenna and those do not go down?'
>
> G. "'My adversaries and foes' [Ps 27:2]: You find that the number of days in the solar year are three hundred sixty-five, but the number of names of Satan are three hundred and sixty-four.
>
> H. "For on all the days of the year, Satan is able to draw up an indictment, but on the Day of Atonement, Satan is not able to draw up an indictment.
>
> I. "Said the Israelites before the Holy One, blessed be He, 'Though a host encamp against me'—the host of the nations of the world,
>
> J. "'My heart shall not fear' [Ps 27:3].
>
> K. "'Though war arise against me'—the war of the nations of the world.
>
> L. "'In this I shall trust' [Ps 27:3].
>
> M. "In this which you have promised me: 'With this will Aaron come' [Lev 16:3] [on the Day of Atonement]."

The Day of Atonement is transformed into the occasion for an act of trust, so that, with the Day of Atonement, Israel is accorded atonement despite its actions during the rest of the year. The nations of the world, enemies of Israel, on that day cannot send their paraclete against Israel.

Idolaters, estranged from God by idolatry, gain no benefit from the heritage of unearned grace that the saints of Israel leave to Israel. There are other means of repentance and atonement besides the Day of Atonement. Deemed comparable to sacrifices, for example, is the death of the righteous or of the sages, and these too accrue to Israel's advantage. Here, too, idolaters with their idolatry cannot participate, and so they have no role in the coming restoration, no task to perform:

Yerushalmi-tractate Yoma 1:1 I:2

> [FF] In the view of R. Yohanan, why is the death of the sons of Aaron called to mind in this context [Lev 16], for they died only in the setting of the rite of consecration?
>
> [GG] Said R. Hiyya bar Ba, "The sons of Aaron died on the first day of Nisan. And why is their death called to mind in connection with the Day of Atonement?

[HH] "It is to indicate to you that just as the Day of Atonement effects expiation for Israel, so the death of the righteous effects atonement for Israel."

The same pertains to the death of Miriam and the death of Aaron:

[II] Said R. Ba bar Binah, "Why did the Scripture place the story of the death of Miriam side by side with the story of the burning of the red cow?

[JJ] "It is to teach you that just as the dirt of the red cow [mixed with water] effects atonement for Israel, so the death of the righteous effects atonement for Israel."

[KK] Said R. Yudan b. Shalom, "Why did the Scripture set the story of the death of Aaron side by side with the story of the breaking of the tablets?

[LL] "It is to teach you that the death of the righteous is as grievous before the Holy One, blessed be He, as the breaking of the tablets."

None of this pertains to idolaters, excluded as they are by their own decision to reject the Torah.

The Temple, uniquely Israel's in the process of repentance and atonement, figures in yet another way. Song, too, constitutes a form of atonement, and the song takes place in the Temple, once more omitting reference to the idolaters:

Yerushalmi-tractate Taanit 4:2 II.3

[L] How do we know that the song [in the Temple] is called a form of atonement?

[M] Hinena. father of Bar Netah, in the name of R. Benaiah: "'To make atonement for the people of Israel'—this refers to the song."

[N] How do we know that the song is indispensable [to the cult]?

[O] R. Jacob bar Aha, R. Bulatah in the name of R. Hinena: "'To make atonement for the people of Israel'—this refers to the song."

Just as the will of humanity, initially of Adam but then localized in Israel, disrupts the world order and stands against the will of God, so God responds to the regeneration of that will in acts of repentance and atonement only as these are carried out by Israel.

Repentance and Resurrection. The Messiah

Once one asks about how repentance forms a principal requirement for the restoration of life over death, in resurrection, and the restoration of Israel over its condition of exile and alienation, the narrative turns to the place of repentance in the end of the world as it now is. Here the message, "Repent for the kingdom of God is near," captures the Rabbinic pattern. The account begins with the figure of the Messiah, an important motif in all discussions of matters of eschatology: the resurrection of the dead, the advent of the world or age to come. Readers already realize that Israel's repentance is a pre-condition for salvation, hence for the coming of the Messiah. None should find surprising, then, that the characterization of the Messiah should stress his humility, as much as the promise of his coming to raise the dead should rest upon Israel's conduct as well.

The theology of the Aggadah delivers in diverse ways its single, fundamental messages concerning world order attained through humility before God. In the present instance the theology takes up the Messiah-theme to make its statement. It says that the true Messiah will be humble, and the false Messiah will be marked as false by his arrogance toward God. What readers already have learned about repentance has made inevitable—indeed urgent—that odd juxtaposition, the contrapuntal relationship of arrogance and repentance, sinfulness and reconciliation. Here is how the false Messiah shows why he cannot save Israel, and in so many words, it is because of his blasphemous arrogance:

> Lamentations Rabbah LVIII:ii.8ff.
> 4. A. Rabbi would interpret the verse, "There shall come forth a star out of Jacob" (Num 24:17) in this way: "Do not read the letters of the word for 'star' as 'star' but as 'deceit.'"
> 5. A. When R. Aqiba saw Bar Koziba, he said, "This is the royal Messiah."
>   B. R. Yohanan b. Torta said to him, "Aqiba, grass will grow from your cheeks and he will still not have come."

The reader is now told why Aqiba is wrong:

> 7. A. Eighty thousand trumpeters besieged Betar. There Bar Koziba was encamped, with two hundred thousand men with an amputated finger.
>   B. Sages sent word to him, saying, "How long are you going to produce blemished men in Israel?"
>   C. He said to them, "And what shall I do to examine them [to see whether or not they are brave]?"
>   D. They said to him, "Whoever cannot uproot a cedar of Lebanon do not enroll in your army."
>   E. He had two hundred thousand men of each sort [half with an amputated finger, half proved by uprooting a cedar].

Now comes the explicit statement of the false Messiah's arrogance toward heaven:

> 8. A. When they went out to battle, he would say, "Lord of all ages, don't help us and don't hinder us!"

B. That is in line with this verse: "Have you not, O God, cast us off? And do not go forth, O God, with our hosts" (Ps 60:12).

It would be difficult to find a passage more directly opposed to the sages' fundamental theological convictions than Bar Kokhba's explicit rejection of God's help in favor of his own strength.

Now a separate story underscores the unsuitable character of this particular Messiah, namely, the mark of arrogance represented by temper. Losing one's temper is a mark of arrogance toward heaven, and here Bar Kokhba does just that:

10. A. For three and a half years Hadrian besieged Betar.
    B. R. Eleazar the Modiite was sitting in sack cloth and ashes, praying, and saying, "Lord of all the ages, do not sit in judgment today, do not sit in judgment today."
    C. Since [Hadrian] could not conquer the place, he considered going home.
    D. There was with him a Samaritan, who said to him, "My lord, as long as that old cock wallows in ashes, you will not conquer the city.
    E. "But be patient, and I shall do something so you can conquer it today."

The first act is one of gossip:

    F. He went into the gate of the city and found R. Eleazar standing in prayer.
    G. He pretended to whisper something into his ear, but the other paid no attention to him.

From slander the conspiracy turns to false witness, taking God's name in vain:

    H. People went and told Bar Koziba, "Your friend wants to betray the city."
    I. He sent and summoned the Samaritan and said to him, "What did you say to him?"
    J. He said to him, "If I say, Caesar will kill me, and if not, you will kill me. Best that I kill myself and not betray state secrets."

The false Messiah proved a false judge as well, rejecting even the testimony in his hands and the plea of the honest sage:

    K. Nonetheless, Bar Koziba reached the conclusion that he wanted to betray the city.
    L. When R. Eleazar had finished his prayer, he sent and summoned him, saying to him, "What did this one say to you?"
    M. He said to him, "I never saw that man."
    N. He kicked him and killed him.

O. At that moment an echo proclaimed: "Woe to the worthless shepherd who leaves the flock, the sword shall be upon his arm and upon his right eye" (Zech 11:17).

P. Said the Holy One, blessed be He, "You have broken the right arm of Israel and blinded their right eye. Therefore your arm will wither and your eye grow dark."

Q. Forthwith Betar was conquered and Ben Koziba was killed.

That God has responded to the arrogance of the Messiah is now underscored. On his own, Hadrian could have accomplished nothing. It was God who killed the Messiah, not Hadrian:

R. They went, carrying his head to Hadrian. He said, "Who killed this one?"

S. They said, "One of the Goths killed him," but he did not believe them.

T. He said to them, "Go and bring me his body."

U. They went to bring his body and found a snake around the neck.

V. He said, "If the God of this one had not killed him, who could have vanquished him?"

W. That illustrates the following verse of Scripture: "If their Rock had not given them over . . ." (Deut 32:30).

The same attitude is set forth in a further story of the arrogance of the army of the Messiah, which repeated the Messiah's plea to heaven, "Let him not help us nor hinder us," and which was defeated not by Hadrian's army but by God:

19. A. There were two brothers in Kefar Haruba, and no Roman could pass by there, for they killed him.

B. They decided, "The whole point of the thing is that we must take the crown and put it on our head and make ourselves kings."

C. They heard that the Romans were coming to fight them.

D. They went out to do battle, and an old mam met them and said, "May the Creator be your help against them."

E. They said, "Let him not help us nor hinder us!"

F. Because of their sins, they went forth and were killed.

G. They went, carrying his head to Hadrian. He said, "Who killed this one?"

H. They said, "One of the Goths killed him," but he did not believe them.

I. He said to them, "Go and bring me his body."

J. They went to bring his body and found a snake around the neck.

K. He said, "If the God of this one had not killed him, who could have vanquished him?"

L. That illustrates the following verse of Scripture: "If their Rock had not given them over . . ." (Deut 32:30).

Arrogance toward God, rather than repentance and remorse, thus characterizes the false Messiah. If, then, Israel wants to bring about the restoration, whether the individual to life or Israel to the land, it will accomplish repentance.

That view is expressed in the statement that when Israel really wants the Messiah to come, he will come. But readers are now aware of the special weight attached to the word, "want" or "will." What Israel must want is only what God wants. What Israel must do is give up any notion of accomplishing on its own, by its own act of will, the work of redemption. It is only through the self-abnegation of repentance that Israel can accomplish its goal. Specifically, when Israel's will conforms to the will of God, then God will respond to the act of repentance by bringing about the time of restoration and eternal life. This is expressed in a colloquy that announces the Messiah will come when all Israel keeps a single Sabbath. And that will take place when Israel wants it to take place. It requires only an act of will on the part of Israel to accept one of the Ten Commandments. Then in a broader restatement of matters, the entire redemptive process is made to depend upon Israel's repentance:

Yerushalmi-tractate Taanit 1:1 II:5

    G. The Israelites said to Isaiah, "O our Rabbi, Isaiah, What will come for us out of this night?"

    H. He said to them, "Wait for me, until I can present the question."

    I. Once he had asked the question, he came back to them.

    J. They said to him, "Watchman, what of the night? What did the Guardian of the ages say [a play on 'of the night' and 'say']?"

    K. He said to them, "The watchman says: 'Morning comes; and also the night. [If you will inquire, inquire; come back again]' (Isa 21:12)."

    L. They said to him, "Also the night?"

    M. He said to them, "It is not what you are thinking. But there will be morning for the righteous, and night for the wicked, morning for Israel, and night for idolaters."

Now comes the main point in the exchange: when will this happen? It will happen when Israel wants. And what is standing in the way is Israel's arrogance, to be atoned for by Israel's remorseful repentance:

    N. They said to him, "When?"

    O. He said to them, "Whenever you want, He too wants [it to be]—if you want it, he wants it."

    P. They said to him, "What is standing in the way?"

    Q. He said to them, "Repentance: 'come back again' (Isa 21:12)."

This is stated in the clearest possible way: one day will do it.

R. R. Aha in the name of R. Tanhum b. R. Hiyya, "If Israel repents for one day, forthwith the son of David will come.

S. "What is the scriptural basis? 'O that today you would hearken to his voice!' (Ps 95:7)."

Now comes the introduction of the Sabbath as a test case:

T. Said R. Levi, "If Israel would keep a single Sabbath in the proper way, forthwith the son of David will come.

U. "What is the scriptural basis for this view? Moses said, 'Eat it today, for today is a Sabbath to the Lord; [today you will not find it in the field]' (Exod 16:25).

V. "And it says, '[For thus said the Lord God, the Holy One of Israel], "In returning and rest you shall be saved; [in quietness and in trust shall be your strength." And you would not]' (Isa 30:15)." By means of returning and [Sabbath] rest you will be redeemed.

The main point, then, is the linkage of repentance to the coming restoration of Israel to the land, the dead to life, by the Messiah. But the advent of the Messiah depends wholly upon Israel's will. If Israel will subordinate its will to God's, all else will follow.

Here is where the Torah's covenant applies. Humanity both complements and corresponds with God, and it is man's freedom, meaning his effective will and power of intentionality, that matches God's will. When these conflict, man's arrogance leads him to rebel against God, sin resulting. And from sin comes the imperfection of world order, change, inequity, imbalance. Punished and remorseful, man gives up his arrogant attitude and conforms his will to God's. By making the covenant with Israel, God responds with mercy, freely accepting the reformation that is freely offered. Then world order restored, that perfection effected at the outset is regained for Israel, which means, for God's part of mankind. Eden, now the Land of Israel, is recovered; Adam, now embodied in Israel, is restored to his place. For the Israelite death dies, humanity rises from the grave to life eternal. For Israel the idolaters' rule comes to an end, and Israel regains the land. Repentance then marks the recovery of the world as God wanted it to be, which is to say, the world in which Israel regains its promised place, realizing the covenant. But then, at the end of days, humanity at large will acknowledge the one true God and so find its place within the Israel that is saved from the grave and rises for eternal life. Rabbinic Judaism promises the eschatological restoration of humanity to God, just as the Hebrew prophets promised.

Turning from the sublime theology of sin, repentance, and atonement to the concretization of the theology of atonement in the Temple sacrifice, the sprinkling of blood on the altar, jolts us back into the particulars of everyday rites. That is what the Halakhah does in its exposition of the atonement rite that accompanies the advent of the Day of Atonement, two of the media of atonement, along with repentance. This account will now bear witness to how the Halakhah formulates matters in a completely different framework, only to end squarely in the center of the theology of atonement through repentance and reconciliation with the other—first, with humanity, then with divinity.

Chapter 4

The Halakhic Theology of Atonement

Law in Narrative Form

The rite of the Day of Atonement, which effects atonement for Israel's sins, in Mishnah-tractate Yoma, amplified by Tosefta-, Yerushalmi-, and Bavli-tractate Yoma, takes the form of a narrative of the rite, rather than exposition of normative rules in abstract form. Only at the end does the Halakhah of Yoma turn from narrative to norms of action and attitude, and then it delivers a message that utterly changes the formulation of the topic.

The sequence of documents over four centuries, from the Mishnah in ca. 200, Tosefta (ca. 300), Yerushalmi (ca. 400), and Bavli (ca. 600) for tractate Yoma in the first seven chapters simply recapitulates the Halakhah of the Written Torah in Leviticus 16. Of the eight chapters of the Mishnah-tractate (which sets the division of the Tosefta, Yerushalmi, and Bavli), the first seven provide a narrative, bearing interpolated materials, of the sacrificial rite of the Day of Atonement. The eighth does little more, taking up the rules of affliction of soul, that is, fasting. But at the end, the Halakhah links atonement to repentance, completely recasting the topic at hand. There the Tosefta, as we shall see, opens the way to a profound reenvisioning of the Day of Atonement. The pertinent verses of Scripture are at Leviticus 16:1-34. Now, by the introduction of a theme invited by, but not present in, the narrative itself, the theme of repentance, the Halakhic exposition of the Mishnah-Tosefta-Yerushalmi-Bavli transforms the topic of atonement. Attitude in the end takes over, the attitude of repentance being the precondition of reconciliation with first humanity, then God.

The two parts of the Torah, written (Leviticus 16) and oral (Mishnah-Tosefta-Yerushalmi-Bavli Yoma), then deliver the message by their coordination. It is by repeating the Written Torah's narrative and then making a striking addition of a Halakhic character to that narrative that the Oral Torah accomplishes its goal. And, we shall see at the end, the Bavli uses the same medium of recapitulation and amplification to make its still more dramatic statement, which, predictably, concerns the centrality of Israel's attitude. The power of the repentant spirit is present in the very heart and center of the cult itself. If we compare the sequence of the Scripture's narrative to the presentation of the Halakhah, meaning in this case, the Halakhah of the Mishnah (which governs the order of exposition of the Tosefta, Yerushalmi, and Bavli)—there being nothing of weight or consequence in the posterior documents of the Halakhah—we see the following pattern (the Mishnah-passages are given below):

Leviticus
16:3   He shall put on the holy linen coat
M. 3:6–7
16:6   Aaron shall offer the bull as a sin-offering
M. 3:8
16:7   Then he shall take the two goats
M. 3:9, 4:1
16:9   Aaron shall present the goat on which the lot fell for the Lord
16:11   Aaron shall present the bull as a sin-offering for himself and for his house
M. 4:2–3
16:12   He shall take a censer full of coals of fire
M. 5:1–2
16:14   He shall take some of the blood of the bull
M. 5:3
16:15   Then he shall kill the goat of the sin-offering which is for the people
M. 5:4
16:18   Then he shall take some of the blood of the bull and of the blood of the goat and put it on the horns of the altar
M. 5:5–6
16:20   Aaron shall lay both his hands on the head of the live goat and confess over him all the iniquities of the people of Israel
M. 6:2–6
16:23   Then Aaron shall offer his burnt-offering and the burnt-offering of the people
M. 6:7–8
16:24   The high priest changes into golden garments and offers the ram and the ram of the people, so completing the offerings of the day
M. 7:3–4
16:31   You shall afflict yourselves
M. 8:1–7

Omitted from this correlation between Scripture and the Mishnah's treatment of the topic are only the materials on Torah-reading, prayer, and atonement, M. 7:1–2. All that the Halakhah adds is the opening unit, the preparation of the high priest for the rite and the daily whole offering, and the closing materials on Torah-reading, prayer, and, above all, atonement. Now let us turn to the pertinent texts.

The Halakhah of Yoma

The exposition of the Halakhah of atonement follows the narrative of Scripture at Leviticus 16 and persists in the same narrative voice, telling what the priest does here, then there, until the final topic, then shifts to the definition of norms of conduct. We start with the preparation of the high priest for the conduct of the Day of Atonement offerings set forth at Leviticus 16. A week before, that is, three days after the New Year or Rosh Hashanah, he is set apart, together with an understudy, to avoid possible sources of uncleanness.

Once more the sources are identified with formatted text so that readers may follow the unfolding of the law from document to document.

The Conduct of the Temple Rite on the Day of Atonement

Preparing the High Priest for the Day of Atonement

> **M. 1:1 Seven days before the Day of Atonement they set apart the high priest from his house to the councilors' chamber. And they [also] appoint another priest as his substitute, lest some cause of invalidation should affect him. R. Judah says, "Also: they appoint another woman as a substitute for his wife, lest [his wife] die. "Since it says, 'And he shall make atonement for himself and for his house' (Lev 16:6). 'His house'—this refers to his wife." They said to him, "If so, the matter is without limit."**

During the week of preparation, the high priest participates in the daily whole offering, an atonement-offering purchased by every Israelite via the half-sheqel Temple-offering in support of the public offering of atonement for Israel's corporate sins presented morning and at dusk

> **M. 1:2 All seven days he tosses the blood, offers up the incense, trims the lamps, and offers up the head and hind leg [of the daily whole offering]. But on all other days, if he wanted to offer it up he offers it up. For a high priest offers up a portion at the head and takes a portion at the head [of the other priests].**

M. 1:3 **They handed over to him elders belonging to the court, and they read for him the prescribed rite of the Day [of Atonement]. And they say to him, "My lord, high priest, you read it with your own lips, lest you have forgotten—or never [even] learned it to begin with." On the eve of the Day of Atonement at dawn they set him up at the eastern gate and bring before him bullocks, rams, and sheep, so that he will be informed and familiar with the service.**

T.   1:1 Why do they set apart the high priest from his house to the councilors' chamber [M. Yoma 1:1]? R. Judah b. Patera explained, "Lest his wife turn out to be in doubt as to whether she is menstruating, and if he has sexual relations with her, he will turn out to be unclean for seven days." R. Judah would call it, "The senators' chamber."

T.   1:2 All chambers in the Temple were exempt from the requirement of having a *mezuzah* on their doorposts, except for the councilors' chamber, for it was the residence of the high priest seven days a year. Said R. Judah, "And was this one the only residence? But any room which is a residence is liable, and any which is not a residence is exempt."

T.   1:3 All the chambers in the Temple were deemed to be private domain so far as the Sabbath is concerned and private domain so far as matters of uncleanness are concerned, except for the chamber for wine and oil, which has two entries, one facing the other, and which is private domain so far as the Sabbath is concerned but public domain so far as matters of uncleanness are concerned. Abba Saul would call it, "The chamber of oil." R. Judah says, "Every chamber in the Temple which has two entries facing each other, for instance the gates of the court-yard, constitutes a private domain so far as the Sabbath is concerned, but public domain so far as matters of uncleanness are concerned."

T.   1:4 Why do they appoint another priest as his substitute? lest some cause of invalidation should overtake him [M. Yoma 1:1B–C], so the other may take his place. R. Hananiah, Prefect of the Priests, says, "For that purpose the prefect was appointed: [So that] in the case of a priest over-taken by some cause of invalidation, the other may take his place." [If the substitute should serve in his place], the high priest returns to the priesthood, and this one who served in his place is subject to all of the religious requirements of the high priesthood," the words of R. Meir. R. Yosé says, "Even though they have said, 'All the religious require-ments of the high priesthood apply to him,' he is valid neither as a high priest nor as an ordinary priest." Said R. Yosé, "Joseph b. Elim of Sepphoris served in the place of the high priest for one hour. And from that time onward he was not valid either as a high priest or as an ordi-nary priest. When he went forth [from his high priesthood of one hour], he said to the king, 'The bullock and ram which were offered today, to whom do they belong? Are they mine, or are they our high priest's?' The king knew what to answer him. He said to him, 'Now what's going on, Son of Elim! It is not enough for you that you have served in the place of the high priest for one hour before Him who spoke and brought the world into being. But do you also want to take over the high priesthood for yourself?' At that moment Ben Elim realized that he had been separated from the priesthood."

The activities of the high priest during the week prior to the Day of Atonement are now specified:

> T. 1:5 How does the high priest take a portion at the head [of the other priests] [M. Yoma 1:2C]? He says, "This sin-offering is mine," "This guilt-offering is mine," "One loaf of the two loaves, four or five loaves of the Show Bread [are mine]." Rabbi says, "I say that this one should take half, since it says, 'And what is left of the cereal-offering shall be for Aaron and for his sons' (Lev 2:10)—that Aaron should be equivalent to his sons [and get half]." Under what circumstances? In the case of Holy Things of the Temple. But in the case of Holy Things of the provinces, all the same are the high priest and the ordinary priest: each gets an equal portion.

The narrative of Scripture is itself enriched with further narratives in a mixture of story and law.

> T. 1:6 It is the religious requirement of the high priest to be greater than his brethren in beauty, strength, wealth, wisdom, and good looks. [If] he is not, how do we know that his brethren should magnify him? Since it says, "And the priest who is higher by reason of his brethren" (Lev 21:10)—that they should make him great. They said about Pinhas of Habbata, on whom the lot fell to be high priest, that the revenuers and supervisors came along and found him cutting wood. So they filled up his woodshed with golden denars. R. Hanina b. Gamaliel says, "Was he not a stonecutter? And was he not our father-in-law? But they found him ploughing, as it says concerning Elisha, 'So he departed from there, and found Elisha the son of Shaphat, who was plowing, with twelve yoke of oxen before him, and he was with the twelfth' (I Kgs 19:19)."
>
> T. 1:7 When [unacceptable] kings became many, they ordained the practice of regularly appointing priests, and they appointed high priests every single year.

The high priest ate properly on all days but the one immediately prior to the Day of Atonement, when he was given only a small volume of food, lest he be made sleepy and, in his sleep, suffer a seminal emission and so contract a mild form of uncleanness. He is then kept awake (M. 1:7). He is sworn to carry out the rite as instructed.

M. 1:4   All seven days they did not hold back food or drink from him. [But] on the eve of the Day of Atonement at dusk they did not let him eat much, for food brings on sleep.

M. 1:5   The elders of the court handed him over to the elders of the priesthood, who brought him up to the upper chamber of Abtinas. And they imposed an oath on him and took their leave and went along. [This is what] they said to him, "My lord, high priest: We are agents of the court, and you are our agent and agent of the court. We abjure you by Him who caused his name to rest upon this house, that you will not vary in any way from all which we have instructed you." He turns aside and weeps. And they turn aside and weep.

M. 1:6   If he was a sage, he expounds [the relevant scriptures]. And if not, disciples of the sages expound for him. If he was used to reading [Scriptures], he reads. And if not, they read for him. And what do they read for him? In Job, Ezra, and Chronicles. Zechariah b. Qebutal says, "Many times I read for him in the book of Daniel."

M. 1:7   [If] he tried to doze off, young priests snap their middle fingers before him and say to him, "My lord, high priest: Stand up and drive off [sleep] by walking on the cold stones."

Why the weeping and the oath require explanation. Here the Rabbinic contempt for the Temple priesthood and its conduct of the rite surfaces. The Tosefta tells the tale of conflict over the procedures and how prior priests tried to impose their opinion of the rite upon the Temple's conduct, over the opposition of the Rabbinic sages, and their reading of the law.

T.   1:8   Why does he turn aside and weep [M. Yoma 1:5F]? Because it is necessary to impose an oath on him. And why do they turn aside and weep [M. Yoma 1:5F]? Because they have to impose an oath on him. And why do they have to impose an oath on him? Because there already was the case of that certain Boethusian, who offered up the incense while he was still outside, and the cloud of incense went forth and frightened the entire house. For the Boethusian maintained that he should burn the incense while he is still outside, as it says, 'And put the incense on the fire before the Lord, that the cloud of the incense may cover the mercy seat which is upon the testimony'" (Lev 16:13). The sages said to them, "Now has it not also been stated, 'And put the incense on the fire before the Lord'? From this it follows that whoever offers up incense offers up incense only inside. If so, why is it said, 'The cloud of the incense may cover'? This teaches that he puts into it something which causes smoke to rise. If therefore he did not put in something which makes smoke rise, he is liable to the death penalty." Now when this Boethusian went forth, he said to his fathers, "In your entire lives you would [merely] expound the Scripture, but you never did the deed properly, until I arose and I went in and did it right." They said to him, "Even though we do expound matters as you say, we do not do things in the way in which we expound them. We obey the words of the sages. I shall be very much surprised at you if you live for very long." Not thirty days passed before they put him into his grave.

The first rite at dawn was to clear ashes from the altar. The Halakhic narrative once more looks backward at happenings in the Temple. The enthusiasm of the young priests for performing the rites, spilling over into violence, made it necessary to ask lots for selecting the priest to perform a given rite.

Clearing the Ashes from the Altar

M. 1:8 Every day at the cock's crow or near it they take up the ashes from the altar, whether before or after it. At the Day of Atonement from midnight, and on festivals at the end of the first watch [they do so]. And never did the cock crow before the courtyard was filled with masses of Israelites.

M. 2:1 At first whoever wants to take up the ashes from the altar does so. And when they are many [who wanted to do so], they run up the ramp. And whoever gets there before his fellow, within four cubits of the altar, has acquired the right to do so. And if the two came at the same time, the one in charge says to them, "Choose up [by raising a finger]." And what do they put forth? One or two. But they did not put out the thumb in the Temple. There was the case of two who got there at the same time, running up the ramp. And one shoved his fellow. And he [the other] fell and broke his foot. When the court saw that the matter was dangerous, they ordained that the right of clearing off the ashes from the altar should be apportioned only by lot. There were four lots, and this was the first of the four.

T. 1:10 How does one cast lots [M. Yoma 2:2D]? They enter the hewn-stone chamber and stand round about it in the form of a spiral figure. And the supervisor comes and takes the miter of one of them. Then they know that from him the lot begins. They did not put forth two by two, but one by one. And individuals among them put out two by two. But they did not count the extra [finger].

The story of the priestly violence spills over into an account of a particular incident, in which one priest killed another. The cutting edge of the story is, the priests and Temple mob were more concerned with cultic cleanness—removing the corpse before the corpse-contamination took effect—than murder, as the narrator explicitly states.

T. 1:12 M'SH B: There were two who got there at the same time, running up
the ramp. One shoved the other [M. Yoma 2:2A–B], within four cubits
[of the altar]. The other then took out a knife and stabbed him in the
heart. R. Sadoq came and stood on the steps of the porch and said,
"Hear me, O brethren of the house of Israel! Lo, Scripture says, 'If in
the land which the Lord your God gives you to possess, any one is
found slain, lying in the open country, and it is not known who killed
him, then your elders and your judges shall come forth, and they shall
measure the distance to the cities which are around him that is slain'
(Deut 21:1-2). Come so let us measure to find out for what area it is
appropriate to bring the calf, for the sanctuary, or for the courts!" All
of them moaned after his speech. And afterward the father of the
youngster came to them, saying, "O brethren of ours! May I be your
atonement. His [my] son is still writhing, so the knife has not yet been
made unclean." This teaches you that the uncleanness of a knife is more
grievous to Israelites than murder. And so it says, "Moreover Manasseh
shed very much innocent blood, till he had filled Jerusalem from one
end to the other" (2 Kgs 21:16). On this basis they have said, "Because
of the sin of murder the Presence of God was raised up, and the sanctuary was made unclean."

We now revert to the narrative of the daily whole offering, with special
attention to the lots taken to assign diverse tasks to the several priests.

M. 2:2 The second lot: Who slaughters the animal, who tosses the blood,
who clears the ashes off the candelabrum, and who brings the
limbs up the ramp: the head, right hind leg, two forelegs, rump,
left hind leg, breast, neck, two flanks, and innards; the fine flour,
the baked cakes [Lev 6:21], and the wine. Thirteen priests acquired
the right to participate in the service. Said Ben Azzai before R.
Aqiba in the name of R. Joshua, "In the way in which it walked it
was offered."

M. 2:3 The third lot: "Those who are new to the burning of the incense,
come and draw lots." The fourth: "Those who are new and those
who are experienced—who will bring up the limbs from the ramp
to the altar itself?"

T. 1:11 R. Judah says, "They did not cast lots for the privilege of carrying the
fire-pan. But whoever won the right to care for the incense-offering
says to the one who is with him, 'You too—for the fire-pan.'" R. Eliezer
b. Jacob says, "There was no lot for carrying the sacrificial fat of the
goat. But whoever took the limbs up the ramp offers them up on the
altar" [cf. M. Yoma 2:4].

T. 1:13 "The superintendent said to them, 'Come and cast lots [to determine]
who executes the act of slaughter, who tosses the blood, who removes
the ashes of the inner altar, who removes the ashes of the candlestick,

who carries up the limbs to the camp, the head, the right hind leg, the two forelegs, the rump, and the left hind leg, the breast, the neck, the two flanks, the innards, the fine flour, the cakes, and the wine [M. Tam. 3:1A–B]," these are the words of R. Simeon of Mispeh. R. Yosé says, "[The order was] the head, the right hind leg, the two forelegs, the breast, the neck, the two flanks, the rump, and the left hind leg." Said Ben 'Azzai to R. Aqiba in the name of R. Joshua, "In the way in which it walked, it was offered."

The daily whole offering is now described in some detail, the priests having been chosen to carry out their particular tasks.

The Daily Whole Offering

M. 2:4 **The daily whole-offering was offered by nine, ten, eleven, or twelve [priests], no less, no more. How so? It itself was offered by nine [priests]. On the Festival [of Tabernacles], in the hand of one [additional priest] was a flask of water—thus ten. At dusk, by eleven: it itself by nine, and two, with two pieces of wood in their hands. And on the Sabbath, by eleven: it itself by nine and two priests, with two dishes of frankincense for the show bread in their hands. And on the Sabbath which coincides with the Festival [of Tabernacles], in the hand of yet another priest was a flask of water. A ram was offered by eleven: the meat by five, the innards, flour, and wine by two each. An ox was offered by twenty-four: the head and the right hind leg—the head by one, and the right hind leg by two; the rump and the left hind leg—the rump by two, and the left hind leg by two; the breast and the neck—the breast by one, and the neck by three; the two forelegs by two; the two flanks by two; the innards, the fine flour, and the wine by three each. Under what circumstances? In the case of public offerings. But in the case of an individual's offering, if [one priest] wanted to offer it up [all by himself], he offered it up. Flaying and cutting up both these and those [offerings] are subject to the same rules.**

T. 1:13 [M. Yoma 2:3E]: the head, the right hind leg, the breast and throat, the two forelegs, the two flanks, the rump, the left hind leg." Thirteen acquire rights to it [M. Yoma 2:3D]. Sometimes thirteen acquire rights to it, sometimes fourteen, sometimes fifteen. A ram was offered by eleven [M. Yoma 2:6]. The lambs offered for the community are offered by eight, for there are no Baked Cakes with them. An ox is offered by twenty-four: the head and the right hind leg [M. Yoma 2:7A–B]: two hold the right hind leg and bring it up to the altar; three hold the dish and offer it up on the altar. Under what circumstances? In the case of public offerings. But in the case of an individual's offering, whoever wanted to offer it up offers it up [M. Yoma 2:4H–J].

> T. 1:14 M'SH B: One of the sons of Martha, daughter of Boethus, could take
> two sides of an ox which cost one thousand zuz and walk with them
> heel to toe and bring them up onto the altar.

The script of the rite is transcribed, now with attention to the time of day.
The daily whole offering of the morning coincided with the dawn.

> **M. 3:1 The supervisor said to them, "Go and see whether the time for
> slaughtering the sacrifice has come." If it has come, he who sees it
> says, "It is daylight!" Matithiah b. Samuel says, "[He says,] 'Has
> the whole east gotten light?' 'To Hebron?' and he says, 'Yes.'"**
> **M. 3:2 And why were they required to do thus? For once the moonlight
> came up, and they supposed that the eastern horizon was bright,
> and so they slaughtered the daily whole offering and had to bring
> it out to the place of burning. They brought the high priest down
> to the immersion hut. This governing principle applied in the
> Temple: Whoever covers his feet [and defecates] requires immer-
> sion, and whoever urinates requires sanctification [the washing] of
> hands and feet.**

The priests immersed, even if they were already in a state of cultic cleanness,
before they came in to perform their labor. They would immerse for times
and sanctify (wash) the hands and feet ten times in the course of the rite.

> **M. 3:3 A person does not enter the courtyard for the service, even if he is
> clean, unless he immerses. Five acts of immersion, and ten acts of
> sanctification of the hands and feet, does the high priest carry out
> on that day. And all of them are in the sanctuary at the Parvah
> chamber, except for this one alone.**

How the high priest immersed is now explained in detail. He wore
golden garments for the offering of the whole offering. He would perform
the blood-rite and another priest finished the butchering of the sacrificial
beast. He then proceeded to the incense-offering and the rest of the rites.

> **M. 3:4 They spread out a linen sheet between him and the crowd. He took
> off his clothes, went down, immersed, came up, and dried off. They
> brought him golden garments, and he put them on, and he sancti-
> fied his hands and feet. They brought him the daily whole-offer-
> ing. He cut [the windpipe and gullet], and another priest
> completed the slaughtering on his behalf. He received the blood
> and tossed it. He went in to offer up the incense-offering of the
> morning, to trim the lamps, and to offer up the head and limbs,
> baked cakes, and wine.**
> T. 1:15 Why does one say, "Is the whole eastern horizon light, up to Hebron?"
> Sometimes the rising column of the sun rises in the usual way, but the

rising column of the moon breaks forth over the entire eastern horizon. Abba Yosé b. Hanan says, "Daylight has broken forth" [cf. M. Yoma 3:1B].

T. 1:16 A high priest who goes out of the courtyard to speak with his fellow and went too far requires immersion [cf. M. Yoma 3:3A]. They asked Ben Zoma, "What is the reason for this immersion?" He said to them, "If one who goes in from one holy area to another, a place not subject to the punishment of extirpation, requires immersion, he who enters from an ordinary area to a holy place, which is subject to punishment of extirpation, surely should require immersion." R. Judah says, "This immersion too was required only because of real dirt. Sometimes an old source of uncleanness clings to one's hands. Because one is going to immerse [to clean up], he remembers that he is unclean and goes along."

The rule if the priest did not immerse and sanctify hands and feet requires specification.

T. 1:17 Priests who did not immerse and did not sanctify their hands and feet, and so too a high priest who did not immerse and did not sanctify his hands and feet between one act of service and the next, between putting on one set of garments and putting on the next, and who performed an act of service—their act of service is valid. But priests who did not immerse at all, or who did not sanctify their hands and feet at all, and so too a high priest who did not immerse at all or did not sanctify his hands and feet at all, in the morning [before beginning their acts of service], and who performed an act of service—their act of service is invalid.

The incense-offering was sandwiched between the rites of offering up the animal.

M. 3:5 The incense-offering of the morning was offered between the tossing of the blood and the offering up of the limbs. That of twilight [was offered up] between the burning of the limbs and the drink-offerings. If the high priest was decrepit or infirm, they heated hot water for him and poured it into the cold water, to relieve the chill.

T. 1:21 In all it was worth thirty maneh [M. Yoma 3:7C]. These funds are taken from the sanctuary. If he wanted to add, he may add out of his own pocket [M. Yoma 3:7E]. M'SH B: Ishmael b. Phiabi's mother made for him a tunic worth a hundred maneh. And he would stand and make offerings on the altar wearing it.

T. 1:22 SWB M'SH B: Eleazar b. Harsom's mother made for him a tunic for twenty thousand, and he would stand and make offerings on the altar while wearing it. But his brethren, the priests, called him down, because [it was so sheer that] he appeared naked while wearing it.

T. 1:23 A woman who made a white tunic—it is valid, on condition that she give it over for public use. All the same is the rule covering the garments of the high priest and those of the ordinary priest: [funds for] them derive from the heave-offering of the sheqel-chamber.

Before the high priest makes the atonement-offering for all Israel, he atones for himself and his family. How that rite for his household is set forth is now explained.

The High Priest's Personal Offering for the Day of Atonement

M. 3:6 **They brought him to the Parvah chamber, and it was in the sanctuary. They spread out a linen sheet between him and the crowd. He sanctified his hands and feet and took off his clothes. R. Meir says, "He took off his clothes, [then] sanctified his hands and feet." He went down, immersed, came up, and dried off. They brought him white clothes. He put them on and sanctified his hands and feet. "At dawn he would put on a garment of Pelusium linen worth twelve manehs, and at dusk, he wore Indian linen worth eight hundred zuz," the words of R. Meir. And the sages say, "At dawn he would put on a garment worth eighteen manehs, and at dusk, one worth twelve manehs. "In all it was worth thirty manehs." These belong to the public. And if he wanted to spend more, he could do so at his own expense.**

Now he does more than slaughter the beast. He offers a prayer beseeching forgiveness for the iniquities, transgressions, and sins committed by himself and his household.

M. 3:7 **He came over to his bullock. Now his bullock was set between the Porch and the Altar. Its head was to the south and its face to the west. And the priest stands at the east, with his face to the west. And he puts his two hands on it and states the confession. And thus did he say, "O Lord, I have committed iniquity, transgressed, and sinned before you, I and my house. O Lord, forgive the iniquities, transgressions, and sins, which I have done by committing iniquity, transgression, and sin before you, I and my house. As it is written in the Torah of Moses, your servant, 'For on this day shall atonement be made for you to clean you. From all your sins shall you be clean before the Lord' (Lev 16:30)." And they respond to him, "Blessed is the Name of the glory of his kingdom forever and ever."**

T. 2:1 How does he state the confession? "O Lord, I have committed iniquity, transgressed and sinned before you, I and my house. O Lord, forgive the iniquities, transgressions, and sins, which I have done in committing iniquity, transgression, and sin before you, I and my house, as it is written in the Torah of Moses, your servant. For on this day shall atonement be made for you to clean you. From all your sins shall you be clean before the Lord" (Lev 16:30) [M. Yoma 3:8F–G]. And the high priest further says, '[And Aaron shall lay both his hands upon the head of the live goat,] and confess over him all the iniquities of the people of Israel and all their transgressions, all their sins' (Lev 16:21)," the words of R. Meir. And the sages say, "Iniquities—these are those done deliberately. "Their transgressions—these are acts of rebellion." "Their sins—these are the misdeeds done inadvertently. Now after he has confessed the deliberate iniquities and the acts of rebellion, shall he go back and confess their inadvertent misdeeds as well? But how does he say the confession? 'O Lord, I have committed iniquity, transgressed, and sinned before you. . . .' And they respond to him, 'Blessed is the name of the glory of his kingdom forever and ever' [M. Yoma 3:8F–H]. For we see that all who confess make confession thus. David said, 'Both we and our fathers have sinned, we have committed iniquity, we have done wickedly' (Ps 106:6). Solomon said, 'We have sinned, we have transgressed, we have done wickedly' (I Kings 8:47). Daniel said, 'we have sinned, we have transgressed, we have done wickedly' (Dan 9:5). Now what is it that Moses said, 'Forgiving iniquity, transgression and sin' (Exod 34:7)? But since he was making confession for deliberate violations of the law and acts of rebellion, it is as if they are deeds done inadvertently before him. And thus did he confess, 'I have sinned, I have transgressed, I have done wickedly before you.'"

T. 2:2   He came to the east side of the courtyard, to the north of the altar [M Yoma 3:9]. There were two goats [M. Yoma 3:9B], with their faces towards the people and their backs toward the sanctuary. The high priest faced the sanctuary. Ten times that day he expresses the Divine Name, six in regard to the bullock, three for the goat, and one for the lots. There also was a box with two lots. They used to be of boxwood, but Ben Gamla made them of gold, and consequently he was remembered with honor [M. Yoma 3:9B–E]. Ben Qatin made twelve stopcocks for the laver, so that twelve priests may sanctify [wash] their hands and feet from it at one time. It had had only two, so that only two priests could sanctify their hands and feet from it at one time. And he is remembered with honor [M. Yoma 3:10A].

Now come the goats that atone for sin, one presented on the altar, the other sent forth to perish in the wilderness, that is, the scapegoat that carries the sins of the community away. The exposition begins with an account of those who provided the utensils for the rite, Ben Qatin, King Monobases of Adiabene and his mother, Helene. Then those who are remembered in contempt are listed, to complete the set. The Tosefta's supplement is particularly rich on this point.

The Two Goats and Other Offerings on the Day of Atonement

M. 3:8 He came to the east side of the courtyard, to the north of the altar, with the prefect at his right hand and the head of the father's house at the left. There were two goats. There also was a box with two lots. They used to be of boxwood, but Ben Gamla made them of gold. Consequently he was remembered with honor. Ben Qatin made twelve stopcocks for the laver, which had had only two. And he too made a mechanism for the laver, so its water should not be invalidated by being kept overnight. King Monobases had handles made of gold for all the vessels used on the Day of Atonement. Helene, his mother, set a golden candlestick over the door of the sanctuary. She also made a golden tablet, on which was written the pericope of the accused wife. As to Nicanor, miracles were done at his doors. And they remembered him with honor.

M. 3:9 But these [were remembered] dishonorably: the members of the household of Garmu did not want to teach others how to make the show bread. The members of the household of Abtinas did not want to teach others how to make the incense. Hygras b. Levi knew a lesson of singing but did not want to teach it to anyone else. Ben Qamsar did not want to teach others how to write. Concerning the first ones listed is stated the following verse: "The memory of the just is blessed" (Prov 10:7). And concerning these [latter ones] is stated the following verse: "But the name of the wicked shall rot."

The Tosefta will now amplify the theme of what noteworthy individuals did that is remembered as a blessing or that is preserved as a disgrace to their names.

T. 2:3 King Monobases had gold handles made for all the knives used on the Day of Atonement, and he is remembered with honor [cf. M. Yoma 3:10C]. Helene, his mother, set a gold candlestick over the door to the sanctuary. She also made a golden tablet on which was written the pericope of the accused wife [M. Yoma 3:10D–E], so that when the sun rises, sparks of golden light sparkle forth from it, so people know that the sun is rising.

T. 2:4 All the gates which were there were covered with gold except for Nicanor's gates, for a miracle was done with them. There are those who say it is because their copper is bright. R. Eliezer b. Jacob says, "It was Corinthian bronze and shown like gold ["it is as pretty as gold"]." Now what is the miracle which was done with them? They say: When Nicanor was bringing them from Alexandria, in Egypt, a gale rose in the sea and threatened to drown them. They took one of them and tossed it into the sea, and they wanted to throw in the other but

Nicanor would not let them. He said to them, "If you throw in the second one, throw me in with it." He was distressed all the way to the wharf at Jaffa. Once they reached the wharf at Jaffa, the other door popped up from underneath the boat. And there are those who say one of the beasts of the sea swallowed it, and when Nicanor came to the wharf at Jaffa, it brought it up and tossed it onto land. And concerning it, it is explicitly stated in tradition, "The beams of our house are cedar, our rafters are pine" (Song of Songs 1:17).

T.   2:5   The members of the household of Garmu were experts in making Show Bread and they did not want to teach others [how to make it] [cf. M. Yoma 3:11 B]. The sages sent and brought experts from Alexandria, in Egypt, who were expert in similar matters, but were not experts in removing it from the oven. The members of the house of Garmu would heat the oven on the outside, and it [the loaf of bread] would be removed [on its own] on the inside. The experts from Alexandria did not do so. And some say this made it get moldy. And when the sages learned of the matter, they said, "The Holy One, blessed be He, created the world only for his own glory, as it is said, "Everyone that is called by my name and whom I have created for my glory" (Isa 43:7), [so we might as well pay the tariff]." They sent for them, and they did not come until they doubled their former salary. They used to take a fee of twelve manehs every day, and now they went and took a fee of twenty-four," the words of R. Meir. R. Judah says, "Twenty-four did they take every day, and now they went and took forty-eight manehs." Said to them the sages, "Now why were you unwilling to teach?" They said, "The members of father's house knew that the Temple is destined for destruction, and they did not want to teach others how to do it, so that they should not be able to do it before an idol in the way in which they do it before the Omnipresent." And on account of this next matter they are remembered with honor: M. For a piece of clean bread was never found in the hands of their sons and daughters under any circumstances, so that people might not say about them, "They are nourished from the Show Bread." This was meant to carry out the following verse: "You shall be clean before the Lord and before Israel" (Num 32:22).

T.   2:6   The members of the house of Abtinas were experts in preparing the incense for producing smoke [cf. M. Yoma 3:11C], and they did not want to teach others how to do so. The sages sent and brought experts from Alexandria, in Egypt, who knew how to concoct spices in much the same way. But they were not experts in making the smoke ascend [as well as the others]. The smoke coming from the incense of the house of Abtinas would ascend straight as a stick up to the beams, and afterward it scattered in all directions as it came down. That of the Alexandrians would scatter as it came down forthwith [not rising properly]. Now when the sages realized this, they said, "The Omnipresent has created the world only for his own glory, as it is said, 'The Lord has made everything for his own purpose' (Prov 16:4)." The sages sent to them [the members of the house of Abtinas], but they declined to come until the sages doubled their wages. They had been receiving twelve manehs every day, and now they went and got twenty-four," the words of R. Meir. R. Judah says, "They had been getting twenty-four every day. Now they went and got forty-eight manehs." The sages said to them, "Now why were you unwilling to teach [others]?" They said to them, "The members of father's house knew that the Temple is destined for destruction, and they did not want to teach others their art, so that people would not burn incense before an idol in the same way in which they burn incense before the Omnipresent." And in this [next] matter, they are remembered for good: A woman of their household never went out wearing perfume at any time, and not only so, but when they would marry into their household a woman from some other place, they made an agreement that she not put on perfume, so that people should not say, "Their women are putting on perfume made up from the preparation of the incense for the Temple." This they did to carry out the following verse, "And you shall be clear before the Lord and before Israel" (Num 32:22).

The sequence of virtuous actions continues, now involving heirs of virtue.

T. 2:7 Said R. Aqiba, "Simeon b. Luga told me, 'A certain child of the sons of their sons and I were gathering grass in the field. Then I saw him laugh and cry. 'I said to him, 'Why did you cry?' 'He said to me, 'Because of the glory of father's house, which has gone into exile.' I said to him, 'Then why did you laugh?' He said, 'At the end of it all, in time to come, the Holy One, blessed be He, is going to make his descendants rejoice.' I said to him, 'Why?' [What did you see to make you think of this?] He said to me, 'A smoke-raiser' in front of me [made me laugh].' I said to him, 'Show it to me.' He said to me, 'We are subject to an oath not to show it to anyone at all.'" Said R. Yohanan b. Nuri, "One time I was going along the way and an old man came across me and said to me, 'I am a member of the house of Abtinas. At the beginning, when the house of father was discreet, they would give their scrolls [containing the prescriptions for frankincense only] to one another. Now take it, but be careful about it, since it is a scroll containing a recipe for spices.' And when I came and reported the matter before R. Aqiba, he said to me, 'From now on it is forbidden to speak ill of these people again.'" On the basis of this story, Ben 'Azzai said, "Yours will they give you, by your own name will they call you, in your place will they seat you. There is no forgetfulness before the Omnipresent. No humanity can touch what is designated for his fellow."

T. 2:8 Agdis b. Levi knew a certain mode of singing, and he did not want to teach it to others [M. Yoma 3:11D]. The sages said to him, "Why did you not want to teach it to others?" He said to them, "The members of father's house knew that the Temple was destined for destruction, and they did not want to teach their mode of singing to others, so that they should not sing before an idol the way in which they say [song] before the Omnipresent." Ben Qamsar knew [the art] of writing, and did not want to teach anyone else [M. Yoma 3:11 E]. They said to him, "Why do you not want to teach anyone else?" He remained silent. These others found an answer to what they said, but Ben Qamsar did not find an answer to what he said. These others sought to increase their own glory and to diminish the glory owing to heaven. Therefore their own glory was diminished, while the glory of heaven was increased. And a good name and a good memorial were not theirs ever. Concerning the first ones, it is said, "The memory of the righteous is for a blessing." But with regard to the latter ones it is said, "But the name of the wicked shall rot" (Prov 10:7).

Now the rite is carried forward. The priest draws lots for each of the two goats, one for the Lord, one for Azazel.

M. 4:1 He shook the box [with the lots] and brought up the two lots. On one was written, "For the Lord," and on one was written, "For Azazel." The prefect was at his right, and the head of the ministering family [father's house] at his left. If the lot "for the Lord" came up in his right hand, the prefect says to him, "My lord, high priest, raise up your right hand." If the one "for the Lord" came up in his left hand, the head of the ministering family says to him, "My lord, high priest, raise up your left hand." He put them on the two goats and says, "For the Lord, a sin-offering." R. Ishmael says, "He did not have to say 'sin-offering,' but only 'For the Lord.'" And they respond to him, "Blessed is the name of the glory of his kingdom forever and ever."

T. 2:9 He shook the box [with the lots] and took up two lots [M. Yoma 4:1A], one in his right hand and one in his left. If it [the one for the Lord] came up in his right hand, all the Israelites were joyful. But if it came up in his left hand, all Israelites were not joyful.

T. 2:10 They asked R. Aqiba, "What about changing it from the left hand to the right?" He said to them, "Don't give the heretics a chance to ridicule you." R. Judah said in the name of R. Eliezer, "The prefect and the high priest put out their two right hands simultaneously. If it came up in the right hand of the high priest, the prefect says to him, 'My lord, high priest, raise up your right hand.' If it came up in the right hand of the prefect, the head of the house of the fathers says to him, 'Prefect, speak in your own behalf.'" And they put them on two goats. He says, "For the Lord." And the prefect says, "For a sin-offering." R.

Ishmael says, "It was not necessary to call it a sin-offering" [M. Yoma 4:1G]. They said to him, "Now has it not already been said, 'And he will make it a sin-offering' (Lev 16:9)?"

The scapegoat is sent away and the goat for the offering is designated. Now the priest confesses the sins of the community at large, beginning with the priesthood itself.

> **M. 4:2** **He tied a crimson thread on the head of the goat which was to be sent forth, and set it up toward the way by which it would be sent out. And on that which was to be slaughtered [he tied a crimson thread] at the place at which the act of slaughter would be made [the throat]. And he came to his bullock a second time [M. 3:8A] and put his two hands on it and made the confession. And thus did he say, "O Lord, I have committed iniquity, transgressed, and sinned before you, I and my house and the children of Aaron, your holy people. O Lord, forgive, I pray, the iniquities, transgressions, and sins which I have committed, transgressed, and sinned before you, I, my house, and the children of Aaron, your holy people, as it is written in the Torah of Moses, your servant, 'For on this day shall atonement be made for you to cleanse you. From all your sins shall you be clean before the Lord' (Lev 16:30)." And they responded to him, "Blessed is the name of the glory of his kingdom forever and ever."**

After the confession, the blood rite is performed, with the blood tossed on the altar.

> **M. 4:3** **He slaughtered it and received its blood in a basin. He handed it over to him who would stir it while he was standing on the fourth terrace of the sanctuary, so that [the blood] would not congeal. He took the fire-pan and went up to the top of the altar. He cleared off coals to either side and scooped up glowing cinders from below. Then he came down and set it down on the fourth terrace of the courtyard.**

The interlude compares the daily rite with that of the Day of Atonement.

> **M. 4:4** **Every day he would scoop out the cinders with a silver fire-pan and empty them into a golden one. But today he would clear out the coals in a gold one, and in that same one he would bring the cinders in[to the inner sanctuary]. On other days he would clear out cinders with one holding four qabs and empty that into one holding three. But today he would clear them out with one holding three qabs, and in that same one he would bring the cinders in[to the inner sanctuary]. R. Yosé says, "Every day he would clear the**

cinders out in one holding a seah and empty it into one holding
three qabs. But today he would clear the cinders in one holding
three qabs, and in that same one he would bring the cinders in."
Every day it was heavy. But today it was light. Every day its handle
was short. But today it was long. "Every day it was of yellow gold,
But today it was of red gold," the words of R. Menahem.

M. 4:5 Every day one would offer up half a maneh of incense at dawn and
half at dusk. But today he would add his two handfuls [of incense].
Every day it was fine. But today it was the finest of the fine. Every
day the priests go up on the east side of the ramp and go down on
the west. But today the high priest goes up right in the middle of
the ramp and goes down right in the middle. R. Judah says, "At all
times the high priest goes up in the middle and goes down in the
middle." Every day the high priest sanctifies his hands and feet
from the laver. Today he does it from a golden jug. R. Judah says,
"At all times the high priest sanctifies his hands and feet from a
golden jug."

M. 4:6 "Every day there were four stacks of wood there. But today there
were five," the words of R. Meir. R. Yosé says, "Every day there were
three, but today there were four." R. Judah says, "Every day there
were two. But today there were three."

T. 2:11 Every day two priests go in, one with the ladle, and one with the fire-
pan. Today he [the high priest alone] takes the fire-pan in his right
hand the ladle in his left hand. Under what circumstances? In the case
of the incense for the inner altar. But as to the incense of the golden
altar, lo, it is deemed equivalent to the rite for the incense of all the
other days of the year. Every day it was heavy, but today it was light.
Every day its handle was short, but today it was long [M. Yoma
4:4G–J], so that its arm would assist him. Every single day it had no
cask, but today it had a cask," the words of the Son of the Prefect. Every
day there were two stacks of wood there, but today three, one for the
large stack of wood, one for the second stack of wood, and one which
they add to the incense which is burned inside," the words of R. Judah
[M. Yoma 4:6E–F]. R. Yosé adds one for maintaining the fire. R. Meir
adds one for [burning up] the limbs and the birds which were not
wholly consumed the preceding evening.

Y. 4:5 I:1 *The compound of incense [was made up of] balm, onycha, galbanum,
and frankincense, each in the quantity of seventy manehs; myrrh, cassia,
spikenard, and saffron, each sixteen manehs by weight; costus, twelve; aromatic rind, three; cinnamon, nine manehs. You turn out to rule. They
weight in all three hundred sixty-five manehs, for the days of the year. And
there were the three of that day. That is in line with that which we have
learned: But today he would add his two handfuls of incense [M. 4:5B].*

The narrative of the rite resumes, now with attention to the incense-offering.

> **M. 5:1 They brought the ladle and fire-pan out to him. And he took hand-
> fuls [of incense from the pan] and put [the incense] into the
> ladle—a large one in accord with the large size [of his hand], or a
> small one in accord with the small size [of his hand], such was the
> required measure [of the ladle]. He took the fire-pan in his right
> hand and the ladle in his left. He then walked through the sanctu-
> ary, until he came to the space between the two veils which sepa-
> rate the holy place from the most holy place, and the space between
> them was a cubit. R. Yosé says, "There was only a single veil there
> alone, since it says, 'And the veil shall divide for you between the
> holy place and the most holy place' (Exod 26:33)."**

> **M. 5:2 The outer [veil] was looped up at the south and the inner one at
> the north. He walks between them until he reaches the northern
> side. [When] he has reached the northern side, he turns around to
> ward the south, walks along with the curtain at his left until he has
> reached the ark. [When] he has reached the ark, he places the fire-
> pan between the two bars [Exod. 25:12]. He piled up the incense
> on the coals, so that the whole house was filled with smoke. He
> came out, going along by the way by which he had gone in. And
> he said a short prayer in the outer area. He did not prolong his
> prayer, so as not to frighten the Israelites.**

The Yerushalmi specifies the short prayer offered with the incense-offering
at the inner sanctum.

> *Y. 5:2 II:1 And he said a short prayer in the outer area [M. 5:2G]. This was the
> prayer of the high priest on the Day of Atonement, when he left the holy
> place whole and in one piece: "May it be pleasing before you, Lord, our
> God of our fathers, that [a decree of] exile not be issued against us, not this
> day or this year, but if a decree of exile should be issued against us, then let
> it be exile to a place of Torah. May it be pleasing before you, Lord, our God
> and God of our fathers, that a decree of want not be issued against us, not
> this day or this year, but if a decree of want should be issued against us,
> then let it be a want of [the performance of] religious duties. May it be
> pleasing before you, Lord, our God and God of our fathers, that this year
> be a year of cheap food, full bellies, good business; a year in which the earth
> forms clods, then is parched so as to form scabs, and then moistened with
> dew, so that your people, Israel, will not be in need of the help of one
> another. And do not heed the prayer of travelers [that it not rain]." Rabbis
> of Caesarea say, "And concerning your people, Israel, that they not exercise
> dominion over one another." And for the people who live in the Sharon
> plain he would say this prayer: "May it be pleasing before you, Lord, our
> God and God of our fathers, that our houses not turn into our graves."*

M. 5:3 **Once the ark was taken away, there remained a stone from the days of the earlier prophets, called Shetiyyah. It was three finger-breadths high. And on it did he put [the fire-pan].**

T. 2:12   He went in and walked in the Sanctuary until he was located standing between the golden altar [at the right] and the candelabrum [at his left]. The altar was further in than he. The table was set to the north, a third of the way inward, two and a half cubits away from the wall. A candelabrum was opposite it at the south, a third of the way inward, two and a half cubits away from the wall. The altar was right in the middle, extending somewhat outward, toward the two bars of the ark, and extending outward to the east. And all of them were situated from the halfway point of the house and inward. Then he walked through the Sanctuary until he came to the space between the two veils which separate the Holy Place from the Most Holy Place, and the space between them was a cubit [M. Yoma 5:1F–G]. This was the place of the sanctuary [*debir*] which Solomon had made. R. Yosé says, "There was only a single veil there alone, since it says, 'And the veil shall divide for you between the Holy Place and the Most Holy Place' (Exod 26:33)" [M. Yoma 5:1H–I]. They said to him, "Why does Scripture then say, Between the Holy Place and the Most Holy Place?" He said to them, "Between the upper Holy Place [on top] and the lower Holy Place [on the bottom]. Another matter: Between Nob, Gibeon, Shilo, and the eternal house."

T. 2:13   The outer one was looped up at the south, and the inner one at the north. He walks between them until he reaches the northern side. When he reaches the northern side, he turns around toward the south, walks along with the curtain at his left until he has reached the ark [M. Yoma 5: IJ–L]. When he reaches the ark, he then pushes the veil aside with his hips And he placed the fire-pan between the two bars and he piled up the incense on the coals, so that the whole house was filled with smoke. He went out, going along by the way by which he went in. And he said a short prayer in the outer area. He did not prolong his prayer, so as not to frighten the Israelites [M. Yoma 5:1M–Q]. M'SH B: A high priest took a long time. They said to him, "Why did you take a long time?" He said to them, "I was praying for you and for the sanctuary of your fathers that it not be destroyed." They said to them, "No matter, you have no right to change the custom."

T. 2:14   A stone was there from the days of the earlier prophets, called Shetiyyah. It was three fingerbreadths high [M. Yoma 5:2A–B]. In the beginning the ark was placed on it. When the ark was taken away, on it they would burn the incense before the innermost altar. R. Yosé says, "From it the world was created, as it says, 'Out of Zion, the perfection of the world' (Ps 50:2)."

T. 2:15 The bottle containing the manna, the flask of the anointing oil, the staff of Aaron, with its almonds and blossoms, and the chest sent as a gift when the Philistines return the Glory to Eli the God of Israel—all of them are in the house of the Most Holy of Holies. When the ark was stored away, they were stored away with it. The two bars of the ark protruded from the ark until they reached the veil, as it is said, "And the poles were so long that the ends of the poles were seen from the holy place before the inner sanctuary" (1 Chron 5:9). Is it possible that they tore a hole in the veil? Scripture says, "But they could not be seen from outside" (2 Chron 5: 9). Is it possible that they could not be seen on the inside? Scripture says, "The ends of the poles were seen from the Holy Place before the inner sanctuary." On this basis one must conclude: they were very long. The poles were very long and reached the veil and pressed against the veil and were seen on the inside. And concerning them it is stated explicitly in tradition, "My beloved is to me a bag of myrrh, that lies between my breasts" (Song of Songs 1:13).

Now the blood rite is performed, with blood tossed on the altar. The synagogue prayers for the Day of Atonement recapitulate these rites in verbal descriptions that recall the Temple activities. But in the end we shall see a different emphasis altogether from that upon the Temple and its sacrificial procedures that preoccupy the Halakhah through chapter 7.

M. 5:4 **He took the blood from the one who had been stirring it. He [again] went into the place into which he had entered and again stood on the place on which he had stood. Then he sprinkled some [of the blood], one time upward and seven times downward. But he did not intentionally toss it upward or downward. But [he did it] like one who cracks a whip. And thus did he count: "One, one and one, one and two, one and three, one and four, one and five, one and six, one and seven." He went out and he set down [the bowl of blood] on the golden stand in the Sanctuary. They brought him the goat. He slaughtered it and received its blood in a basin. He went into that same place into which he had entered, and stood on that same place on which he had stood. And he sprinkled some [of the blood], one time upward and seven times downward. But he did not intentionally sprinkle upward or downward. But he [did it] like one who cracks a whip. And thus did he count: "One, one and one, one and two," etc. He went out and he set it on the second stand which was in the Sanctuary. R. Judah says, "There was only one stand there alone. He took the blood of the bullock and set down the blood of the goat in its place," and sprinkled some of it on the veil toward the ark outside. [He sprinkled some of the blood] one time upward and seven times downward. But he did not** intentionally sprinkle upward or downward. But he did it like one who cracks a whip. And thus did he count: "One, one and one, one and two," etc. He took the blood of the goat and set down the blood of the bullock, and he sprinkled some of it on the veil toward the ark, on the outside of the veil, one time upward and seven times downward. But he did not intentionally sprinkle upward or downward. But he did it like one who cracks a whip. And thus did he count: "One, one and one, one and two," etc. Then he emptied the blood of the bullock into the blood of the goat, and poured the contents of the full basin into the empty one. "And he went out toward the altar which is before the Lord" (Lev 16:18). This refers to the golden altar.

M. 5:5   He began to purify [the altar] [by sprinkling the blood] in a downward gesture. From what point does he start? From the northeastern corner, then to the northwestern, southwestern, and southeastern ones. At the place at which he begins in the process of purification on the outer altar, at that point does he complete doing the same at the inner altar. R. Eliezer says, "He stood right where he was and purified [the altar by sprinkling the blood of purification]." And at every one he sprinkled the horn from below to above, except for this one which was before him, on which he would sprinkle [the blood] from above to below.

M. 5:6   He tossed the blood on the top of the altar seven times. Then did he pour out the residue of the blood [used on the inner altar] onto the western base of the outer altar. And that [the residue of the blood sprinkled on] the outer altar he poured out on the southern base. The two streams of blood then mingled together in the [flow of the] surrounding channel and flowed down into the Qidron brook. They are sold to gardeners for fertilizer. And the law of sacrilege applies to them [until the sale].

T. 2:16   He took the blood from the one who was stirring it. He [again] went into the place into which he had entered [earlier] and again stood on the place on which he had stood [M. Yoma 5:3A–B]. Then he sprinkled some of it [M. Yoma 5:4C] on the Mercy Seat toward the two bars of the ark, one time upwards and seven times downwards. But he did not intentionally sprinkle upwards or downwards. But he did it like one who cracks a whip [M. Yoma 5:3C–E]. And thus did he count, "One, one and one, one and two, one and three, one and four, one and five, one and six, one and seven" [M. Yoma 5:3F]. R. Judah said in the name of R. Eliezer, "Thus did he count: 'One, one and one, two and one, three and one, four and one, five and one, six and one, seven and one.'" He went out to his left, along the veil. And he did not touch the veil. But if he touched it, he touched it. Said R. Eleazar b. R. Yosé, "I myself saw it in Rome and there were drops of blood on it. And he told me, 'These are from the drops of blood of the Day of Atonement'" [cf. M. Yoma 5:4J].

T. 3:1   He came to circumambulate the altar. From what point does he start? From the northeastern corner, then to the northwestern, the southwestern, and the southeastern corners [M. Yoma 5:5D–E]. At the place at which he begins the process of purification, on the outer altar, at that point does he complete doing the same at the inner altar [M. Yoma 5:5F]. And at the place at which he begins preparing the burnt-offering on the outer altar, there he completes the sin-offering on the inner altar. At every one he sprinkled the horn from below to above, except for the one which was before him, on which he would sprinkle the blood from above to below [M. Yoma 5:5H–J]. R. Judah said in the name of R. Eliezer, "He stood right where he was and purified the altar. And at every one he put the blood sprinkled the horn from below to above, except for the one diagonally before him, on which he would sprinkle the blood from above to below" [M. Yoma 5:5G, H–J].

The order of the actions is strictly regulated, and one component cannot be performed out of its proper position. If the blood of the goat was tossed before that of the bullock, he has to repeat the rite afterward.

M. 5:7   **The entire rite of the Day of Atonement stated in accord with its proper order—if [the high priest] did one part of the rite before its fellow—he has done nothing whatsoever. [If for instance] he took care of the blood of the goat before the blood of the bullock, let him go and sprinkle some of the blood of the goat after he has sprinkled the blood of the bullock. And if before he had completed the acts of placing the blood on the inner altar, the blood was poured out, let him bring other blood and go and sprinkle it to begin with on the inner altar [M. 5:3–4]. And so [is the rule] in the case of the sanctuary [M. 5:5], and so in the case of the golden altar [M. 5:5], for each of them constitutes an act of atonement unto itself [and need not be repeated]. R. Eleazar and R. Simeon say, "From the place at which he broke off, from there he begins once more."**

T. 3:3   The entire rite of the Day of Atonement, stated in accord with its proper order—if one did one part of the rite before its fellow, he has done nothing whatsoever [M. Yoma 5:7A–B], except for taking out the ladle and fire-pan, for if he did one deed before its fellow, what he has done is done.

T. 3:4   Said R. Judah, "Under what circumstances? In the case of deeds done inside, while the high priest is wearing white garments. But as to things done outside, while the high priest is wearing golden garments, even if he did one deed before its fellow, and repeated any one of all the rites, what he has done is done."

T. 3:5 [If] he put some of the placings of blood inside and then the blood was
poured out, let him bring new blood and begin afresh inside. R. Eleazar
and R. Simeon say, "He begins at the place at which he stopped" [cf.
M. Yoma 5:7H]. [If] he completed the placings of blood inside and put
some of the placings of blood outside and then the blood was poured
out, let him bring fresh blood and begin at the beginning outside. R.
Eleazar and R. Simeon say, "He begins at the place at which he
stopped."

We revert to the scapegoat and the rite of sending it off into the wilderness.
We start with a law and proceed to the narrative.

The Scapegoat and its Rule

M. 6:1 **The two goats of the Day of Atonement—the religious requirement
concerning them is that the two of them be equivalent in appearance, height, and value, and that they be purchased simultaneously.
But even though they are not equivalent [in these regards], they are
valid. [If] one purchased one this day and the other one the next,
they are valid. If one of them died, if before the casting of the lots
it died, let [the priest] purchase a mate for the survivor. But if after
the casting of the lots it died, let one get another mate and cast lots
for them as at the outset. And he says, "If the one belonging to the
Lord died, then this one upon which the lot 'For the Lord' has come
up is to stand in its stead. And if the one which was for Azazel has
died, this one upon which the lot 'For Azazel' has come up will
stand in its stead." And the second one is to be put out to pasture
until it is blemished, and then it is sold, and the money received for
it is to fall to a freewill-offering. For a sin-offering of the community is not left to die. R. Judah says, "It is left to die." And further
did R. Judah say, "[If] its blood is poured out, let the one who is to
be sent forth be left to die. If the one which is to be sent forth died,
let its [the other's] blood be poured out."**

T. 3:9 The bullock and goat for the Day of Atonement which were lost, and
one set apart other animals in their stead, and he did not suffice to offer
them up before the animals first set aside were found—Let them be set
out to pasture until they suffer a blemish, then be sold, and their proceeds fall for a freewill-offering.

T. 3:10 The religious requirement of the two goats of the Day of Atonement is
to be subject to lots. [If] one did not cast lots for it, even so it is valid.
The casting of lots for them is to be by Aaron [a high priest]. Even [if
it is done] by an ordinary priest, they are valid. The two goats of the
Day of Atonement—before one has cast lots for them, he is permitted
to designate them for some other purpose. Once he has cast lots for
them, he is not permitted to designate them for some other purpose [cf.
M. Yoma 6:1F–G].

T. 3:11 A Passover-offering which is not offered on the first [festival] is to be
         offered on the second. [If] it was not offered on the second, it is to be
         offered on the third. Coins not [used for] an offering on the first should
         be [used for] an offering on the second. [If] they are not used for an
         offering on the second, they should be [used for] an offering on the
         third. A festal offering which is not offered on the first should be
         offered on the second. [If] it is not offered on the second, it should be
         offered on the third. [If] it is not offered on the third, it should be
         offered at some point in the future.

T. 3:12 Goats set aside for the festival which are not offered on the festival
         should be offered on the New Month. [If] they are not offered on the
         New Month, let them be offered on the Day of Atonement. [If] they
         are not offered on the Day of Atonement, let them be offered on the
         next festival. For to begin with they were set apart as public offerings
         only so as to be offered on the outer altar. [If] the goat which is to be
         sent forth died before the blood of the first [goat] was sprinkled on the
         altar, even though he has not recited the confession over it, he has ful-
         filled his obligation, since it says, 'He shall bring forth the live goat'
         (Lev 16:20). How long is it required to be kept alive? Until 'he finishes
         making atonement for the holy' (Lev 16:20)," the words of R. Judah.
         R. Simeon says, "Until the time of confession." M. R. Yosé says, "Thus
         he says, 'Your people, the house of Israel, have sinned, transgressed, and
         done iniquity.'"

The goat that carries away the sins of Israel to the wilderness is presented
along with a confession, now covering the house of Israel.

**M. 6:2 He comes to the goat which is to be sent forth and lays his two
hands on it and makes the confession. And thus did he say, "O
Lord, your people, the house of Israel, has committed iniquity,
transgressed, and sinned before you. Forgive, O Lord, I pray, the
iniquities, transgressions, and sins, which your people, the house
of Israel, have committed, transgressed, and sinned before you, as
it is written in the Torah of Moses, your servant, 'For on this day
shall atonement be made for you to clean you. From all your sins
shall you be clean before the Lord' (Lev 16:30)." And the priests
and people standing in the courtyard, when they would hear the
Expressed Name [of the Lord] come out of the mouth of the high
priest, would kneel and bow down and fall on their faces and say,
"Blessed be the name of the glory of his kingdom forever and ever."**

Then the dispatch of the goat for Azazel is carried out. Even an ordinary
Israelite, not of the caste-status of the priest, was permitted to do so, but the
priests kept the rite in their own hands.

M. 6:3 He gave [the scapegoat] over to the one who was to lead it out. All are valid to lead it out. But high priests made it a practice of not letting Israelites lead it out. Said R. Yosé, "M'SH W: Arsela led it out, and he was an Israelite."

M. 6:4 They made a ramp for it, on account of the Babylonians, who would pull out its hair and say, "Take and go, take and go." The eminent people of Jerusalem used to accompany him to the first booth. There were ten booths from Jerusalem to the ravine, a distance of nine ris—seven and a half to a [Roman] mil. At each booth they say to him, "Lo, here is food, here is water." And they accompany him from one booth to the next, except for [the man in] the last [tabernacle] among them, who does not go along with him to the ravine. But he stands from a distance and observes what he does.

T. 3:13 They make a ramp for it, because of the Alexandrians, who pull out its hair, and say to it, "Take and go, take and go." The best people of Jerusalem accompany it to the first tabernacle [M. Yoma 6:4A–C]. For there were ten tabernacles within a distance of twelve miles," the words of R. Meir. R. Judah says, "There were nine tabernacles in a distance of ten miles." R. Yosé says, "There were five tabernacles in a distance of ten miles." And they share an 'erub [commingling the boundaries for the Sabbath] with one to the other [so that they in the tabernacles may accompany the man]. Said R. Yosé, son of R. Judah, "I can arrange them in two tabernacles [only]."

The rite of the goat for Azazel now culminates in pushing the beast off a cliff and into a ravine.

M. 6:5 Now what did he do? He divided the crimson thread. Half of it he tied to a rock, and half of it he tied between its horns. He then pushed it over backward, and it rolled down the ravine. And it did not reach halfway down the mountain before it broke into pieces. He came and sat himself down under the last tabernacle until it got dark. At what time does the one who takes the goat impart uncleanness to garments [Lev 16:26]? Once he has gone forth from the wall of Jerusalem. R. Simeon says, "Once he has pushed it into the ravine."

T. 3:14 They asked R. Eliezer, "Lo, if the goat which is to be sent fell sick, what is the law as to carrying it?" He said to them, "Can he carry others?" [If] the one who sends him fell sick, what is the law as to sending him with someone else?" He said to them, "Thus may you and I be in peace." [If] he pushed it down and it did not die, what is the law as to going down after it and killing it?" He said to them, "Thus be the fate of the enemies of the Omnipresent." And the sages say, "[If] it fell ill,

he carries it. [If] the one who sends it fell ill, one sends it with someone else." [If] one pushed it down and it did not die, one should go
down after it and kill it."

The narrative of the scapegoat breaks off and reverts to what was happening in the Temple while the goat for Azazel was being led into the wilderness to its death. This was reported to the high priest.

M. 6:6 [Meanwhile, the high priest] came to the bullock and goat which
are to be burned. He tore them open and removed their innards.
He put them onto a dish and offered them up on the altar. He then
twisted [the limbs of the beasts] on poles, and they carried them
out to the place of burning. And when do they impart uncleanness
to clothing [who carry out the limbs of the goat and bullock]?
Once they have gone past the wall of the courtyard. R. Simeon
says, "Once the fire has taken hold of the greater part of [the
beasts' carcasses]."

M. 6:7 They said to the high priest, "The goat has reached the wilderness." Now how did they know that the goat had come to the
wilderness? They made sentinel posts, and waved flags, so they
might know that the goat had reached the wilderness. Said R.
Judah, "Now did they not have a more impressive sign than that?
From Jerusalem to Bet Hiddudo is three miles. They can walk a
mile, come back a mile, and wait sufficient time to walk a mile, and
so they will know that the goat has reached the wilderness." R.
Ishmael says, "Now did they not have another sign? There was a
crimson thread tied to the door of the sanctuary. When the goat
had reached the wilderness, the thread would turn white, as it says,
'Though your sins be as scarlet, they shall be as white as snow' (Isa
1:18)."

T. 3:15 "The goat which is sent forth, even though it does not impart uncleanness to clothing, imparts uncleanness to food," the words of R. Meir.
The sages say, "It does not impart uncleanness to food or drink,
because it is alive, and what is alive does not impart uncleanness to food
or drink." At what point does it impart uncleanness to clothes? Once
it has gone beyond the wall of Jerusalem," the words of R. Meir. R.
Judah says, "When it has reached the ravine." R. Simeon says, "From
the time of its being pushed into the ravine" [cf. M. Yoma 6:6G–H].

T. 3:16 "Bullocks which are to be burned and goats which are to be burned,
even though they do not impart uncleanness to clothing, impart
uncleanness to food and drink," the words of R. Meir. And the sages
say, "The [red] cow and cows which are to be burned impart uncleanness to food and drink. But the goat which is to be sent forth does not
impart uncleanness to food and drink, because it is alive, and a living
being does not impart uncleanness to food and drink." At what point

do they impart uncleanness to clothing? Once they have gone beyond the wall of the courtyard," the words of R. Meir. R. Judah says, "Once one has thrown them into the fire." R. Simeon says, "Once the fire has caught hold of the greater part of them" [M. Yoma 6:7G].

T. 3:17 Where do they burn them? In the great house of ashes, outside of Jerusalem, north of Jerusalem, beyond the three camps. Rows of priests were set up around the fire, because of the crush of the crowd, so that they should not push to see and fall into the fire. All the same is the one who burns and the one who helps out at the time of the burning— they impart uncleanness. But the one who arranges the wood on the pyre and who kindles the fire with a torch does not impart uncleanness to [their] clothing.

The animal offerings having been completed, the liturgy turns to the declamation of the Torah and to prayer.

The Rite Concludes with Reading from the Torah and with Prayer

M. 7:1 The high priest came to read [the Torah portion for the day in the women's court]. If he wanted to read while wearing linen garments, he reads [wearing them]. If not, he reads wearing his own white vestment. The beadle of the community takes the scroll of the Torah and gives it to the head of the community, and the head of the community gives it to the prefect [of the priests], and the prefect gives it to the high priest. The high priest rises and receives it and reads, "After the death" (Lev 16), and "Howbeit on the tenth day" (Lev 23:26-32). Then he rolls up the Torah and holds it to his heart and says, "More than what I have read out before you is written here." "And on the tenth" (Num 29:7-11) which is in the book of Numbers he reads by heart. Then he says eight blessings over it: ". . . for the Torah, . . .for the Temple service, . . . for the confession, . . . for the forgiveness of sin, . . . for the sanctuary (by itself), for Israel (by themselves), . . . and for the priests (by themselves), and for the rest of the Prayer." He who can see the high priest when he is reading cannot see the bullock and goat which are burned. And he who can see the bullock and goat when they are burned cannot see the high priest when he is reading. But this is not because he is not permitted to do so, but because it was quite a distance. The rites concerning both of them were done simultaneously.

T. 3:18 Eight blessings does he say over them on that day: For the Torah—just as they say a blessing over the Torah in the synagogue; for the Temple service, for the confession, for the forgiveness of sin, in their usual order. For the sanctuary, a blessing unto itself; for Israel, a blessing unto itself; for the priests, a blessing unto itself; and the remainder of the prayer— a supplication: and a prayer, "For your people Israel need salvation from you." And he seals the prayer with, ". . . who hears prayer." All of the people read from their own scroll, to show their worthiness in public.

Now there is a final rite of purification and the high priest goes home. Israel has atoned for its sin, through the rite of atonement and the effect of the Day of Atonement itself.

> **M. 7:2** **If [the high priest] reads [the Scriptures] wearing linen garments, he sanctified his hands and feet, took them off, descended, immersed, came up, and dried off. They brought him the golden garments. He put them on and sanctified his hands and feet. "Then he went out and prepared his ram and the ram of the people [Lev 16:24], and the seven unblemished lambs a year old [Num 29:8]," the words of R. Eliezer. R. Aqiba says, "They were offered with the daily whole-offering made at dawn. "And the bullock, burnt-offering, and goat offered outside [Num 29:11] were offered with the daily whole-offering made at dusk." He sanctified his hands and feet and took off his clothes and went down and immersed and came up and dried off. They brought him white garments, and he put them on, and sanctified his hands and feet. He went in to bring out the ladle and fire-pan. He sanctified his hands and feet, took off his clothes, went down and immersed, came up and dried off. They brought him golden garments and he put them on. He sanctified his hands and feet, and entered in to offer up the incense made at dusk, to trim the lamps. Then he sanctified his hands and feet, and took off his clothes. They brought him his own clothing and he put it on. Then they accompany him all the way home. And they celebrate a festival for all his friends when he has come forth whole from the sanctuary.**

> T. 3:19 R. Eliezer says, "Thus is the order of the offerings [which] they offered up: The bullock which is a whole-offering, and the goat which is prepared outside were offered with the whole-offering of the morning, and afterward the bullock and goat which are prepared inside, and afterward the ram of the people, and afterward seven unblemished rams." R. Aqiba says, "The bullock which is a whole-offering and the seven unblemished rams were afterward with the whole-offering of the morning, as it is said, "Beside the burnt-offering in the morning, which is for a continual burnt-offering" (Num 28:23), and afterward the bullock and goat which are prepared inside, and afterward the goat which is prepared outside, as it is said, "Beside the sin-offering of atonement and the continual burnt-offering and its meal-offering and drink-offering" (Num 29:11). And afterward his ram and the ram of the people." R. Judah says in the name of R. Eliezer, "One is offered with the daily whole-offering of the morning and six are offered with the daily whole-offering of dusk" [cf. M. Yoma 7:3D–F].

T. 3:20 A holiday does he make for his friends, when he has gone forth whole [M. Yoma 7:4]. M'SH B: Simeon b. Qimhit went forth to speak with an Arab king, and spit spurt out of his [the king's] mouth and fell on his clothes. His brother went in and served in his stead as high priest. The mother of these [men] witnessed two [officiating] high priests [who were her sons] on the same day.

M. 7:3 The high priest serves in eight garments, and an ordinary priest in four: tunic, underpants, head covering, and girdle. The high priest in addition wears the breastplate, apron, upper garment, and frontlet. By these did they receive inquiries for the Urim and Thummim. And they received inquiry only from the king, the court, or from someone in the service of the public.

Y. 7:3 II:2 R. Simon in the name of R. Jonathan of Bet Gubrin: "For two matters was there no atonement, but the Torah provided atonement for them, and these are they: gossiping and killing someone inadvertently. For gossiping there was no atonement, but the Torah provided atonement for it in the bells on the garment. 'And it shall be upon Aaron when he ministers, and its sound shall be heard when he goes into the holy place before the Lord, and when he comes out, lest he die' (Exod 28:35). Let the sound of the bell come and atone for the sound [of the gossip's tongue]. For killing inadvertently there was no mode of atonement, but the Torah provided atonement in the death of the high priest. 'And the congregation shall rescue the manslayer from the hand of the avenger of blood, and the congregation shall restore him to his city of refuge, to which he had fled, and he shall live in it until the death of the high priest who was anointed with the holy oil'" (Num 35:25).

[Y. 7:3 II:3 It has been taught: R. Eliezer b. Jacob says, "Atonement is noted with regard to the inner altar, and atonement is noted with regard to the outer altar. Just as atonement stated with regard to the inner altar involves atonement provided by an animal taken from the herd for those who shed blood, so atonement stated with regard to the outer altar involves atonement provided by an animal taken from the herd for those who shed blood. In the one case, however, it is for an act done inadvertently, and in the other case it is for an act done deliberately. The heifer whose neck is broken is different, however, since it atones for a killing whether it was done inadvertently or deliberately."

Y. 7:3 III:1 As to the frontlet [M. 7:3C]: There is he who wishes to propose that it is for the sins of those who blaspheme, and there is he who wishes to propose that it is for the sins of those who are presumptuous.

The exposition of the rite through the narrative, which is the preferred medium of expression in the Halakhah for the presentation of Temple rituals, has come to an end. It is comprehensible only in the context of Leviticus 16. It embodies no theological principles, treats the Day of Atonement as a celebration, not a day of remorse, and ignores the obligation to afflict the soul as part of the atonement rite for the Day of Atonement. The final chapter of Mishnah-tractate Yoma and its continuators in the Tosefta, Yerushalmi, and Bavli take up that matter and introduce the theme of repentance for sin, transforming the context in which the rite is performed.

The Laws of the Day of Atonement

We begin with rules governing refraining from eating and drinking, now expressed in the exemplary general rules and case-law that dominate in the Halakhic discourse of the Mishnah and its commentaries.

Not Eating, Not Drinking

M. 8:1 **On the Day of Atonement it is forbidden to eat, drink, bathe, put on any sort of oil, put on a sandal, or engage in sexual relations. But a king and a bride wash their faces. "And a woman who has given birth may put on her sandal," the words of R. Eliezer. And the sages prohibit.**

T. 4:1   On the Day of Atonement it is forbidden to eat, drink, bathe, anoint, put on sandals, [and] have sexual relations [M. Yoma 8:1A]. [It is not permitted to put on] even felt shoes. Minors are permitted to do all of them except putting on sandals, for appearance's sake.

T. 4:5   A man should not put on a nail-studded shoe and walk about his house, even from one bed to another [cf. M. Yoma 8:1]. But Rabban Simeon b. Gamaliel permits. And so did Rabban Simeon b. Gamaliel say, "If one's hands were dirty with mud or excrement, he may rinse them off in water, so that they will not dirty his clothes." [If] he was going to receive his father, master, [or] disciple, he crosses over the sea or river in the normal way, even up to his neck, and need not scruple. Male and female Zabs immerse in their normal way on the night [prior to] the Day of Atonement. Menstruating women and women who have given birth immerse in their normal way on the night [prior to] the Day of Atonement. R. Yosé b. R. Judah says, "From the twilight onward, one should not immerse, until it gets dark." R. Yosé says, "Priests immerse in the normal way at dusk, so that they may eat food in the status of heave-offering in the evening."

The Halakhah, as is its way, asks questions of definition: how much food or drink add up to eating or drinking? Do diverse foods join together to form that volume of prohibited food?

M. 8:2 **He who eats a large date's bulk [of food], inclusive of its pit—he who drinks the equivalent in liquids to a mouthful—is liable. All sorts of foods join together to form the volume of the date's bulk,**

and all sorts of liquids join together to form the volume of a mouthful. He who eats and he who drinks—[these prohibited volumes] do not join together [to impose liability for eating or for drinking, respectively].

If one is unaware that it is the Day of Atonement and eats and drinks for several hours, the rule is different. He is liable for a single sin-offering to expiate the protracted sin he has committed. But if he went through a number of spells of inadvertence, each distinct from the others, his liability is for a corresponding number of offerings to expiate the sin inadvertently committed. This is a standard inquiry of the Halakhah, dealing as it does with the many and the one.

M. 8:3 **[If] one ate and drank in a single act of inadvertence, he is liable only for a single sin-offering. [If] he ate and did a prohibited act of labor, he is liable for two sin-offerings. If he ate foods which are not suitable for eating, or drank liquids which are not suitable for drinking—[if] he drank brine or fish brine—he is exempt. As to children, they do not impose a fast on them on the Day of Atonement. But they educate them a year or two in advance, so that they will be used to doing the religious duties.**

T. 4:3 He who eats on the Day of Atonement [food] in the volume of a large dried fig, as is with its pit—that produced in the Land of Israel—is liable [M. Yoma 8:2A]. R. Simeon b. Eleazar says, "Even of the type of dried fig produced in Namarin." [If] he ate leaves of reeds, vines, dates, carobs, or anything not suitable for eating, he is exempt. [If he ate] lettuce leaves, vetches' leaves, onion sprouts, vegetable foliage, or anything which is suitable for eating, he is liable [M. Yoma 8:3C–G]. [If he ate, went and ate again, went and ate again, if the interval elapsed from the start of the first act of eating to the conclusion of the last act of eating is sufficient to eat a half-loaf of bread, [the food eaten in the several acts of eating] joins together [to impose liability]. And if not, it does not join together. [If] he drank, went and drank again, if the interval elapsed from the start of the first act of drinking to the conclusion of the last act of drinking is sufficient to drink a quarter-log [of liquid], [the liquid drunk in the several acts of drinking] joins together [to impose liability]. And if not, it does not join together [M. Yoma 8:3A]. Just as eating [is culpable] in an olive's-bulk [of food], so is drinking [culpable] in an olive's bulk [of liquid]. He who drinks brine or fish-brine is exempt [M. Yoma 8:3F–G]. M. R. Eleazar says, "He who drinks a mouthful of liquid is liable."

T. 4:2 Children nearing puberty—they educate them a year or two in advance, so that they get used to keeping their religious duties [M. Yoma 8:4B]. R. Aqiba would conclude [the prayer] in the study house

for the children, so their parents may feed them. M'SH B: Shammai
the Elder did not want to feed his son. They decreed that he feed him
with his own hand.

The Halakhah takes up the special cases of the pregnant woman and the
sick humanity on the Day of Atonement. They are to be taken care of, given
food and drink, and not to be subjected to the disciplines of the day. On the
Sabbath or the Day of Atonement, described in Scripture as the Sabbath of
Sabbaths, one is obligated to save and preserve life, and in case of doubt, to
violate the law of the Sabbath or Day of Atonement. That is made explicit
at M. 8:5.

> M. 8:4 A pregnant woman who smelled food [and grew faint]—they feed
> her until her spirits are restored. A sick person—they feed him on
> the instruction of experts. If there are no experts available, they
> feed him on his own instructions, until he says, "Enough."
>
> M. 8:5 He who is seized by ravenous hunger—they feed him, even unclean
> things, until his eyes are enlightened. He who was bitten by a crazy
> dog—they do not feed him a piece of its liver's lobe. And R. Mattia
> b. Harash permits doing so. Further did R. Mattia b. Harash say,
> "He who has a pain in his throat—they drop medicine into his
> mouth on the Sabbath, because it is a matter of doubt as to danger
> to life. And any matter of doubt as to danger to life overrides the
> prohibitions of the Sabbath." He upon whom a building fell
> down—it is a matter of doubt whether or not he is there, it is a
> matter of doubt whether [if he is there], he is alive or dead, it is a
> matter of doubt whether [if he is there and alive he is a gentile or
> an Israelite—they clear away the ruin from above him. [If] they
> found him alive, they remove the [remaining] ruins from above
> him. But if they found him dead, they leave him be [until after the
> Sabbath].
>
> T. 4:4 He who was seized by blinding hunger [M. Yoma 8:6A]—they feed
> him [that which violates the law in] least [possible measure]. How so?
> [If] there were before him untithed produce and produce of the
> Seventh Year, they feed him produce of the Seventh Year. [If there were]
> untithed produce and carrion, they feed him carrion . . . carrion and
> heave-offering—they feed him heave-offering . . . heave-offering and
> produce of the Seventh Year, they feed him produce of the Seventh
> Year—until he gains the light [M. Yoma 8:6A]. How do they know that
> he has regained the light? Sufficient so that he knows the difference
> between good and bad. R. Judah says, "A pregnant woman who smells
> [and craves] produce of the Seventh Year—they hand over to her a
> spindleful. [If] she smelled and craved food in the status of heave-
> offering, they hand over to her a spit-full" [cf. M. Yoma 8:5A].

Now comes the climax of the Rabbinic system: the conception of the relationship of repentance to atonement. Without repentance, atonement through the blood rite of the Temple is null. One deliberately cannot sin and stipulate that atonement will be made by the Day of Atonement; preemptive atonement is not an option, atone first, then sin. Above all, atonement begins in relationships with one's fellow. One has to regain the good will of the one he has harmed or offended before the process of atonement and heaven's forgiveness can get underway. Nothing in the first seven chapters of Mishnah-tractate Yoma has suggested such a stipulation.

Repentance and Atonement

M. 8:6 **A sin-offering and an unconditional guilt-offering atone. Death and the Day of Atonement atone when joined with repentance. Repentance atones for minor transgressions of positive and negative commandments. And as to serious transgressions, [repentance] suspends the punishment until the Day of Atonement comes along and atones.**

T. 4:5 The sin-offering and unconditional guilt-offering effect atonement for what is written in their connection. Death and the Day of Atonement effect atonement along with repentance. Repentance effects atonement for minor transgressions of positive and negative commandments [M. Yoma 8:8B–C], except for a violation of the commandment not to take [the name of the Lord in vain]. And what are major transgressions? [Those punishable by] extirpation and death at the hands of an earthly court, and 'not taking [the name of the Lord in vain]' counts with them. R. Judah says, "For everything from 'not taking [the name of the Lord in vain]' and beneath, repentance effects atonement. For everything from 'not taking [the name of the Lord in vain]' and above, inclusive of 'not taking [the name of the Lord in vain],' repentance suspends the punishment, and the Day of Atonement effects atonement."

T. 4:6 R. Ishmael says, "There are four kinds of atonement." [This passage is cited in chapter 3.]

M. 8:7 **He who says, "I shall sin and repent, sin and repent"—they give him no chance to do repentance. "I will sin and the Day of Atonement will atone,"—the Day of Atonement does not atone. For transgressions done between humanity and the Omnipresent, the Day of Atonement atones. For transgressions between humanity and humanity, the Day of Atonement atones, only if the humanity will regain the good will of his friend. This exegesis did R. Eleazar b. Azariah state: "'From all your sins shall you be clean before the Lord' (Lev 16:30)—for transgressions between humanity and the Omnipresent does the Day of Atonement atone. For transgressions between humanity and his fellow, the Day of**

Atonement atones, only if the humanity will regain the good will of his friend."

The entire conception of purification from sin, not from cultic uncleanness, is now linked to prophecy: God is the source of Israel's purification and atonement, and the matter of sin and uncleanness is joined. There is a play on the word for immersion-pool, used for removing cultic uncleanness, and the word for "hope," and God is the immersion-pool/hope of Israel, purifying them from sin and from uncleanness. Ezekiel and Jeremiah are invoked in conclusion.

> Said R. Aqiba, "Happy are you, O Israel. Before whom are you made clean, and who makes you clean? It is your Father who is in heaven, as it says, 'And I will sprinkle clean water on you, and you will be clean' (Ezek 36:25). And it says, 'O Lord, the hope [*miqweh* = immersion pool] of Israel' (Jer 17:13)—Just as the immersion pool cleans the unclean, so the Holy One, blessed be He, cleans Israel."

T. 4:9 The sin-offering, guilt-offering, and Day of Atonement all effect atonement only along with repentance. since it says, But on the tenth day of the seventh month [is a Day of Atonement] (Lev 23:27). If [the sinner] repents, atonement is effected for him, and if not, it is not effected for him. R. Eleazar says, "'Forgiving [iniquity, transgression, and sin]' (Exod 34:7)—He forgives iniquity to penitents, but he does not forgive iniquity to those who do not repent." R. Judah says, "Death and the Day of Atonement effect atonement along with repentance. Repentance effects atonement with death. And the day of death—lo, it is tantamount to an act of repentance."

The Tosefta's amplification of the theme of the Mishnah vastly extends the boundaries of the law. First, the issue of bestowing merit, winning divine favor for the community, or of causing the community to sin, is raised. The Mishnah's presentation of the Halakhah of repentance and atonement has not hinted at the matter.

T. 4:10 Whoever bestows merit on the community—they never suffice him to commit a transgression, lest his disciples [the community] inherit the world [to come] while he descends to Sheol. As it is said, "For you will not leave my soul in hell" (Isa 16:10).

T. 4:11 Whoever brings sin on the community—they never suffice him to effect repentance, lest his disciples [the community] descend to Sheol, while he inherits the world [to come], as it is said, "A humanity who does violence to any person shall flee to the pit, let no humanity stay him" (Prov 28:17).

T. 4:12 They bring about merit in behalf of a meritorious person, to assign to him passages worthy of being told about him [e.g., the story of the daughters of Zelophehad], and demerit in behalf of a disreputable person, to assign to him passages worthy of being told about him. They make public hypocrites' [evil deeds] on account of the desecration of the divine name, as it is said, "When a righteous humanity turns from his righteousness and commits iniquity and I lay a stumbling block before him, he shall die" (Ezek 3:20)—to make public his [hypocrisy].

Second, repeated sinning is taken into account. Scripture is clear that recidivism is taken into account.

T. 4:13 R. Yosé says, "[If] a man sins two or three times, they forgive him. [But on the] fourth, they do not forgive him, as it says, 'Forgiving iniquity, transgression, and sin, but he will by no means clear the guilty' (Exod 34:7). Up to this point he clears [him]. From this point forward he will not clear [him], since it says, 'For three transgressions of Israel—but for four, I will not turn away the punishment' (Amos 2:6). And it says, '[He will deliver his soul from going into the pit. All these things does God do two or three times for a man' (Job 33:28-29). And it says, 'Withdraw your foot from your neighbor's house lest he be weary of you' (Prov 25:16)."

Second, the Tosefta defines the confession for sin that is recited by the individual Israelite. This is to be recited repeatedly at each prayer service of the Day of Atonement.

T. 4:14 The religious duty of saying the confession [applies] at the eve of the Day of Atonement at dusk. But the sages have said, "A man should say the confession before eating and drinking, lest he be distracted while eating and drinking. And even though he has said the confession before eating and drinking, he has to say the confession after eating and drinking, lest some untoward manner have affected the meal. And even though he has said the confession after eating and drinking, he has to say the confession in the evening [prayer]. And even though he has said the confession in the evening [prayer], he has to say the confession in the morning [prayer]. And even though he has said the confession in the morning [prayer], he has to say the confession in the additional prayer. And even though he has said the confession in the additional prayer, he has to say the confession in the afternoon prayer. And even though he has said the confession in the afternoon prayer, he has to say the confession in the prayer for the closing of the gates—lest some untoward matter have affected any part of the entire day [of atonement]. At what point in the service does he say the [confession]? After the Prayer. The one who passes before the ark says it in the fourth [benediction]. R. Meir says, "He prays seven [benedictions] and concludes the confession [with a blessing]." And the sages say, "He prays seven [benedictions]. And if he wanted to conclude the confession with a blessing, he does. And he has to specify each individual sin," the words of R. Judah b. Patera, as it is said, "O Lord, these people have sinned a great sin land have made a god of gold (Exod 32:31)." R. Aqiba says, "It is not necessary [to list each sin]. If so, why does it say, 'And made a god of gold'? But: thus did the Omnipresent say, 'Who made you make a god of gold? It is I, who gave you plenty of gold.'"

Third, the confession is specific to the person that recites it, it is not a fixed formula.

> T. 4:15 Matters concerning which one has said confession on the preceding Day of Atonement, one does not have to include in the confessions of the coming Day of Atonement, unless he did those same transgressions [in the intervening year]. [If] he committed those transgressions, he must include them in the confession. [If] he did not commit those transgressions, but he included them in his confession—concerning such a person the following is said: "As a dog returns to his vomit, so a fool returns to his folly" (Prov 26:11). R. Eliezer b. Jacob says, "Lo, such a person is praiseworthy, since it is said, 'For I acknowledge my transgressions'" (Ps 51:3).
>
> T. 4:16 R. Eleazar b. R. Simeon says, "A strict rule applies to the goat [for Azazel] which does not apply to the Day of Atonement, and to the Day of Atonement which does not apply to the goat. For the Day of Atonement effects atonement [even if] no goat [is offered]. But the goat effects atonement only along with the Day of Atonement.
>
> T. 4:17 "A more strict rule applies to the goat. For the goat's sacrifice [takes effect] immediately, but the Day of Atonement [takes effect only] at dusk."

The shift in tone and focus from the narrative of the sacrificial rite to the exposition of the laws of repentance and atonement is noteworthy. Now we ask what it all means and how the Halakhah relates to the Aggadah of repentance that we met in chapter 3.

Religious Principles of Yoma

Only at the concluding statements of the Halakhah does the presentation of the topic move beyond the Halakhic reprise of the Torah's narrative at Leviticus 16, cited at the outset. And then the presentation of the Halakhah tells us what is at stake, which is the *prophetic* reading of the cult. The sages understood the prophets' critique not as repudiation of the cult but as refine-ment of it, and in the very context of their account of the blood-rite they therefore invoke the prophets' norms alongside the Torah's. Jeremiah's call to repentance, Ezekiel's insistence on purity of spirit, Isaiah's prophecy of for-giveness of sin—these flow into the exposition of the Halakhah. Above all, the sages underscore God's explicit promise to purify Israel, the promise set forth in Isaiah's, Ezekiel's and Jeremiah's prophecies. So the Halakhah recasts the entire category of the Day of Atonement, taking the theme of atonement to require an account of repentance, on the one side, and a doctrine of God's power to forgive and purify from sin, on the other. The main point is, the rites of atonement do not work *ex opere operato* but only conditionally. And the attitude and intention of the Israelite set that condition.

Two fundamental messages register. First, the rites atone and so does death—but only when joined with repentance, and repentance reaches its climax in the cleansing effect of the occasion, the Day of Atonement itself, when a sin-offering and an unconditional guilt-offering atone. Death and the Day of Atonement atone when joined with repentance. Repentance atones for minor transgressions of positive and negative commandments. And as to serious transgressions, repentance suspends the punishment until the Day of Atonement comes along and atones. But the entire system real-izes its promise of reconciliation with God only on one condition: the Israelite must frame the right attitude, one of sincerity and integrity. He who says, "I shall sin and repent, sin and repent"—they give him no chance to do repentance. "I will sin and the Day of Atonement will atone,"—the Day of Atonement does not atone. Preemptive atonement—first suffer, then sin—is dismissed as null. Intentionality makes all the difference.

These statements involve attitude. They pertain not to the Day of Atonement nor even to the rites of penitence, but to the spirit in which the person acts when he commits a sin. If in the commission of the sin he declares his conviction that his attitude makes no difference—I shall do what I want, and then repent in impunity—that attitude nullifies the possibility of repentance and the Day of Atonement to do their part in the work of rec-onciliation. The Halakhah carries the matter still further, when it insists that, in the end, the attitude of the repentant sinner does not complete the trans-action; the sinner depends also upon the attitude of the sinned-against. One cannot think of a more eloquent way of saying that the entire condition of Israel depends upon the inner integrity of Israel: the intentionality that moti-vates its actions, whether with God or with humanity.

How the Halakhah of Yoma Reached Judaism

In Judaism as set forth by the Rabbinic sages in the Mishnah, and the Talmuds, the Day of Atonement, which the Torah lays out as principally a Temple occasion, overspreads the world. Israel's virtue, the virtue of self-affliction through fasting, can win heaven's cordial response, analogous to the provision of manna in the wilderness. That is because Israel's ordinary life compares with the Temple's sanctification; even as the Temple space is sanctified, so Israel's space is marked off by signs of the holy. The righteousness represented by a life fearful of sin and rich in repentance, which comes to its climax on the Day of Atonement, infuses the entire people of Israel, not only the priesthood in the Temple on that same holy day.

The Mishnah's presentation of the Day of Atonement with its recapitulation of the themes of Leviticus 16 in the proportions of Scripture's treatment of that topic, is both replicated and revised. But the framers of the Mishnah invited this revision, for it is they who introduced the theme of repentance into the rite of atonement and insisted upon the centrality of the human will in the process of reconciliation. Atonement depends upon the world beyond the sanctuary and what happens there. But the Halakhic theologians have not strayed far from the message that God himself revealed to the prophets, Jeremiah, Ezekiel, Isaiah, and the rest. All they have done is see things whole and in proportion.

What for Leviticus and the first seven chapters of Mishnah-tractate Yoma forms a cultic occasion, in which Israel participates as bystanders, emerges in the Halakhic presentation of the Mishnah and the Tosefta and Bavli-tractate Yoma as an event in the life of holy Israel, in which all Israel bears tasks of the weight and consequence that, on that holy day, the High Priest uniquely carries out. On the Day of Atonement, holy Israel joins the high priest in the Holy of Holies; this they do on that day by afflicting themselves through fasting and other forms of abstinence, as the Written Torah requires. The Day of Atonement, the occasion on which the high priest conducts the rite in the privacy of the Holy of Holies, emerges transformed: the rites are private, but the event is public; the liturgy is conducted in the holy Temple, with sins sent forth through the scapegoat, but the event bears its consequences in holy Israel, where sins are atoned for in the setting of the everyday and the here and now. What is singular and distinct—the rites of atonement on the holiest day of the year in the holiest place in the world—now makes its statement about what takes place on every day of the year in the ordinary life of holy Israel.

The Halakhah then takes shape within its own logic, the logic emergent in the dialectic of the Written Torah's and the prophets' contrasting but complementary teachings, both this and that. That is the logic—joining rite to right—discerned by the sages of the Halakhah of the Oral Torah, first in the Mishnah and the Tosefta. And that is how the Day of Atonement would make its way through time, not the sacrificial rite of the high priest in the Temple, but the atonement-celebration of all Israel in the world. What mattered to the compilers of Leviticus and the Mishnah alike was the timeless performance of atonement through the bloody rites of the Temple. What captured the attention of the framers of the Tosefta's amplification, by contrast, was the personal discipline of atonement through repentance on the Day of Atonement and a life of virtue and Torah-learning on the rest of the days of the year. They took out of the Holy of Holies and brought into the homes and streets of the holy people that very mysterious rite of atonement that the Day of Atonement called forth. In Mishnah-tractate Yoma chapter 8 the Rabbinic sages transformed the presentation the day and its meaning, transcending its cultic limits. And it was their vision, and not the vision of Leviticus 16 and the Mishnah-tractate's amplification in seven chapters, that would prove definitive.

The irony comes to expression in the fact that, from antiquity to our own day, the Day of Atonement would enjoy the loyalty of holy Israel come what may, and everywhere, gaining the standing of Judaism's single most widely observed occasion. That fact attests to the power of the distinctive ideas set forth by the framers of the Torah and the prophets, then the Mishnah-Tosefta to transform a sacerdotal narrative into a medium of the inner, moral sanctification for Israel, the holy people in utopia entering into the status of the holy priest and the locus of the Temple's inner sanctum.

So much for Israel and its encounter with the outside world of idolatry, Israel, and the interior realm of encounter with God. We have seen how the Aggadah and the Halakhah work together to realize the covenantal nomism that defines normative Judaism. But the two cases on which we have focused constitute only examples of that covenantal nomism of which E. P. Sanders speaks. Let us turn to a survey of other important instances that show the working of covenantal nomism: how, within the Halakhah itself, the Aggadah is embedded and acted out.

Chapter 5

Law and Theology, Halakhah and Aggadah

Covenantal nomism is realized in rules of conduct that act out norms of conviction. Chapters 1 and 2, 3 and 4, have twice illustrated that fact, the first set for the relationship of Israel and the idolaters, the second, of Israel and God. But that claim to this point has rested on showing the match between the Aggadic structure and the Halakhic system. The disjuncture of chapters 3 and 4—atonement in theology, atonement in practice—raises the question of whether the Halakhah on its own, not in juxtaposition with the Aggadah, embodies theological convictions, and whether it responds to the mythic monotheism of Scripture's narrative. Or perhaps a script is always required to link conduct to conviction, to articulate the attitude supposedly inherent in the action.[4] This premise carries us to the final exercise, how the law in its concrete and particular formulation constitutes the acting out of an implicit theological statement. We shall see that no script is required for the drama of the Halakhah to take place.

This chapter sets forth a variety of cases in which the law itself, in its very details, embodies the animating theology of monotheism in its narrative formulation by Scripture. It addresses laws that express the covenantal relationship between Israel and God (sections 1 and 2), within Israel's social order (section 3), and how Israel and God meet within the Israelite household, with special attention to sacred time in the form of the Sabbath (section 4), Passover (section 5), and Tabernacles (section 6). Here covenantal conduct takes Halakhic form: readers do not have to turn to the Aggadah to articulate the theology through narrative. The hard details of the Halakhah on their own make the theological statement.

Between Israel and God:
The Halakhah of Shebi'it, the Sabbatical Year

The Torah represents God as the sole master of creation, the Sabbath as testimony to God's pleasure with, and therefore sanctification of, creation. Tractate Shebi'it, on the Sabbatical year and the rest accorded to the land every seventh year, sets forth the law that in relationship to the Land of Israel embodies that conviction. The law systematically works through Scripture's rules, treating [1] the prohibition of farming the land during the seventh year; [2] the use of the produce in the seventh year solely for eating, and [3] the remission of debts. During the Sabbatical year, Israel relinquishes its ownership of the Land of Israel. At that time Israelites in farming may do nothing that in secular years effects the assertion of ownership over the land.[5] Just as one may not utilize land he does not own, in the Sabbatical year, the farmer gives up ownership of the land that he does own.

So much for the topic. One wonders what defines the particular problems that attract the sages' attention. The problematic of the Halakhic tractate is the interplay between the Land of Israel, the People of Israel dwelling on the Land of Israel, and God's Sabbath, and what imparts energy to the analysis of the law is the particular role accorded to humanity's—Israelite humanity's—intentionality and attitude. These form the variable, to be shown able to determine what is, or is not, permitted in the holy time of the seventh year. Specifically, the focus of the law of Shebi'it as set forth in the Mishnah centers upon the role of human will in bringing about the reordering of the world (of which readers will hear more in the next section). By laying emphasis upon the power of the human will, the sages express the conviction that the Israelite has the power by an act of will to restore creation to its perfection. That is why the details of the law time and again spin out the implications of the conviction at hand, that all things depend upon humanity's intentionality in a given action or humanity's likely perception of an action.

If the problematic of the Halakhah generates small-scale inquiries into large-bore principles, then, as a matter of fact, the reason that questions of a particular order dominate in the exposition of the law of a specific topic requires attention. Specifically, readers wonder why the sages identified for sustained inquiry questions of the sort they have found urgent, meaning, why they have defined the problematic of the law in the way that they have?

Not only did they have the choice of answering questions of another order entirely. They also had reason to select this particular topic to make the statement that they have made—this and no other.

To understand the answer, one turns first of all to Avery-Peck's and Newman's introductions to the Halakhah of Shebi'it,[6] which, in both cases, turn to Scripture for perspective on how the Mishnah (one should say, how the Halakhah) treats the topic at hand. Both make the move from the problematic of human intentionality (in this case: how people will make sense of appearances), a problematic that can and does animate discussion of a variety of topics, to the particular topic of Shebi'it. The Written Torah leaves no doubt that the Sabbatical year finds its place in the context of creation and God's conduct thereof: perfecting the world order of creation, sanctifying the order of creation, then, celebrating the Sabbath in response thereto.

> In modeling their lives on the perfected character of the universe that once existed, Israelites make explicit their understanding that this order will exist again, that God's plan for the Israelite people still is in effect . . . Israelites themselves, through their actions, participate in the creation of that perfected world. They do this through their intentions and perceptions in defining proper observance of the Sabbatical year,[7]

so Avery-Peck, providing a fine statement of the paramount religious principle of the Halakhah of Shebi'it.

The Sabbatical Year recovers that perfect time of Eden when the world was at rest, all things in place. Before the rebellion, man did not have to labor on the land; he picked and ate his meals freely. And, in the nature of things, with Adam and Eve in charge, everything belonged to everybody; private ownership in response to individual labor did not exist, because man did not have to work anyhow in the way that he did afterward. Reverting to that perfect time, the Torah maintains that the land will provide adequate food for everyone, including the flocks and herds, even if people do not work the land. But that is on condition that all claim of ownership lapses; the food is left in the fields, to be picked by anyone who wishes, but it may not be hoarded by the landowner in particular. Avery-Peck states this matter as follows:

> Scripture thus understands the Sabbatical year to represent a return to a perfected order of reality, in which all share equally in the bounty of a holy land that yields its food without human labor. The Sabbatical year provides a model through which, once every seven years, Israelites living in the here-and-now may enjoy the perfected order in which God always intended the world to exist and toward which, in the Israelite worldview, history indeed is moving. . . . The release of debts [unsecured by the prosbol] accomplishes for Israelites' economic relationships just what the

agricultural Sabbatical accomplishes for the relationship between the people and the land. Eradicating debt allows the Israelite economy to return
to the state of equilibrium that existed at the time of creation, when all
shared equally in the bounty of the land.[8]

The Holiness Code expresses that same concept when it arranges for the
return, at the Jubilee Year, of inherited property to the original family ownership: "You shall count off seven weeks of years, so that the period of seven
weeks of years gives you a total of forty-nine years / . . . You shall proclaim
release throughout the land for all its inhabitants. It shall be a jubilee for you;
each of you shall return to his holding and each of you shall return to his
family" (Lev 25:8-10). The Jubilee Year is observed as is the Sabbatical year,
meaning that for two successive years the land is not to be worked. The
Halakhah establishes that when land is sold, it is for the span of time remaining to the next Jubilee Year. That then marks the reordering of landholding
to its original pattern, when Israel inherited the land to begin with and commenced to enjoy its produce.

Just as the Sabbath commemorates the completion of creation, the perfection of world order, so does the Sabbatical year. So too, the Jubilee year
brings about the restoration of real property to the original division. In both
instances, Israelites so act as to indicate they are not absolute owners of the
land, which belongs to God and which is divided in the manner that God
arranged in perpetuity. Avery-Peck states the matter in the following way:

> On the Sabbath of creation, during the Sabbatical year, and in the Jubilee
> year, diverse aspects of Israelite life are to return to the way that they were
> at the time of creation. Israelites thus acknowledge that, in the beginning,
> God created a perfect world, and they assure that the world of the here-
> and-now does not overly shift from its perfect character. By providing
> opportunities for Israelites to model their contemporary existence upon a
> perfected order of things, these commemorations further prepare the peo-
> ple for messianic times, when, under God's rule, the world will perma-
> nently revert to the ideal character of the time of creation.[9]

Here readers find the Halakhic counterpart to the restorationist theology
that the Oral Torah sets forth in the Aggadah. Israel matches Adam, the
Land of Israel, Eden, and, readers now see, the Sabbatical year commemorates the perfection of creation and replicates it.

A further striking point emerges from the sages' reading of the law of
Shebi'it in the written part of the Torah. That reading is worked out in Sifra,
a commentary to the book of Leviticus produced ca. 300 C.E. It makes the
point that the Sabbatical year takes effect at the moment of Israel's entry into

the land. Then Israel reenacts the drama of creation, the seventh day marking the perfection of creation and its sanctification, so, here too, the Sabbath is observed for the land as much as for humanity. Observing the commandments of the Sabbatical year marks Israel's effort at keeping the land like Eden, six days of creation, one day of rest, and so too here:

Sifra CCXLV:I.2

    A. "When you come [into the land which I give you, the land shall keep a Sabbath to the Lord]:"

    B. Might one suppose that the Sabbatical year was to take effect once they had reached Transjordan?

    C. Scripture says, "into the land."

    D. It is that particular land.

Now comes the key point: the Sabbatical year takes effect only when Israel enters the land, which is to say, Israel's entry into the land marks the counterpart to the beginning of the creation of Eden. But a further point will register in a moment. It is when Eden/the land enters into stasis, each family receiving its share in the land, that the process of the formation of the new Eden comes to its climax; then each Israelite bears responsibility for his share of the land. That is when the land has reached that state of order and permanence that corresponds to Eden at sunset on the sixth day:

    E. Might one suppose that the Sabbatical year was to take effect once they had reached Ammon and Moab?

    F. Scripture says, "which I give you,"

    G. and not to Ammon and Moab.

    H. And on what basis do you maintain that when they had conquered the land but not divided it, divided it among familiars but not among fathers' houses so that each individual does not yet recognize his share—

    I. might one suppose that they should be responsible to observe the Sabbatical year?

    J. Scripture says, "[Six years you shall sow] your field,"

    K. meaning, each one should recognize his own field.

    L. " . . . your vineyard":

    M. meaning, each one should recognize his own vineyard.

    N. You turn out to rule:

    O. Once the Israelites had crossed the Jordan, they incurred liability to separate dough-offering and to observe the prohibition against eating the fruit of fruit trees for the first three years after planting and the prohibition against eating produce of the new growing season prior to the waving of the sheaf of new grain [that is, on the fifteenth of Nisan].

P. When the sixteenth of Nisan came, they incurred liability to wave the sheaf of new grain.

Q. With the passage of fifty days from then they incurred the liability to the offering of the Two Loaves.

R. At the fourteenth year they became liable for the separation of tithes.

The Sabbatical year with its prohibitions takes over only when the Israelite farmers have asserted their ownership of the land and its crops. Then the process of counting the years begins.

S. They began to count the years of the Sabbatical cycle, and in the twenty-first year after entry into the land, they observed the Sabbatical year.

T. In the sixty-fourth year they observed the first Jubilee [T. Men. 6:20].

What, exactly, imposes limits on the analogy of the Sabbath for the land remains to be seen. Whether one treats the Sabbath of the land as equivalent in all ways to the Sabbath observed by Israel demands attention. The answer is no; the metaphor has its limits:

3. A. ". . . the land shall keep a Sabbath to the Lord":

   B. might one suppose that the Sabbath should involve not digging pits, ditches, and wells, not repairing immersion-pools?

   C. Scripture says, "you shall not sow your field or prune your vineyard"—

   D. I know that the prohibition extends only to sowing.

   E. How do I know that it covers also sowing, pruning, ploughing, hoeing, weeding, clearing, and cutting down?

   F. Scripture says, "your field you shall not . . . your vineyard . . . you shall not":

   G. none of the work that is ordinarily done in your field and in your vineyard.

4. A. And how do we know that farmers may not fertilize, prune trees, smoke the leaves or cover over with powder for fertilizer?

   B. Scripture says, "your field you shall not . . . "

5. A. And how do we know that farmers may not trim trees, nip off dry shoots, trim trees?

   B. Scripture says, "your field you shall not . . ."

6. A. Since Scripture says, "you shall not sow your field or prune your vineyard,"

   B. might one suppose that the farmer also may not hoe under the olive trees, fill in the holes under the olives trees, or dig between one tree and the next?

   C. Scripture says, "you shall not sow your field or prune your vineyard"—

   D. sowing and pruning were subject to the general prohibition of field labor. Why then were they singled out?

E. It was to build an analogy through them, as follows:

F. what is distinctive in sowing and pruning is that they are forms of labor carried on on the ground or on a tree.

G. So I know that subject to the prohibition are also other forms of labor that are carried on on the ground or on a tree, [excluding from the prohibition, therefore, the types of labor listed at B].

So much for the systematic exploration of the enlandisement of Eden in the Land of Israel, the formulation of Israel's relationship with God through Israel's use of the Land of Israel and its produce, in a way analogous to Adam's use of Eden—and abuse thereof.

In relationship to God, the Land of Israel, as much as the People of Israel, emerges as a principal player. The land is treated as a living entity, a participant in the cosmic drama, as well it should, being the scene of creation and its unfolding. If the perfection of creation is the well-ordered condition of the natural world, then the Land of Israel, counterpart to Eden, must be formed into the model of the initial perfection, restored to that initial condition. So the Sabbath takes over and enchants the Land of Israel as much as it transforms Israel itself. Newman expresses this view in the following language:

> For the priestly writer of Leviticus, the seventh year, like the seventh day, is sanctified. Just as God rested from the work of creation on the seventh day and sanctified it as a day of rest, so too God has designated the seventh year for the land's rest. Implicit in this view is the notion that the Land of Israel has human qualities and needs. It must 'observe a Sabbath of the Lord' because, like the people of Israel and God, it too experiences fatigue and requires a period of repose. The Land of Israel, unlike all other countries, is enchanted, for it enjoys a unique relationship to God and to the people of Israel. That is to say, God sanctified this land by giving it to his chosen people as an exclusive possession. Israelites, in turn, are obligated to work the land and to handle its produce in accordance with God's wishes. . . .[10]

The counterpart in the matter of the remission of debts works out the conception that all Israelites by right share in the land and its gifts, and if they have fallen into debt, they have been denied their share; that imbalance is righted every seven years.

Now one has to relate the problematic that directs the exposition of details of the law to the particular religious convictions inherent in the topic of the law, as promised in the Preface. The Halakhah outlines where and how humanity participates in establishing the sanctity of the Sabbatical year, expanding the span of the year to accommodate humanity's intentionality in working the land now for advantage then. It insists that humanity's perceptions of the facts, not the facts themselves, govern: what looks like a law violation is a law violation. In these and other ways the Halakhah of Shebi'it works out the problematics of humanity's participation in the sanctification of the land in the Sabbatical year. The topic of the law, restoring the perfection of creation, joins with the generative problematic of the Halakhah to make one point. Israel has in its power the restoration of the perfection of creation. It can order all things to accord with the condition that prevailed when God declared creation. The topic served as an obvious, ideal medium to state that Israel, by a fulfilled act of will, possessed the capacity to attain the perfection of the world. The reason is that Israel's perception of matters—and its actions consequent upon those perceptions—made all the difference. The Halakhah of Shebi'it did not define the sole arena for the detailed and practical working out of that statement. Readers will find themselves many times in the same framework of discussion. The Halakhah of Shebi'it framed a fitting occasion to show how, in small things, that large conception was to be realized.

That brings us to the interiorities of Israel's relationship with God. The blatant affirmation that God pays the closest attention to Israel's attitudes and intentions pervades the tractate. Otherwise there is no way to explain the priority accorded to Israelite perception of whether or not the law is kept, Israelite intention in cultivating the fields in the sixth year, and other critical components of the governing, generative problematic. God furthermore identifies the Land of Israel as the archetype of Eden and model of the world to come. That is why God treats the land in its perfection just as he treats Eden, by according to the land the Sabbath rest. He deems the union of Israel and the Land of Israel to effect the sanctification of the land in its ascending degrees, corresponding to the length of the term of Israel's possession. Finally, he insists, as the ultimate owner of the land, that at regular intervals, the possession of the land be relinquished, signaled as null, and that at those same intervals ownership of the produce of the land at least in potentiality be equally shared among all its inhabitants.

God therefore relates to Israel through the land and the arrangements that he imposes upon the land. In that context God relates to the land in response to Israel's residence thereon. But God relates to the land in a direct way, providing for the land, as he provides for Israel, the sanctifying moment of the Sabbath. So a web of relationships, direct and indirect, hold together God, land, and Israel. That is for the here-and-now, all the more so for the world to come. And if that is how God relates to Israel, Israel relates to God in one way above all, and that is, by exercising in ways that show love for

God and acceptance of God's dominion the power of free will that God has given humanity.

Between Israel and God: The Halakhah of 'Orlah, Fruit of a Tree in the Fourth Year of its Planting

As a statement of religious attitudes on how Israel relates to God, much that has been said in connection with tractate Shebi'it pertains here—even if that is only in general terms, and not in the distinctive and particular ones that concern the Sabbatical year. That God responds to Israel's attitudes and intentions does not shape the exegesis of the topic or generate a rich program of problem-framing and problem-solving.

Further, one point should register even though it is not particular to our topic. God as the ultimate owner of the land sets the terms of Israel's utilization of the land, and the rules that he imposes form the condition of Israel's tenure there, as Scripture states explicitly, "not be eaten. In the fourth year all its fruit shall be set aside for jubilation before the Lord, and only in the fifth year may you use its fruit, that its yield to you may be increased: I am the Lord your God." The yield of the land responds to Israel's obedience to God's rules for cultivating the land, and that having been said, why this particular rule carries with it the stated consequence hardly matters. The religious premise of the treatment of the topic of 'Orlah is the same as the one that sustains tractate Shebi'it: God relates to Israel through the land and the arrangements that he imposes upon it. What happens to Israel in the land takes the measure of that relationship.

But apart from these traits that characterize all Halakhah of enlandisement, the Halakhah of 'Orlah makes points particular to the topic at hand— and accessible, indeed, possible, only within the framework of that topic. The specificities of the law turn out to define with some precision a message on the relationship of Israel to the Land of Israel and to God. If readers turn to Sifra CCII:I.1, their attention is drawn to a number of quite specific traits of the law of 'Orlah, and these make explicit matters of religious conviction that readers might otherwise miss.

The first is that the prohibition of 'Orlah-fruit applies solely within the Land of Israel and not to the neighboring territories occupied by Israelites, which means that, once again, it is the union of Israel with the Land of Israel that invokes the prohibition:

Sifra CCII:I.1.
    A. "When you come [into the land and plant all kinds of trees for food, then you shall count their fruit as forbidden; three years it shall be

forbidden to you, it must not be eaten. And in the fourth year all their fruit shall be holy, an offering of praise to the Lord. But in the fifth year you may eat of their fruit, that they may yield more richly for you: I am the Lord your God" (Lev 19:23–25).]
B. Might one suppose that the law applied once they came to Transjordan?
C. Scripture says, ". . . into the land,"
D. the particular Land [of Israel].

What that means is that some trait deemed to inhere in the Land of Israel and no other territory must define the law, and a particular message ought to inhere in this law.

This same point registers once more: it is only trees that Israelites plant in the land that are subject to the prohibition, not those that idolaters planted before the Israelites inherited the land:

Sifra CCII:I.2
A. "When you come into the land and plant":
B. excluding those that idolaters have planted prior to the Israelites' coming into the land.
C. Or should I then exclude those that idolaters planted even after the Israelites came into the land?
D. Scripture says, "all kinds of trees."

A further point of special interest requires that the Israelite plant the tree as an act of deliberation; if the tree merely grows up on its own, it is not subject to the prohibition. So Israelite action joined to Israelite intention is required:

Sifra CCII:I.4
A. ". . . and plant . . .":
B. excluding one that grows up on its own.
C. ". . . and plant . . .":
D. excluding one that grows out of a grafting or sinking a root.

The several points on which Sifra's reading of the Halakhah and the verses of Scripture that declare the Halakhah alert us to a specific religious principle embedded in the Halakhah of 'Orlah.

First, the law takes effect only from the point at which Israel enters the land. That is to say, the point of Israel's entry into the land marks the beginning of the land's consequential fecundity. In simpler language, the fact that trees produce fruit matters only from Israel's entry onward. To see what is at stake, readers recall that the entry of Israel into the land marks the restoration of Eden (and will again, within the restorationist theology), so there is no missing the point. The land bears fruit of which God takes cognizance only when the counterpart-moment of creation has struck. The Halakhah has no better way of saying the entry of Israel into the land compares with the moment at which the creation of Eden took place—and in no other way does the Halakhah make that point. In this way, moreover, the law of Shebi'it finds its counterpart. Shebi'it concerns telling time, marking off seven years to the Sabbath of creation, the one that affords rest to the land. The Halakhah of 'Orlah also means telling time. Specifically, 'Orlah-law marks the time of the creation of produce from the moment of Israel's entry into the land. Israel's entry into the land marks a new beginning, comparable to the very creation of the world, just as the land at the end matches Eden at the outset.

Second, Israelite intentionality is required to subject a tree to the 'Orlah-rule. If an Israelite does not plant the tree with the plan of producing fruit, then the tree is not subject to the rule. If the tree grows up on its own, not by the act and precipitating intentionality of the Israelite, the 'Orlah-rule does not apply. If an Israelite does not plant the tree to produce fruit, the 'Orlah-rule does not apply. And given the character of creation, which marks the norm, the tree must be planted in the ordinary way; if grafted or sunk as a root, the law does not apply. In a moment, this heavy emphasis upon Israelite intentionality will produce a critical result. But first let us ask some more fundamental questions.

Third, the issue of the counterpart to Israelite observance of the restraint of three years arises. And what requires explanation is why Israelite intentionality plays so critical a role, since, as Sifra itself notes, the 'Orlah-rule applies even to trees planted by idolaters. The answer becomes obvious when, in line with the generative hermeneutics announced with the word "enlandisement," readers try to think of any other commandments concerning fruit-trees in the land that—the sages say time and again—is Eden. Of course they can: "Of every tree of the garden you are free to eat; but as for the tree of knowledge of good and evil, you must not eat of it" (Gen 2:16). But the Halakhah of 'Orlah imposes upon Israel a more demanding commandment. Of no tree in the new Eden may Israel eat for three years. That demands considerable restraint.

Fourth, it is Israel's own intentionality—not God's—that imposes upon every fruit-bearing tree—and not only the one of Eden—the prohibition of three years. So once Israel wants the fruit, it must show that it can restrain its desire and wait for three years. By Israel's act of will, Israel has imposed upon itself the requirement of restraint. Taking the entry-point as their guide, readers may say that, from the entry into the land and for the next three years, trees that Israelites value for their fruit and plant with the produce in mind must be left untouched. And, for all time thereafter, when Israelites plant fruit trees, they must recapitulate that same exercise of self-restraint, that is, act as though, for the case at hand, they have just come into the land.

To find the context in which these rules make their statement, readers consider details, then the main point. First, readers will ask why three years in particular. Fruit trees were created on the third day of creation. Then, when Israel by intention and action designates a tree—any tree—as fruit-bearing, Israel must wait for three years, as creation waited for three years.

Then the planting of every tree imposes upon Israel the occasion to meet once more the temptation that the first Adam could not overcome. Israel now recapitulates the temptation of Adam then, but Israel, the New Adam, possesses, and is possessed by, the Torah. By its own action and intention in planting fruit trees, Israel finds itself in a veritable orchard of trees like the tree of knowledge of good and evil. The difference between Adam and Israel—permitted to eat all fruit but one, Adam ate the forbidden fruit, while Israel refrains for a specified span of time from fruit of all trees—marks what has taken place, which is the regeneration of humanity. The enlandisement of the Halakhah bears that special message, and it is difficult to imagine another way of making that statement through law than in the explicit concern the sages register for the fruit trees of the Land of Israel. No wonder, then, that 'Orlah-law finds its position, in the Holiness Code, in the rules of sanctification.

When Israel enters the land, in exactly the right detail Israel recapitulates the drama of Adam in Eden, but with this formidable difference. The outcome is not the same. By its own act of will Israel addresses the temptation of Adam and overcomes the same temptation, not once but every day through time beyond measure. Adam could not wait out the week, but Israel waits for three years—as long as God waited in creating fruit trees. Adam picked and ate. But here too there is a detail not to be missed. Even after three years, Israel may not eat the fruit wherever it chooses. Rather, in the fourth year from planting, Israel will still show restraint, bringing the fruit only "for jubilation before the Lord" in Jerusalem. That signals that the once forbidden fruit is now eaten in public, not in secret, before the Lord, as a moment of celebration. That detail, too, recalls the Fall and makes its comment upon the horror of it. That is, when Adam ate the fruit, he shamefully hid from God for having eaten the fruit. But when Israel eats the fruit, it does so proudly, joyfully, before the Lord. The contrast is not to be missed, so too the message. Faithful Israel refrains when it is supposed to, and so it has every reason to cease to refrain and to eat "before the Lord." It has nothing to hide, and everything to show.

And there is more. In the fifth year Israel may eat on its own, the time of any restraint from enjoying the gifts of the land having ended. That sequence provides fruit for the second Sabbath of creation, and so through time. How that is so demands explanation. Placing Adam's sin on the first day after the first Sabbath, thus Sunday, then calculating the three forbidden years as Monday, Tuesday, and Wednesday of the second week of creation, reckoning on the jubilation of Thursday, readers come to the Friday, eve of the second Sabbath of creation. So now, a year representing a day of the Sabbatical week, just as Leviticus says so many times in connection with the Sabbatical year, the three prohibited years allow Israel to show its true character, fully regenerate, wholly and humbly accepting God's commandment, the one Adam broke. And the rest follows.

Here, then, is the theology message embedded in the 'Orlah-Halakhah, the statement that only through the details of the laws of 'Orlah as laid out in both parts of the Torah, written and oral, the Halakhah could hope to make. By its own act of restraint, the New Adam, Israel, in detailed action displays its repentance in respect to the very sin that the Old Adam committed, the sin of disobedience and rebellion. Facing the same opportunity to sin, Israel again and again over time refrains from the very sin that cost Adam Eden. So by its manner of cultivation of the land and its orchards, Israel manifests what in the very condition of humanity has changed by the giving of the Torah: the advent of humanity's second chance, through Israel. Only in the land that succeeds Eden can Israel, succeeding Adam, carry out the acts of regeneration that the Torah makes possible.

Enlandisement encompasses the restoration of Israel to the land as it was meant by God to be, Israel's role in the repair of the creation. The next part of the Halakhic statement on acts that embody Israel's relationship with God takes up further chapters of the life of enlandised Israel, first the collaboration of Israel with God as proprietors of the land, then Israel's service to God through the yield of the land.

Within Israel's Social Order: The Halakhah of Sanhedrin-Makkot, Israel's (Theoretical) Criminal Justice System

The most profound question facing Israelite thinkers concerns the fate of the Israelite at the hands of the perfectly just and profoundly merciful God. Since essential to their thought is the conviction that all creatures are answerable to their Creator, and absolutely critical to their system is the fact that at the end of days the dead are raised for eternal life, the criminal justice system encompasses deep thought on the interplay of God's justice and God's mercy. How these are reconciled in the case of the sinner or criminal requires attention.

Within Israel's social order the Halakhah addresses from a theological perspective the profound question of social justice that concerns the Israelite sinner or criminal. Specifically, the sin or crime, which has estranged him from God, may or may not close the door to life eternal. If it does, then justice is implacable and perfect. If it does not, then God shows his mercy—but justice loses out. One can understand the answer only if he keeps in mind that the Halakhah takes for granted the resurrection of the dead, the final judgment, and the life of the world to come beyond the grave. From that perspective, death becomes an event in life but not the end of life. And, it must follow, the death penalty, too, does not mark the utter annihilation of the person of the sinner or criminal. On the contrary, because he pays for his crime or sin in this life, he situates himself with all of the rest of supernatural Israel, ready for the final judgment. Having been judged, he will "stand in judgment," meaning, he will find his way to the life of the world to come along with everyone else. Within the dialectics formed by those two facts—punishment now, eternal life later on—one may identify as the two critical passages in the Halakhah of Sanhedrin-Makkot M. Sanhedrin 6:2 and 10:1: Achan pays the supreme penalty but secures his place in the world to come, all Israel, with only a few exceptions, is going to stand in judgment and enter the world to come, explicitly including all manner of criminals and sinners.

That is what defines the stakes in this critical component of the sages' account of God's abode in Israel. What the Halakhah wishes to explore is how is the Israelite sinner or criminal rehabilitated, through the criminal justice system, so as to rejoin Israel in all its eternity. The answer is that the criminal or sinner remains Israelite, no matter what he does—even though he sins—and the death penalty exacted by the earthly court is the medium of atonement. So the Halakhah of Sanhedrin embodies these religious principles: [1] Israel endures forever, encompassing (nearly) all Israelites; [2] sinners or criminals are able to retain their position within that eternal Israel by reason of the penalties that expiate the specific sins or crimes spelled out by the Halakhah; [3] it is an act of merciful justice when the sinner or criminal is put to death, for at that point, he is assured of eternity along with everyone else. God's justice comes to full expression in the penalty, which is instrumental and contingent; God's mercy endures forever in the forgiveness that follows expiation of guilt through the imposition of the penalty.

That explains why the governing religious principle of Sanhedrin-Makkot is the perfect, merciful justice of God, and it accounts for the detailed exposition of the correct form of the capital penalty for each capital sin or crime. The punishment must fit the crime within the context of the Torah in particular so that, at the resurrection and the judgment, the crime will have been correctly expiated. Because the Halakhah rests on the premise that God is just and that God has made humanity in his image, after his likeness, the Halakhah cannot deem sufficient that the punishment fit the crime. Rather, given its premises, the Halakhah must pursue the issue of the sinner once he has been punished. And the entire construction of the continuous exposition of Sanhedrin-Makkot aims at making this simple statement: the criminal, in God's image, after God's likeness, pays the penalty for his crime in this world but like the rest of Israel will stand in justice and, rehabilitated, will enjoy the world to come.

Accordingly, given their conviction that all Israel possesses a share in the world to come, meaning, nearly everybody will rise from the grave, the sages took as their task the specification of how, in this world, criminals-sinners would receive appropriate punishment in a proper procedure, so that, in the world to come, they would take their place along with everyone else in the resurrection and eternal life. So the religious principle that comes to expression in Sanhedrin-Makkot concerns the meaning of humanity's being in God's image. That means that it is in humanity's nature to surpass the grave. And how, God's being just, the sinner or criminal survive his sin or crime requires an answer. It is by paying with his life in the here and now, so that at the resurrection, he may regain life, along with all Israel. That is why the climactic moment in the Halakhah comes at the end of the long catalogue of those sins and crimes penalized with capital punishment. It is with ample reason that the Bavli places at the conclusion and climax of its version the ringing declaration, "all Israel has a portion in the world to come, except. . . ." And the exceptions pointedly do not include any of those listed in the long catalogues of persons executed for sins or crimes.

The sole exceptions, indeed, pertain to persons who classify themselves entirely outside of the criminal justice system: those who deny that the resurrection of the dead is a teaching of the Torah or (worse still) that the Torah does not come from God. Now, as readers realize, these classes of persons hardly belong in the company of the sinners and criminals catalogued here. Then come specified individuals or groups: three kings (Jeroboam, Ahab, and Manasseh) and four ordinary folk (Balaam, Doeg, Ahitophel, and Gehazi) have no portion in the world to come. There follows the standard trilogy: the generation of the flood, the generation of the dispersion, the generation of Sodom and Gomorrah. One notes the difference between the individual who commits an act of idolatry and the entire community (the townsfolk of the apostate town) that does so. God punishes and forgives the individual, but not an entire generation, not an entire community. That is the point at which the criminal justice system completes its work.

That the two religious principles just now specified play a critical role in the formulation and presentation of the Halakhah of Sanhedrin-Makkot is made explicit in the context of legal exposition itself. The rite of stoning involves an admonition that explicitly declares the death penalty the means of atoning for all crimes and sins, leaving the criminal blameless and welcome into the kingdom of heaven:

M. Sanhedrin 6:2

    A. [When] he was ten cubits from the place of stoning, they say to him, "Confess," for it is usual for those about to be put to death to confess.

    B. For whoever confesses has a share in the world to come.

    C. For so we find concerning Achan, to whom Joshua said, "My son, I pray you, give glory to the Lord, the God of Israel, and confess to him, [and tell me now what you have done; hide it not from me.]" And Achan answered Joshua and said, "Truly have I sinned against the Lord, the God of Israel, and thus and thus I have done" (Josh 7:19). And how do we know that his confession achieved atonement for him? For it is said, "And Joshua said, Why have you troubled us? The Lord will trouble you this day" (Josh 7:25)—This day you will be troubled, but you will not be troubled in the world to come.

    D. And if he does not know how to confess, they say to him, "Say as follows: 'Let my death be atonement for all of my transgressions.'"

So within the very center of the Halakhic exposition comes the theological principle that the death-penalty opens the way for life eternal. It follows that at stake in the tractate Sanhedrin-Makkot is a systematic demonstration of how God mercifully imposes justice upon sinners and criminals, and also of where the limits to God's mercy are reached: rejection of the Torah, the constitution of a collectivity—an "Israel"—that stands against God. God's merciful justice then pertains to private persons. But there can be only one Israel, and that Israel is made up of all those who look forward to a portion in the world to come: who will stand in justice and transcend death. In humanity, idolators will not stand in judgment, and entire generations who sinned collectively as well as Israelites who broke off from the body of Israel and formed their own Israel do not enjoy that merciful justice that reaches full expression in the fate of Achan: he stole from God but shared the world to come. And so will all of those who have done the dreadful deeds catalogued here.

The upshot should not be missed. It is not merely that through the Halakhah at hand the sages make the statement that they make. One may claim much more, specifically: the religious principle expressed here—God's perfect, merciful justice, correlated with the conviction of the eternity of holy Israel—cannot have come to a systematic statement in any other area of the Halakhah. It is only in the present context that the sages can have linked God's perfect, merciful justice to the concrete life of ordinary Israel, and it is only here that they can have invoked the certainty of eternal life to explain the workings of merciful justice.

The sages insist that without mercy, justice cannot function. Now that readers have seen how, in the Halakhah, that statement is made, let us explore some of the counterpart formulations of the same principle in the Aggadah.

Genesis Rabbah XII:XV.1

A. "The Lord God [made earth and heaven]" (Gen 2:4):

B. The matter [of referring to the divinity by both the names, Lord, which stands for mercy, and God, which stands for justice] may be compared to the case of a king who had empty cups. The king said, "If I fill them with hot water, they will split. If I fill them with cold water, they will contract [and snap]."

C. What did the king do? He mixed hot water and cold water and put it into them, and the cups withstood the liquid.

D. So said the Holy One, blessed be He, "If I create the world in accord with the attribute of mercy, sins will multiply. If I create it in accord with the attribute of justice, the world cannot endure.

E. "Lo, I shall create it with both the attribute of justice and the attribute of mercy, and may it endure!"

F. "Thus: The Lord [standing for the attribute of mercy] God [standing for the attribute of justice] [made the earth and heavens]" (Gen 2:4).

Just as too much justice will destroy the world, but too much mercy ruin its coherence, so throughout, each set of traits achieving complementarity must be shown, like dancers, to move in balance one with the other. Then, and only then, are excesses avoided, stasis in motion attained. That brings about the world of justice at rest that the sages deemed God to have created in the beginning, to have celebrated on the original Sabbath, and to intend to restore in the end. But when the Aggadah makes its statement, it speaks in generalities, and, further, it addresses the world at large. It is the Halakhah that formulates the matter not only in specificities but well within the limits of holy Israel. Seeing how the Halakhah and the Aggadah make the same statement, readers once more see the way in which the Halakhah portrays the interiorities of Israelite life.

But there is more. The sages recognize that, in the setting of this life, the death penalty brings anguish, even though it assures the sinner or criminal expiation for what he has done. That matter is stated in so many words:

Mishnah-tractate Sanhedrin 6:5

    A. Said R. Meir, "When a person is distressed, what words does the Presence of God say? As it were: 'My head is in pain, my arm is in pain.'

    B. "If thus is the Omnipresent distressed on account of the blood of the wicked when it is shed, how much the more so on account of the blood of the righteous!"

God is distressed at the blood of the wicked, shed in expiation for sin or crime, so too humanity. So while the sages recognize the mercy and justice that are embodied in the sanctions they impose, they impute to God, and express in their own behalf, common sentiments and attitudes. They feel the same sentiments God does.

That fact alerts us to the fundamental principle embodied in the Halakhah: man is responsible for what he does, because man is like God. That is the basis for penalizing sins or crimes, but it also is the basis for the hope for eternal life for nearly all Israel. Like God, man is in command of, and responsible for, his own will and intentionality and consequent conduct. The very fact that God reveals himself through the Torah, which man is able to understand, there to be portrayed in terms and categories that man grasps, shows how the characteristics of God and humanity prove comparable. The first difference between humanity and God is that humanity sins, but the one and the just God, never; connecting "God" and "sin" yields an unintelligible result. And the second difference between creature and Creator, humanity and God, is that God is God.

It is not an accident that in the setting of the category-formation of Sanhedrin-Makkot, the sages set forth how God's emotions correspond with humanity's. Like a parent faced with a recalcitrant child, he takes no pleasure in humanity's fall but mourns. In addition, even while he protects those who love him, Israel, from his, and their, enemies, he takes to heart that he made all humanity; he does not rejoice at the Sea when Israel is saved, because, even then, his enemies are perishing. This is said in so many words in the context of a discussion on whether God rejoices when the wicked perish:

Bavli-tractate Sanhedrin 4:5 VI.1/39b

    A. Therefore man was created alone [4:5J]:

    B. "And there went out a song throughout the host" (1 Kgs 22:36) [at Ahab's death at Ramoth in Gilead].

    C. Said R. Aha b. Hanina, "'When the wicked perish, there is song' (Prov 11:10).

    D. "When Ahab, b. Omri, perished, there was song."

Does God sing and rejoice when the wicked perish? Not at all:

E. But does the Holy One, blessed be He, rejoice at the downfall of the wicked?

F. Is it not written, "That they should praise as they went out before the army and say, 'Give thanks to the Lord, for his mercy endures forever' (2 Chr 20:21),

G. and said R. Jonathan, "On what account are the words in this psalm of praise omitted, 'Because he is good'? Because the Holy One, blessed be He, does not rejoice at the downfall of the wicked."

Now readers revert to the conduct of God at the very moment of Israel's liberation, when Israel sings the Song at the Sea:

H. For R. Samuel bar Nahman said R. Jonathan said, "What is the meaning of the verse of Scripture [that speaks of Egypt and Israel at the sea], 'And one did not come near the other all night' (Exod 14:20)?

I. "At that time, the ministering angels want to recite a song [of rejoicing] [the angels' daily song] before the Holy One, blessed be He.

J. "Said to them the Holy One, blessed be He, 'The works of my hands are perishing in the sea, and do you want to sing a song before me?'"

Now the matter is resolved:

K. Said R. Yosé bar Hanina, "He does not rejoice, but others do rejoice. Note that it is written, '[And it shall come to pass, as the Lord rejoiced over you to do good, so the Lord] will cause rejoicing over you by destroying you' (Deut 28:63)—and not 'so will the Lord [himself] rejoice.'"

L. That proves the case.

God's emotions correspond, then, to those of a father or a mother, mourning at the downfall of their children, even though their children have rebelled against them. Even at the moment at which Israel first meets God, with God's act of liberation at the Sea, God cannot join them in their song. God and Israel then correspond, the eternal God in heaven, Israel on earth, also destined for eternal life. Israel forms on earth a society that corresponds to the retinue and court of God in heaven. The Halakhah in its way, in Sanhedrin-Makkot, says no less. But it makes the statement, as readers have seen, in all of the intimacy and privacy of Israel's interior existence: when (in theory at least) Israel takes responsibility for its own condition. Sanhedrin-Makkot, devoted to the exposition of crime and just punishment, turns out to form an encompassing exercise in showing God's mercy, even, or especially, for the sinner or criminal who expiates the sin or crime: that concludes the transaction, but a great deal will follow it—and from it. In the context of the Torah, one cannot think of any other way of making that statement

stick than through the Halakhah of Sanhedrin-Makkot: this sin, this punishment—and no more.

Inside the Walls of the Israelite Household: The Halakhah of Shabbat-Erubin, Time and Space Sanctified on the Sabbath

The Halakhah set forth principally by tractate Erubin focuses on the verses,
that link the act of eating with the locus of residence on the Sabbath: "See!
The Lord has given you the Sabbath, therefore on the sixth day he gives you
bread for two days; remain every one of you in his place; let no man go out
of his place on the seventh day. So the people rested on the seventh day"
(Exod 16:29-30). The juxtaposition of a double supply of bread for Friday
and Saturday and remaining in place leaves no doubt that [1] one stays
home, on the one hand, and that [2] home is where one eats, on the other.

Tractate Shabbat deals with the law of the Sabbath, with special reference
to the prohibition of acts of labor on that day, and Erubin with the law that
prohibits transporting objects from private to public domain on that day and
other Sabbath prohibitions. Now, the paramount question before us is, why
the sages devote their reading of the law of Shabbat-Erubin above all to differentiating public from private domain. All of Erubin devoted to fusing real
estate into a common domain for use on the Sabbath, and a fair component
of Shabbat, devoted to the prohibition of servile labor on the Sabbath, focus
upon that matter, which stands at the head of the first of the two tractates
and at the conclusion of the second. To revert to the Halakhah of Shabbat
once more, the definition of an act of labor that is culpable when performed
on the Sabbath raises another question that demands attention. Why do the
sages formulate the principle that they do, that the act of labor prohibited
on the Sabbath is one that fully constitutes a completed act of labor—beginning, middle, and end—in conformity with the intentionality of the actor?

The answer to both questions derives from the governing theology of the
Sabbath. The Written Torah represents the Sabbath as the climax of creation.
The theology of the Sabbath put forth in the Mishnah's Halakhah derives
from a systematization of definitions implicit in the myth of Eden that
envelopes the Sabbath. The sages' thinking about the Sabbath invokes in the
formation of the normative law defining the matter the model of the first
Sabbath, the one of Eden in Genesis 1 and 2. The two paramount points of
concern—[1] the systematic definition of private domain, where ordinary
activity is permitted, and [2] the particular definition of what constitutes a
prohibited act of labor on the Sabbath—precipitate deep thought and ani-

mate the handful of principles brought to concrete realization in the two tractates. "Thou shalt not labor" of the Commandments refers in a generic sense to all manner of work; but in the Halakhah of Shabbat, "labor" bears particular meanings and is defined in a specific, and odd, manner. One can make sense of the Halakhah of Shabbat-Erubin only by appeal to the story of Creation, the governing metaphor derived therefrom.

When approaching the theme and problem of the Sabbath, the sages chose to answer two questions: what it means to remain "in his place," and what constitutes the theory of forbidden activity, the principles that shape the innumerable rules and facts of the prohibition.

One must work back from the large structures of the Halakhah to the generative thought—how the sages thought, and about what they thought— that gives definition to those structures. Among available formulations, they gave priority to the creation story of Genesis 1:1–2:3, which accounts for the origin of the Sabbath. As readers shall see, the foci of their thinking are what is implicit and subject to generalization in that story. The Halakhah realizes in detailed, concrete terms generalizations that the sages locate in and derive from the story of creation. What they find is a metaphor for themselves and their Israel, on the one hand, and the foundation for generalization, out of the metaphor, in abstract terms susceptible to acute concretization, on the other. That is to say, the Sabbath of Eden forms the model: like this, so all else. And the sages, with their remarkable power to think in general terms but to convey thought in examples and details, found it possible to derive from the model the principles that would accomplish their goal: linking Israel to Eden through the Sabbath, the climax of their way of life, the soul of their theological system.

Our task, then, is first of all to identify the Halakhah that best states in detail some of the principles that the sages derived from their reading of the story of the Genesis of Eden. Building on the definition of the Halakhah that supplies to the Sabbath its program of legislation—the things subjected to acute exegesis, the things treated as other than generative—we may then construct an encompassing theory to find a position, within a single framework, for all of the principal Halakhic constructions. Clearly, the Halakhah of Erubin is not the place, since that body of Halakhah takes for granted layers of profound thought and speculation that have already supplied foundations for the matter at hand. Nor, for the same reason, will the Halakhah of Shabbat help, for its framers know as established principles a set of conceptions, e.g., about the definition of forbidden activity, that presuppose much but articulate, in this context, remarkably little. Accordingly, when it comes to decoding the sages' reading of the story of creation culminating in the Sabbath of Eden, there is no reading the Halakhah of Shabbat or of Erubin out of the context of the Sabbath as the sages defined that context.

In Shabbat the sages know that the division of the world on the Sabbath into public and private domain precipitates the massive exegetical task undertaken both there and in Erubin. Further, they have in mind a powerful definition of the meaning of an act of labor—of what labor consists—but those facts on their own give little direction. For neither Shabbat nor Erubin defines its context; both presuppose analogies and metaphors that are not articulated but constantly present. Only when readers know what is supposed to take place on the Sabbath—in particular in the model of the Sabbath that originally celebrated creation, to the exclusion of the model of the Sabbath that focuses the Halakhah upon the liberation of slaves from Egypt (Deuteronomy's version) or the cessation of labor of the household, encompassing animals and slaves (Exodus's version)—will readers find the key to the entire matter of the Sabbath of the Halakhah of the Oral Torah. Then they may identify the setting in which the rules before them take on meaning and prove to embody profound religious thinking.

The Halakhah that presents the model of how the sages think about the Sabbath and accounts for the topical program of their thought—the fully articulated source of the governing metaphor—is Shebi'it. We recall that that tractate describes the observance of the Sabbath that is provided every seventh year for the Land of Israel itself. The land celebrates the Sabbath, and then, Israel in its model. The land is holy, as Israel is holy, and the Priestly Code leaves no doubt that for both, the Sabbath defines the rhythm of life with God: the seventh day for Israel, the seventh year for the land. For both, moreover, to keep the Sabbath is to be like God. And, specifically, that is when God had completed the work of creation, pronounced it good, sanctified it—imposed closure and permanence, the creation having reached its conclusion. God observed the Sabbath, whose definition is the celebration and commemoration of God's own action. This is what God did, this is what is now done.

What God did concerned creation, what Israel does concerns creation. And all else follows. The Sabbath then precipitates the imitation of God on a particular occasion and for a distinctive purpose. And given what has been identified as the sages' governing theology—the systematic account of God's perfect justice in creation, yielding an account and explanation of all else—readers find themselves at the very center of the system. The meeting of time and space on the seventh day of creation—God having formed space and marked time—finds its counterpart in the ordering of Israelite space at the advent of time, the ordering of that space through the action and inaction of the Israelites themselves.

In stating what is at stake, we have gotten ahead of the story. The traits that the Sabbath precipitates for the land guide in interpreting the considerations that govern the rules of Shabbat-Erubin but do not suffice to place into context those rules and their principles. Therefore, we must turn to the Halakhah of Shebi'it.

Erubin, with its sustained exercise of thought on the commingling of possession of private property for the purpose of Sabbath observance and on the commingling of meals to signify shared ownership, accomplishes for Israel's Sabbath what Shebi'it achieves for the land's. On the Sabbath inaugurated by the Sabbatical Year, the land, so far as it is otherwise private property, no longer is possessed exclusively by the householder. So too, the produce of the land consequently belongs to everybody. It follows that the Halakhah of Erubin realizes for the ordinary Sabbath of Israel the very same principles that are embodied in the Halakhah of Shebi'it. That Halakhah defines the Sabbath of the land in exactly the same terms: the land is now no longer private, and the land's produce belongs to everybody. The Sabbath that the land enjoys marks the advent of shared ownership of the land and its fruit. Sharing is so total that hoarding is forbidden, and what has been hoarded has now to be removed from the household and moved to public domain, where anyone may come and take it.

Here one finds the Sabbath of creation overspreading the Sabbath of the land, as the Priestly Code at Genesis 1 and at Leviticus 25 define matters. The latter states,

> "When you enter the land that I am giving you, the land shall observe a Sabbath of the Lord. Six years you may sow your field and six years you may prune your vineyard and bather in the yield. But in the seventh year the land shall have a Sabbath of complete rest, a Sabbath of the Lord; you shall not sow your field or prune your vineyard. You shall not reap the aftergrowth of your harvest or gather the grapes of your untrimmed vines; it shall be a year of complete rest for the land. But you may eat whatever the land during its Sabbath will produce—you, your male and female slaves, the hired-hand and bound laborers who live with you, and your cattle and the beasts in your land may eat all its yield" (Lev. 25:1-8).

The Sabbatical year bears the message, therefore, that on the Sabbath, established arrangements as to ownership and possession are set aside, and a different conception of private property takes over. What on ordinary days is deemed to belong to the householder and to be subject to his exclusive will on the Sabbath falls into a more complex web of possession. The house-holder continues to utilize his property but not as a proprietor does. He gives up exclusive access thereto, and gains in exchange rights of access to other peoples' property. Private property is commingled; everybody shares in everybody else's. The result is, private property takes on a new meaning, different from the secular one. So far as the householder proposes to utilize his private property, he must share it with others, who do the same for him. To own then is to abridge ownership in favor of commingling rights thereto, to possess is to share. And that explains why the produce of the land belongs to everyone as well, a corollary to the fundamental postulate of the Sabbath of the land.

Now the Halakhah of Shebi'it appeals to the metaphor of Eden, and, along those same lines, if readers wish to understand how the sages thought about the Sabbath, they have here to follow suit. But that is hardly to transgress the character of the evidence in hand, the story of the first Sabbath as the celebration of the conclusion and perfection of creation itself. Since, accordingly, the Sabbath commemorates the sanctification of creation, readers cannot contemplate Sabbath-observance outside of the framework of its generative model, which is Eden. What the sages add in the Halakhah of the Oral Torah becomes self-evident: Eden provides the metaphor for imagining the Land of Israel, and the Sabbath, the occasion for the act of metaphorization.

Then, hermeneutics in hand, the exegesis of the Halakhah becomes possible. Specifically, the governing question to which the details of the law respond has been identified, specifically, what *about* Eden on the Sabbath defines the governing metaphor from which the principles of the Halakhah work. Working back from the details to the organizing topics, and from the topics to the principles that govern, one is able to frame the right question.

The question concerns the qualities of Eden that impress the sages. With the Halakhah as the vast corpus of facts, one must focus upon two matters: [1] time and space, [2] time and activity. The question is how space is demarcated at the specified time and how activity is classified at that same time. The former works itself out in a discussion of where people may move on the Sabbath and how they may conduct themselves (carry things as they move). The latter finds its definition in the model of labor that is prohibited. With Eden as the model and the metaphor, one may take a simple sighting on the matter. First, Adam and Eve are free to move in Eden where they wish, possessing all they contemplate. God has given it to them to enjoy. If Eden then belongs to God, he freely shares ownership with Adam and Eve. And—all the more so—the produce of Eden is ownerless. With the well-known exception, all the fruit is theirs for the taking. As readers we find ourselves deep within the Halakhah of Shebi'it.

The Halakhah of Shebi'it sets forth in concrete terms what is implicit in the character of Eden. In the Sabbatical Year the land returns to the condition characteristic of Eden at the outset: shared and therefore accessible, its produce available to all. The Sabbatical Year recovers that perfect time of Eden when the world was at rest, all things in place. Before the rebellion, humanity did not have to labor on the land; he picked and ate his meals freely. And, in the nature of things, everything belonged to everybody; private ownership in response to individual labor did not exist, because humanity did not have to work anyhow. Reverting to that perfect time, the Torah maintains that the land will provide adequate food for everyone, including the flocks and herds, even if people do not work the land. But that is on condition that all claim of ownership lapses; the food is left in the fields, to be picked by anyone who wishes, but it may not be hoarded by the landowner in particular.

The Priestly Code expresses that same concept when it arranges for the return, at the Jubilee Year, of inherited property to the original family ownership (Lev 25:8-10). The Jubilee year is observed as is the Sabbatical year, meaning that for two successive years the land is not to be worked. The Halakhah moreover establishes that when land is sold, it is for the span of time remaining to the next Jubilee Year. Then it reverts to the original owner. That then marks the reordering of land-holding to its original pattern, when Israel inherited the land to begin with and commenced to enjoy its produce. Just as the Sabbatical Year commemorates the completion of creation, the perfection of world order, so does the Sabbath.

So too, the Jubilee year brings about the restoration of real property to the original division. In both instances, Israelites so act as to indicate they are not absolute owners of the land, which belongs to God and which is divided in the manner that God arranged in perpetuity. Here readers find the Halakhic counterpart to the restorationist theology that the Oral Torah sets forth in the Aggadah. Israel matches Adam, the Land of Israel, Eden, and, they now see, the Sabbatical year commemorates the perfection of creation and replicates it. If the perfection of creation is the well-ordered condition of the natural world, then the Land of Israel, counterpart to Eden, must be formed into the model of the initial perfection, restored to that initial condition.

It is in this context that one may return to the Halakhah of Shabbat-Erubin, with special reference to the division of the world into private and public domain, the former the realm of permitted activity on the Sabbath, the latter not. If one may deal with an 'erub-fence or an 'erub meal, one must interpret what is at stake in these matters. It in both instances is to render private domain public through the sharing of ownership. The 'erub-fence for its part renders public domain private, but only in the same sense that private domain owned by diverse owners is shared, ownership being commingled. The 'erub-fence signals the formation for purposes of the sanctification of time of private domain—but with the ownership commingled. What is "private" about "private domain" is different on the Sabbath from in secular time. By definition, for property to be private in the setting of the Sabbath, it must be shared among householders. On the Sabbath, domain that is totally private, its ownership not commingled for the occasion, becomes a prison, the householder being unable to conduct himself in the normal manner in the courtyard beyond his door, let alone in other courtyards in the same alleyway, or in other alleyways that debouch onto the same street. And the Halakhah makes provision for those—whether Israelite or gentile—who do not offer their proprietorship of their households for commingling for the Sabbath.

What happens, therefore, through the 'erub-fence or 'erub meal is the redefinition of proprietorship: what is private is no longer personal, and no one totally owns what is his, but then everyone (who wishes to participate, himself and his household together) owns a share everywhere. So much for the "in his place" part of "each humanity in his place." His place constitutes an area where ordinary life goes on, but it is no longer "his" in the way in which the land is subject to his will and activity in ordinary time. If constructing a fence serves to signify joint ownership of the village, now turned into private domain, or constructing the gateway, of the alleyway and its courtyards, one then asks what about the meal. The 'erub-meal signifies the shared character of what is eaten. It is food that belongs to all who wish to share it. But it is the provision of a personal meal, also, that allows an individual to designate for himself a place of Sabbath residence other than the household to which he belongs.

So the Sabbath loosens bonds, those of the householder to his property, those of the individual to the household. It forms communities, the householders of a courtyard into a community of shared ownership of the entire courtyard, the individual into a community other than that formed by the household to which he belongs—now the community of disciples of a given sage or the community of a family other than that in residence in the household, to use two of the examples common in the Halakhah. Just as the Sabbath redefines ownership of the land and its produce, turning all Israelites into a single social entity, "all Israel," which, all together, possesses the land in common ownership, so the Sabbath redefines the social relationships of the household, allowing persons to separate themselves from the residence of the household and designate some other, some personal, point of residence instead.

The main point of the law of private domain in Shabbat and Erubin seen in the model of Shebi'it then is to redefine the meaning of "private domain," where each man is to remain in "his" place. The law aims to define the meaning of "his," and to remove the ownership of the land and its produce from the domain of a householder, rendering ownership public and collective. Taking as our model Shebi'it, readers note that in the year that is a Sabbath, the land is held to be owned by nobody and everybody, and the produce of the land belongs to everyone and no one, so that one may take and eat but thank only God. It is no one's, so everyone may take; it is everyone's, so everyone may eat, and God alone is to be acknowledged. Since, on the Sabbath, people are supposed to remain within their own domain, the counterpart to Shebi'it will provide for the sharing of ownership, thus for extending the meaning of "private domain" to encompass all the partners in a shared locus. "Private domain," his place, now bears a quite different meaning from the one that pertains in profane time. The Sabbath recapitulates the condition of Eden, when Adam and Eve could go where they wished and eat what they wanted, masters of all they contemplated, along with God. Israel on the Sabbath in the land, like Adam on the Sabbath of Eden that celebrates Creation, shares private domain and its produce.

Israel on the Sabbath in the land like God on the Sabbath of Eden rests from the labor of creation. And that brings us to the question of that other principle of the Sabbath, the one set forth by the Halakhah of Shabbat. The richly detailed Halakhah of Shabbat defines the matter in a prolix, yet simple way. It is that on the Sabbath it is prohibited deliberately to carry out in a normal way a completed act of constructive labor, one that produces enduring results, one that carries out one's entire intention: the whole of what one planned, one has accomplished, in exactly the proper manner. That definition takes into account the shank of the Halakhah of Shabbat as set forth in the Mishnah-tractate, and the amplification and extension of matters in the Tosefta and the two Talmuds in no way revises the basic principles. Here there is a curious, if obvious, fact: it is not an act of labor that itself is prohibited (as the Ten Commandments in Exodus and Deuteronomy would have it), but an act of labor of a very particular definition.

No prohibition impedes performing an act of labor in an other-than-normal way. In theory, one may go out into the fields and plough, if he does so in some odd manner. He may build an entire house, so long as it collapses promptly. The issue of activity on the Sabbath therefore is removed from the obvious context of work, conventionally defined. Now the activity that is forbidden is of a very particular sort, modeled in its indicative traits after a quite specific paradigm. A person is not forbidden to carry out an act of destruction, or an act of labor that produces no lasting consequences. He may start an act of labor if he does not complete it. He may accomplish an act of labor in some extraordinary manner. None of these acts of labor are forbidden, even though, done properly and with consequence, they represent massive violations of the Halakhah. Nor is part of an act of labor that is not brought to conclusion prohibited. Nor is it forbidden to perform part of an act of labor in partnership with another person who carries out the other requisite part. Nor does one incur culpability for performing an act of labor in several distinct parts, e.g., over a protracted, differentiated period of time. A person may not willingly carry out the entirety of an act of constructive labor, start to finish. The issue is not why not, since readers know the answer: God has said not to do so. The question concerns whence the particular definition at hand.

Clearly, a definition of the act of labor that is prohibited on the Sabbath has taken over and recast the commonsense meaning of the commandment not to labor on the Sabbath. For considerations enter that recast matters from an absolute to a relative definition. One may tie a knot—but not one that stands. One may carry a package, but not in the usual manner. One may build a wall, only if it falls down. And one may do pretty much anything without penalty—if he did not intend matters as they actually happened. The metaphor of God in Eden, as the sages have reflected on the story of Creation, yields the governing principles that define forbidden labor. What God did in the six days of creation provides the model.

Let us review the main principles item by item. They involve the three preconditions. The act must fully carry out the intention of the actor, as creation carried out God's intention. The act of labor must be carried out by a single actor, as God acted alone in creating the world. An act of labor is the like of one that is required in the building and maintenance of God's residence in this world, the tabernacle. The act of labor prohibited on the Sabbath involves two considerations. The act must be done in the ordinary way, just as Scripture's account leaves no doubt, God accomplished creation in the manner in which he accomplished his goals from creation onward, by an act of speech. And, weightier still, the forbidden act of labor is one that produces enduring consequences. God did not create only to destroy, but he created the enduring world. And it goes without saying, creation yielded the obvious consequences that the act was completely done in all ways, as God himself declared. The act was one of consequence, involving what was not negligible but what man and God alike deemed to make a difference. The sages would claim, therefore, that the activity that must cease on the Sabbath finds its definition in the model of those actions that God carried out in making the world.

That such a mode of thought is more than a mere surmise, based on the congruence of the principles by which labor forbidden on the Sabbath spin themselves out of the creation story, emerges when readers recall a striking statement. It is the one that finds the definition of forbidden labor in those activities required for the construction and maintenance of the tabernacle, which is to say, God's residence on earth. The best statement, predictably, is the Bavli's:

> Bavli Sanhedrin 4:2 I.4/49B
>> People are liable only for classifications of labor the like of which was done in the tabernacle. They sowed, so you are not to sow. They harvested, so you are not to harvest. They lifted up the boards from the ground to the wagon, so you are not to lift them in from public to private domain. They lowered boards from the wagon to the ground, so you must not carry anything from private to public domain. They transported boards from wagon to wagon, so you must not carry from one private domain to another.

The sages found in the analogy of how, in theory, the tabernacle was maintained, the classifications of labor that pertain. In the tabernacle these activities are permitted, even on the Sabbath. In God's house, the priests and Levites must do for God what they cannot do for themselves—and the identification of acts of labor forbidden on the Sabbath follows.

The details of the Halakhah then emerge out of a process in which two distinct sources contribute. One is the model of the tabernacle. What man may do for God's house he may not do for his own—God is always God, the Israelite aspires only to be "like God," to imitate God, and that is a different thing. The other is the model of the creation of the world and of Eden. Hence to act like God on the Sabbath, the Israelite rests; he does not do what God did in creation. The former source supplies generative metaphors, the like of which may not be done; thus acts like sowing, harvesting, lifting boards from public to private domain, and the like, are forbidden. The latter source supplies the generative principles, the abstract definitions involving the qualities of perfection and causation: intentionality, completion, the normality of the conduct of the action, and so on. The mode of analogical thinking governs, but, a double metaphor pertains, the metaphor of God's activity in creation, the metaphor of the priests' and Levites' activity in the tabernacle. Creation yields those large principles that have been identified:

the traits of an act of labor for God in creation define the prohibited conditions of an act of labor on the Sabbath. By appeal to those two metaphors, one can account for every detail of the Halakhah.

What then takes place inside the walls of the Israelite household when time takes over space and revises the conduct of ordinary affairs requires an explanation. Then—so the Sabbath provides—Israel goes home to Eden. There is no better way to make the statements that the land is Israel's Eden, that Israel imitates God by keeping the Sabbath, meaning, not doing the things that God did in creating the world but ceased to do on the Sabbath. To restore its Eden, Israel must sustain its life—nourish itself—where it belongs. To set forth those most basic convictions about God in relationship to humanity and about Israel in relationship to God, it is difficult to imagine a more eloquent, a more compelling and appropriate, medium of expression than the densely detailed Halakhah of Shebi'it, Shabbat, and Erubin. Indeed, outside of the setting of the household, its ownership, utilization, and maintenance, one cannot think of any other way of making that statement stick. In theory implausible for its very simplicity (as much as for its dense instantiation), in Halakhic fact, compelling, the Oral Torah's statement accounts for the human condition. Israel's Eden takes place in the household open to others, on the Sabbath, in acts that maintain life, share wealth, and desist from creation.

The key words, therefore, are in the shift from the here and now of time in which one works like God, to the *then* and *there* when one desists from working, just as God did at the moment the world was finished, perfected, and sanctified. Israel gives up the situation of humanity in ordinary time and space, destructive, selfish, dissatisfied, and doing. Then, on the Sabbath, and there, in the household, with each one in place, Israel enters the situation of God in that initial, that perfected and sanctified then and there of creation: the activity that consists in sustaining life, sharing dominion, and perfecting repose through acts of restraint and sufficiency.

Inside the Walls of the Israelite Household: The Halakhah of Pesahim, The Passover Festival

For the Halakhah as for the Aggadah, Passover marks the advent of Israel's freedom, which is to say, the beginning of Israel. The liturgy for the occasion makes that matter explicit, and that represents a Halakhic statement of a norm: "Passover . . . the season of our freedom." But that only focuses the question of the Halakhah: what is that freedom that Israel gained at Passover, freedom from what? And to what, in the Halakhic framework, had Israel been enslaved?

Alas, on the surface the Halakhah in its classical formulation is not only remarkably reticent on that question but lays its emphasis elsewhere altogether. What makes Israel into Israel, and what defines its trait as Israel, so far as the Halakhah is concerned, are two matters: [1] the preparation of the home for the festival through the removal of leaven, which may not be consumed or seen at that time; and [2] the preparation and presentation of the Passover-offering and the consumption of its meat in the household.

These define the topics of Halakhic interest in tractate Pesahim, and no others pertinent to the festival register. So the celebration of Israel's freedom turns into the transformation of Israel into a kingdom of priests and a holy people, celebrating its birth by recapitulating the blood-rite that marked the separation of Israel from Egypt and the redemption of Israel for life out of death, Israel's firstborn being saved from the judgment visited upon Egypt's. That defines the focus of the Halakhah: the act of sanctification unto life that marks, and re-marks every year, the advent of Israel out of the nations. The freedom that is celebrated is freedom from death.

Its message for the occasion of Israel's beginning as a free people focuses upon Israel's sanctification, and that message comes to the fore in the Halakhah's stress upon the analogy of the Israelite household and the Temple in Jerusalem, an analogy that takes effect on Passover in particular. The upshot is that Passover marks the celebration of Israel's redemption, meaning its separation from Egypt—the separation being marked off by blood rites on both sides—and its entry into the condition of cleanness so that a Temple-offering may be eaten in the very household of the Israelite. True enough, the Temple-offering is one of the very few—the offering of the red cow for the preparation of ashes for the purification water (Num. 19:1-20) is another—that may be conducted in a state of uncleanness. The second Passover explicitly provides for that circumstance. But the point of the Halakhah should not be lost: conforming with God's explicit instructions in the Written Torah, on Passover Israel differentiates itself from the nations (Egypt) and chooses as the signification of its identity the attainment of the condition of cleanness in the household, such that Temple meat may be eaten there.

Like the Halakhah of Yoma, as readers have seen, most of which is devoted to the Temple rite on that occasion, the Halakhah of Pesahim therefore stresses the cultic aspect of the occasion: the disposition of the Passover-offering. In volume nearly half of the Halakhah readers have exam-

ined is devoted to that one theme—Mishnah-tractate Pesahim 5:1–9:11—
and in complexity, by far the best articulated and most searching Halakhic
problems derive from that same theme. But the Halakhah of Pesahim
belongs to the realm of the Israelite household and yields a statement on the
character of that household that the Halakhah of Yoma does not even contemplate. The household is made ready to serve as part of the cult by the
removal of leaven and all marks of fermentation; now man eats only that
same unleavened bread that is God's portion through the year. The household is further made the locus of a rite of consuming other specified foods
(bitter herbs, for example). But the main point is that the offering sacrificed
in the Temple yields meat to be eaten in the household, at home, not only
in the Temple courtyard.

That rule pertains only to Lesser Holy Things—the peace-offerings and
the festal offering, for example—and to the Passover:

M. Zebahim 9:14
> Most Holy Things were eaten within the veils [of the Temple], Lesser
> Holy Things and second tithe within the wall [of Jerusalem].

Among offerings eaten in Jerusalem in the household but outside of the
Temple walls, the Passover-offering is the only one precipitated by the advent
of a particular occasion (as distinct from peace- and festal offerings). The festivals of Tabernacles and Pentecost, by contrast, do not entail a home-
offering of a similar character, nor does the celebration of the New Month.
For its part, the Halakhah of Yoma describes an occasion that is celebrated
at the Temple or in relationship to the Temple. In this context, then, the
Halakhah of Pesahim alone sets forth an occasion in the life of all Israel that
commences in the Temple but concludes at home. Its message, then, is that
for Passover in particular—"season of our freedom"—the home and the
Temple form a single continuum. That is why the advent of Israel's freedom
from Egypt is characterized as an occasion of sanctification: the differentiation through a blood rite in particular of Israel from the nations, represented
by Egypt.

On what basis, then, the Halakhah before us pertains to the world
within the walls of the Israelite household in a way in which the Halakhah
of Yoma, the counterpart, does not, requires consideration. Why the sages
have treated in a single tractate so distinct a set of venues as the home and
the Temple, rather than leaving the exposition of the Passover-offering to
take its place in tractate Zebahim, the general rules of the cult, where the
Passover makes its appearance in context, requires an explanation. Once the
question is framed in that way, the obvious answer emerges. The sages

through their emphases transformed the festival of freedom into the celebration of Israel's sanctification, embodied here and now in the act of eating the Passover-offering at home, in a family, natural or fabricated, that stands for the Israelite household. As God abides in the Temple, so on this occasion God's abode extends to the household. That is why the Passover-offering takes place in two locations, the Temple for the blood-rite, the home for the consumption of the meat assigned to the sacrifiers—those who benefit from the offering, as distinct from the sacrificers, those who perform the rite itself.

The law is explicit that people bring the animals to the Temple, where the beasts are sacrificed, the blood collected and the sacrificial portions placed on the altar-fires. Then the people take the remaining meat home and roast it. Passover is represented as a pilgrim festival alone; the home ritual hardly rates a single penetrating Halakhic inquiry, being presented as a set of inert facts. It follows that, on the occasion at hand, the household (at least in Jerusalem) forms a continuum with the Temple. That means, also, that the Passover sacrifice then stands in an intermediate situation, not an offering that takes place in a state of uncleanness, like the offering of the red cow, which takes place outside of the Temple (Num 19:1-20); nor an offering that is presented and eaten in the Temple in a state of cleanness, with the meat eaten by the priests in the Temple itself, like the sin-offering and other Most Holy Things. As to where the sacrifier eats his share of the Passover-offering (and its comparable ones), the Halakhah takes for granted it is in a state of cleanness. So far as the Passover is concerned, it is not eaten in the Temple but at home or in a banquet hall, which by definition must be in Jerusalem. That consideration gains weight when one takes into account the unleavened character of the bread with which the meat is eaten, in the model of nearly all meal-offerings:

Mishnah-tractate Menahot 5:1
"All meal offerings are brought unleavened [Lev 2:4-5, 6:7-9], except for the leaven[ed cakes] in the thank offerings [M 7:1] and the two loaves of bread [of Shabuot], which are brought leavened [Lev 7:13, 23:17]."

By treating the sacrifice in that intermediate realm—the sacrifice in the Temple, the meat eaten at home—the Halakhah takes into account the requirement of the Written Torah, which, read as a harmonious statement, dictates that the Passover take place in two locations, the home and the Temple. Deuteronomy 16:1-8 places the rite in the Temple in Jerusalem. It is explicit that only in the Temple is the Passover-offering to be sacrificed, and nowhere else. It is to be boiled and eaten in the same place, not at home, and in the morning the people are to go home. With that statement in hand, one should treat the Passover-offering as a Temple rite, as much as the sacrifice for the Day of Atonement is a Temple rite.

Then we wonder where the altar is in the home. Exodus 12:1-28 treats the offering as a rite for the home, with the blood tossed on the lintel of the house as a mark of an Israelite dwelling. The lintel then serves as the counterpart to the altar. That is where the blood rite takes place, where the blood of the sacrifice is tossed. Here readers find as clear a statement as is possible that the Israelite home compares to the Temple, the lintel to the altar, the abode of Israel to the abode of God. Why readers wonder, the lintel? It is the gateway, marking the household apart from the world beyond. Inside the walls of the Israelite household conditions of genealogical and cultic cleanness pertain, in a way comparable to the space inside the contained space of the Temple courtyard.

What contribution the Oral Torah makes to the Halakhah of Passover emerges when readers ask to what offering they may then compare the Passover. The answer is, to the sin-offering. This is stated explicitly at Mishnah-tractate Zebahim 1:1 below. But first, to advance the argument, one asks for the foci of the analogy. It is temporal and occasional, not permanent and spatial. True, the Halakhah treats the lintel of the Israelite home to the altar, the contained space of the Israelite household as comparable to the Temple courtyard, the household serving as the venue for an offering comparable to the sin-offering. But that analogy takes effect only at a very specific moment, just as the household compares to Eden only at the specific moment of the Sabbath day, the invisible wall descending to mark of the temporal Eden in the particular space consecrated by the Israelite abode. The advent of the first new moon after the vernal equinox then compares with the advent of sunset on the sixth day, the beginning of the Sabbath comparing, then, to the beginning of the lunar calendar marked by the first new moon of spring. The Sabbath places Israel in Eden. The fifteenth of Nisan places the Israelite household into a continuum with the Temple, the lintel with the altar (in the Written Torah's reading).

With Passover the Israelite, in the Halakhic theory of the Oral Torah, carries his offering to the Temple and brings home the sacrificial parts to be consumed by himself and his family (or the surrogate family formed by an association organized for that particular purpose), so treating the household as an extension of the Temple for the purpose at hand. That same conception extends to other Lesser Holy Things, eaten in Jerusalem but not in the Temple; but Passover among festivals is unique in having its own offering,

celebrating its own specific event in the natural year and in the rhythm of
Israel's paradigmatic existence as well.

The Passover, moreover, may be subject to the rules of Lesser Holy
Things but bears its own very particular signification. Some of the Lesser
Holy Things are interchangeable, in that if an animal is designated for one
purpose but offered for another, it may serve, e.g., as a freewill-offering. But
in the case of the Passover in particular, the law deals with a Lesser Holy
Thing that is not interchangeable. The Halakhah stresses that the rite is analogous to the sin-offering, in that the animal that is designated for the rite
must be offered for that purpose—and for that particular sacrifier. If it is designated for the benefit of a given party (sacrifier) and offered for some other
sacrifier and it is not possible to clarify the situation, the animal is simply
disposed of, so, readers recall, M. Pesahim 9:9 for example:

> An association, the Passover-offering of which was lost, and which said to
> someone, "Go and find and slaughter another one for us," and that one
> went and found and slaughtered [another], but they, too, went and
> bought and slaughtered [one for themselves]—if his was slaughtered first,
> he eats his, and they eat with him of his. But if theirs was slaughtered first,
> they eat of theirs, and he eats of his. And if it is not known which of them
> was slaughtered first, or if both of them were slaughtered simultaneously,
> then he eats of his, and they do not eat with him, and theirs goes forth to
> the place of burning, but they are exempt from having to observe the sec-
> ond Passover.

The stress on the specificity of identification of the beast and sacrifier aligns
the Passover-offering with the sin-offering, not with peace- or freewill-
offerings.

That analogy is stated explicitly at M. Zeb 1:1:

> "All animal offerings that were slaughtered not for their own name are
> valid [so that the blood is tossed, the entrails burned], but they do not go
> to the owner's credit in fulfillment of an obligation, except for the
> Passover and the sin-offering—the Passover at its appointed time [the
> afternoon of the fourteenth of Nisan], and the sin-offering of any time."

The theory of the matter is explained in the argument of Eliezer that the
guilt-offering should be subject to the same rule: "The sin-offering comes on
account of sin, and the guilt-offering comes on account of sin. Just as the
sin-offering is unfit [if it is offered] not for its own name, so the guilt-offering is unfit [if offered] not for its own name]." Eliezer's statement takes for
granted that the sin-offering is brought in expiation of (inadvertent) sin, and

it must follow, the Halakhah in general must concur that the same category encompasses also the Passover-offering. That matches the story of the blood on the lintel, an offering that expiates Israel and atones for those sins for which, on the same moment, Egypt will atone through the offering of the firstborn among men and cattle alike. Within that theory, one finds in the account of the offering the basis for treating it as comparable to the sin-offering, which is offered to expiate inadvertent sin. Since the Passover-offering signals that Israel is to be spared the judgment of the Lord executed against the first-born of Egypt, it is reasonable to suppose that the blood of the Passover lamb, placed on the lintel, not only marks the household as Israelite but also expiates inadvertent sin carried out in that household.

True, the Written Torah itself imposed the requirement of celebrating Passover in two places, Deuteronomy in the Temple, the meat consumed in Jerusalem, Exodus at home, the meat consumed there. But in joining the two conceptions, with its rules for the household wherever it is located, the Halakhah has made a statement of its own out of the disharmonious facts received from Scripture. That statement is in two parts. First, the Israelite abode is treated as comparable to the Temple not merely in the aspect of cultic cleanness but in the aspect of cultic activity: the place where the sacrificial meat was consumed, within the unfolding of the rite of expiation of inadvertent sin itself. It is that analogy, between the Passover on the fourteenth of Nisan and the sin-offering at any time, that forms the critical nexus between the Israelite abode and the Temple altar. So the question arises concerning why that particular analogy, and to what effect. What conclusions one draws from the fact that the Passover-offering is comparable to the sin-offering demands an answer.

The answer derives from the occasion itself, Israel on the eve of the Exodus from Egypt, at the threshold of its formation into a kingdom of priests and a holy people. When God executed judgment on Egypt, exacting the first-born of humanity and beast as the sanction, he saw the blood, which—the Halakhah now tells us—compared with the blood of the sin-offering. Israel then had expiated its inadvertent sin and attained a state of atonement, so entering a right relationship with God. On the eve of Israel's formation, the Passover offered at home, with the blood on the lintel, marked Israel as having expiated its sin. The sinless people were kept alive at the time of judgment—just as, at the end of days, nearly all Israel will stand in judgment and pass on to life eternal.

Sin and atonement, death and life—these form the foci of Passover. If the sages had wished to make the theological statement that Israel differs from the Egyptians as does life from death, and that what makes the difference is that Israel is sanctified even—or especially—within its household walls, not only within the Temple veils, there is no better way to say so then through the Halakhah of Passover. Eat unleavened bread as God does in the meal-offerings, consume the meat left over from the blood rite of the Passover-offering, analogous to the sin-offering in its very particular identification with a given family-unit, and the actions speak for themselves. These are the two facts out of the repertoire of the data of Passover that the Halakhic statement from the Mishnah through the Bavli chooses to explore and articulate. It is the Written Torah that sets forth the facts, the Oral Torah that explores their implications for the norms of conduct, while, in doing so, imparting its sense for the proportion, therefore the meaning and significance, of the whole.

One must explain why these two topics in particular. The sages will assuredly have maintained they said no more than the Written Torah implied, and, as readers have seen, that claim enjoys powerful support in the content of the Halakhah. But the sages are the ones who framed the law, chose its points of proportion and emphasis. In doing so, they shaped the law into a statement congruent with the stresses of their system as a whole. Theirs was a theology of restoration, Israel to the land standing for mankind to Eden. To such a statement the fact that fully half of the Halakhic formulations were monumentally irrelevant to the practical affairs made no difference. The sages knew full well that all Israel was resident outside of Jerusalem; in the time that the Halakhic statement was being formulated, Israel could not enter Jerusalem, let alone sacrifice on the ruined, ploughed-over Temple mount. But to the realities of the moment the sages chose to make no statement at all; these meant nothing of enduring consequence to them. For the situation of Israel in the here and now did not define the focus of the Halakhah, only its venue.

For the sages, at stake in the Halakhah is the transformation of Israel by time and circumstance, the reconciliation of Israel and God by rites of atonement for sin, and the location of Israel and God into a single abode: the household now, Eden then. What is at stake in the Halakhah of innermost Israel, the Israel embodied in the abode of the household, is readily seen. It is what takes place in the Holy of Holies on the Day of Atonement: the encounter of Israel, its sins atoned for, its reconciliation in the aftermath of the fall from Eden complete—the encounter of Israel with God, the occasion of eternity, the moment at which, for now, death is transcended. Scripture said no less, the sages no more: "It is the Lord's Passover. For I will pass through the land of Egypt that night, and I will smite all the first-born in the land of Egypt, both man and beast; and on all the gods of Egypt I will execute judgments; I am the Lord. The blood shall be a sign for you, upon the houses where you are; and when I see the blood I will pass over you, and no plague shall fall upon you to destroy you, when I smite the land of Egypt." The Halakhah makes the statement that the freedom that Passover celebrates is Israel's freedom from death. Where Israel lives, there life is lived that transcends the grave. When, as is the custom, some people at the Passover Seder wear their burial garment, the gesture says no less than that.

Inside the Walls of the Israelite Household: The Halakhah of Sukkah, the Festival of Tabernacles

The temporary abode of the Israelite, suspended between heaven and earth, the *Sukkah* or tabernacle, hut, in its transience matches Israel's condition in the wilderness, wandering between Egypt and the land, death and eternal life. Just as Passover marks the differentiation of Israel, expiating sin through the Passover-offering and so attaining life, from Egypt, expiating sin through the death of the first-born, so Sukkot addresses the condition of Israel. It is, readers must remind themselves, the generation of the wilderness with which they deal, that is, the generation that must die out before Israel can enter the land. Entering the Sukkah reminds Israel not only of the fragility of its condition but also—in the aftermath of the penitential season—of its actuality: yet sinful, yet awaiting death, so that a new generation will be ready for the land. So it is that interstitial circumstance, between death in Egypt and eternal life in the land,[11] that the Festival recapitulates. The now-abode of Israel-in-between is the house that is not a house, protected by a roof that is open to the elements but serves somewhat: Israel en route to death (for those here now) and then eternal life (for everyone then).

It is at the Sukkah itself that one finds the center of the Halakhic repertoire concerning the Festival. Israel in the wilderness, replicated annually from the first new moon after the autumnal equinox, lived in houses open to the rain and affording protection only from the harsh sunlight, shade if not continuous shadow such as a roof provides. Their abode was constructed of what was otherwise useless, bits and pieces of this and that, and hence, as readers noted in examining the generative problematic of the Halakhah, insusceptible to uncleanness. And, readers note, that is the abode in which Israel is directed to take up residence. The odd timing should not be missed. It is not with the coming of the spring and the dry season, when the booth serves a useful purpose against the sun, but at the advent of the autumn and the rainy one, when it does not protect against the rain.

Now it is an abode that cannot serve in the season that is coming, announced by the new moon that occasions the festival. Israel is to take shelter, in reverting to the wilderness, in any random, ramshackle hut, covered with what nature has provided but in form and in purpose what humanity otherwise does not value. Israel's dwelling in the wilderness is fragile, random, and transient—like Israel in the wilderness. Out of Egypt Israel atoned and lived, now, after the season of repentance, Israel has atoned and lived—but only in the condition of the wilderness, like the generation that, after all, had to die out before Israel could enter the land and its intended eternal life.

Reminding Israel annually by putting the Israelites into booths that Israel now lives like the generation of the wilderness then, sinful and meant to die, the Halakhah underscores not only transience. It emphasizes the contemporaneity of the wilderness-condition: the Sukkah is constructed fresh, every year. Israel annually is directed to replicate the wilderness generation—Scripture says no less. The dual message is not to be missed: Israel is en route to the land that stands for Eden, but Israel, even beyond the penitential season, bears its sin and must, on the near term, die, but in death enjoys the certainty of resurrection, judgment, and eternal life to come. What readers are dealing with here is a redefinition of the meaning of Israel's abode and its definition. All seven days a person treats his Sukkah as his regular dwelling and his house as his sometime dwelling. On the occasion of the Festival, Israel regains the wilderness and its message of death but also transcendence over death in the entry into the land. Only in the context of the New Year and the Day of Atonement, only as the final act in the penitential season and its intense drama, does Sukkot make sense. It is the Halakhah that draws out that sense, in the provisions that define the valid Sukkah upon which such heavy emphasis is laid.

True, the Written Torah tells more about the observance of the Festival of Sukkot than about the occasion for the Festival. But viewed from the perspective of this study, what it does say—"that your generations may know that I made the people of Israel dwell in booths when I brought them out of the land of Egypt"—suffices. The reversion to the wilderness, the recapitulation of the wandering, the return to Israel's condition outside of the land and before access to the land, the remembrance of the character of that generation, its feet scarcely dry after passing through the mud of the Red Sea when it has already built the Golden Calf—that is the other half of the cycle that commences at Passover and concludes at Sukkot. Who can have missed the point of the Festival, with Scripture's words in hand, "that I made the people of Israel dwell in booths"? The Rabbis of the Halakhah certainly did not.

Let us return to the eternal present established by the Halakhah and compare the provisions for the principal Halakhic moments, Pesahim and Sukkah. Viewing the Festival of Tabernacles in the model of the Festival of Passover, readers find that three elements require attention, in two divisions: what happens in the home, what happens in the Temple, and what happens in the home that connects the home to the Temple. Passover has the home cleansed of leaven, with the result that the bread of the holiday corresponds to the bread served to God in (most of) the meal-offerings. What happens in the Temple is the sacrifice of the Passover-offering. What happens in the home that connects the home to the Temple is the eating of the portions of the Passover-offering that the ordinary Israelite on Passover eats, just as the priest in the Temple eats portions of the sin-offering (among other Most Holy Things). So, as readers have seen, Passover marks the moment at which the home and the Temple are made to correspond, the whole taking place within the walls of Jerusalem.

That perspective turns out to clarify the divisions of the Halakhah of Sukkah as well: what happens in the Temple is a celebratory rite involving the utilization of certain objects (*lulab*, *etrog*) and the recitation of the Hallel-Psalms. What happens in the home is that the home is abandoned altogether, a new house being constructed for the occasion. During the Festival, the Israelite moves out of his home altogether, eating meals and (where possible) sleeping in the Sukkah, making the Sukkah into his regular home, and the home into the random shelter. Just as, in the wilderness, God's abode shifted along with Israel from place to place, the tabernacle being taken down and reconstructed time and again, so, in recapitulating the life of the wilderness, Israel's abode shifts, losing that permanence that it ordinarily possesses. What happens in the home that connects the home to the Temple is, at first glance, nothing, there being no counterpart to the Passover Seder. But a second look shows something more striking. To see the connection readers must recall that during the Festival a huge volume of offerings is presented day by day. There he will consume the festal-offering (Hagigah) and other sacrificial meat, e.g., from the freewill-offering. Israel removes to the housing of the wilderness to eat the Festival meat, doing in the Sukkah what God did in the Tabernacle in that epoch.

To find the religious meaning of the Halakhah of Sukkot, therefore, readers must ask, what, then, the abode in the wilderness represents. To answer that question within the framework of the Halakhah, readers have to introduce two well-established facts. First, one cannot overstress that as the Halakhah knows Sukkot, the Festival continues the penitential season commencing with the advent of Elul, reaching its climax in the season of judgment and atonement of the Days of Awe, from the first through the tenth of the month of Tishré: Rosh Hashanah, the New Year, and Yom Hakkippurim, the Day of Atonement. Sukkot finds its place in the context of a season of sin and atonement. And since, as the rites themselves indicate, it celebrates the advent of the rainy season with prayers and activities meant to encourage the now conciliated God to give ample rain to sustain the life of the land and its people, the message cannot be missed. Israel has rebelled and sinned, but Israel has also atoned and repented: so much for the first ten days of the season of repentance.

At the new moon following, having atoned and been forgiven, Israel takes up residence as if it were in the wilderness. That is because in the wilderness, en route to the land, still sinful Israel depended wholly and completely on God's mercy and good will and infinite capacity to forgive in response to repentance and atonement. Israel depends for all things on God, eating food he sends down from heaven, drinking water he divines in rocks—and living in fragile booths constructed of worthless shards and remnants of this and that. Even Israel's very household in the mundane sense, its shelter, now is made to depend upon divine grace: the wind can blow it down, the rain prevent its very use. Returning to these booths, built specifically for the occasion (not last year's), manipulating the sacred objects owned in particular by the Israelite who utilizes them, as the rainy season impends, the particular Israelite here and now recapitulates his total dependence upon God's mercy.

Accordingly, requiring that everything be renewed for the present occasion and the particular person, the Halakhah transforms commemoration of the wandering into recapitulation of the condition of the wilderness. The Sukkah makes the statement that Israel of the here and now, sinful like the Israel that dwelt in the wilderness, depends wholly upon, looks only to, God. Israelites turn their eyes to that God whose just now forgiveness of last year's sins and acts of rebellion and whose acceptance of Israel's immediate act of repentance will recapitulate God's on-going nurture that kept Israel alive in the wilderness. The Halakhah's provisions for the Sukkah underscore not so much the transience of Israel's present life in general as Israel's particular condition. The Halakhah renders Israel in the Sukkah as the people that is en route to the land, which is Eden. Yes, Israel is en route, but it is not there. A generation comes, a generation goes, but Israel will get there, all together at the end.

So in defining the Sukkah as it does, the Halakhah also underscores the giving of God's providence and remarkable forbearance. In a negative way the Halakhah says exactly that at M. 2:9: "[If] it began to rain, at what point is it permitted to empty out [the Sukkah]? From the point at which the porridge will spoil. They made a parable: To what is the matter comparable? To a slave who came to mix a cup of wine for his master, and his master threw the flagon into his face." No wonder, then, that in the Aggadah Sukkot is supposed to mark the opportunity for the Messiah to present himself and raise the dead—an appropriate point at which to conclude this narrative of how the Halakhah makes its own statement of the covenant in its own language of purely normative deeds: covenantal nomism.

Epilogue

Covenantal Conduct
The Outcome of Performing Israel's Faith

Law without theology conveyed in lore—exegesis, narrative, topical exposition—yields legalism. It does not fully express Israel's partnership with God, omitting as it does the theological convictions that animate action. Stated simply: Halakhah without Aggadah—rules without convictions—produces robots, automatons of the law. Theology without law conveyed in rules of normative conduct—Aggadah without Halakhah, beliefs without corresponding behavior—yields not a covenanted community but a radically isolated individual. Theology without social norms does not embody that same partnership, omitting as it does the essential aspect of realizing the covenant in actualities of the workaday world. Covenantal conduct contains imperatives of attitude and belief ("You will love the Lord your God with all your heart, soul, and might") and action and behavior ("Love your neighbor as yourself").

We have examined massive testimonies in support of E. P. Sanders's view of covenantal nomism. He argues against the idea of Judaism as "a petty legalism, according to which one had to earn the mercy of God by minute observance of irrelevant ordinances." The relationships between the narrative and theology of idolaters and Israel and between the narrative and theology of repentance and atonement have shown the relevance of ordinances in responding to the grace of God set forth in the Torah. The narrative accounts for the idolaters and their standing and task in world history, the law translates the matter into everyday performance of the faith. The narrative of sin and repentance, atonement and forgiveness, defines the context for the text of the Temple rite, faithfully preserved in synagogue liturgy for the Day of

Atonement even to this very day. The message at the end—repentance begins in the here and now of seeking the forgiveness of those one has sinned against—provides the Judaic setting for the prayer, "Forgive us our trespasses, as we forgive those that trespass against us." The characterization of Judaism as a petty legalism conflicts with the law and theology of covenantal conduct set forth in these pages out of the authoritative documents of the Torah, written as mediated by the oral tradition.

We are further struck by evidence amassed in chapter 5 of the power of the law in its own framework, not in the framework of narrative, to speak in its own behalf of theological things. The law on its own delivers its message, as Ithamar Gruenwald says, without an accompanying script, which became clear in chapter 5. The systematic exposition of the law of the Seventh Year, of the law of the disposition of the fruit of a tree in the first three years and then the fourth year after it is planted show that the law is anything but petty and irrelevant. Rather, it allows the faithful Israelite to act out God's design for creation with its climax at the Sabbath. The laws of Shabbat-Erubin underscore the sanctifying power of the Sabbath over time and space. The laws of Passover and of Tabernacles sanctify the households of Israel in the model of the Temple. So too the criminal justice system portrayed in Sanhedrin-Makkot embodies the conviction of God's passionate love for humanity: his provision for eternal life through the expiation and atonement of sin through death, as through the provisional media of repentance and the Day of Atonement and the rites of atonement.

The law is commonly represented as formal and superficial, the theology conveying the spirit, which gives life. But here we have seen that the law directs itself toward the interior of life, the lore, to externals. That paradox should not be missed. When readers examine matters in detail, they see that the Aggadah's structure and system and those of the Halakhah address a single topic, but from different angles of vision of Israel's existence, the one, outward-looking and the other, inner-facing. But both engaged by relationships, the one transitive ones and the other intransitive. It is the Aggadah, fully set forth, that affords perspective on the Halakhah—and vice versa. The Halakhah in its way makes exactly the same statement about the same matters that the Aggadah does in its categories and terms. But the Aggadah speaks in large and general terms to the world at large, while the Halakhah uses small and particular rules to speak to the everyday concerns of ordinary Israelites.

The Aggadah, accordingly, addresses exteriorities, the Halakhah, interiorities, of Israel in relationship with God. Categorically, the Aggadah faces outward, toward humanity in general and correlates, shows the relationship of, humanity in general and Israel in particular. The theological system of a just world order answerable to one God that animates the Aggadah, specifically, sets forth the parallel stories of humanity and Israel, each beginning with Eden (Israel: the Land of Israel), marked by sin and punishment (Adam's, Israel's respective acts of rebellion against God, the one through disobedience, the other through violating the Torah), and exile for the purpose of bringing about repentance and atonement (Adam from Eden, Israel from the land). The system therefore takes as its critical problem the comparison of Israel with the Torah and the nations with idolatry. It comes to a climax in showing how the comparable stories intersect and diverge at the grave. For from there Israel is destined to the resurrection, judgment, and eternity (the world to come), the nations (that is, the idolators to the end) to death. When readers examine the category-formation of the Halakhah, by contrast, what they see is an account of Israel not in its external relationship to the nations but viewed wholly on its own. The lines of structure impart order from within. Each formation responds to the rules of construction of the same social order—God's justice—but the Aggadic one concerns Israel's social order in the context of God's transaction with humanity, the other, Israel's social order articulated within its own interior architectonics, the one, transitive, the other, intransitive.

The outward-facing theology that coheres in the Aggadic documents investigates the logic of creation, the fall, the regeneration made possible by the Torah, the separation of Israel and the Torah from the nations and idolatry, the one for life through repentance and resurrection, the other for death, and the ultimate restoration of creation's perfection attempted with Adam at Eden, but now through Israel in the Land of Israel.

Encompassing the whole of humanity that knows God in the Torah and rejects idolatry, Israel encompasses nearly the whole of mankind, along with nearly the whole of the Israel of the epoch of the Torah and of the Messiah that has preceded. That is why one may say that the Aggadah tells about Israel in the context of humanity, and hence speaks of exteriorities. Its perspectives are taken up at the border between outside and inside, the position of standing at the border inside and looking outward—hence [1] God and the world, [2] the Torah, and [3] Israel and the nations. That other perspective, the one gained by standing at the border, inside and turning, looking still deeper within, responds to the same logic, seeking the coherence and rationality of all things. That perspective focuses upon relationships, too. But now they are not those between God and mankind or Israel and the nations, but the ones involving [1] God and Israel, [2] Israel in its own terms, and

[3] the Israelite in his own situation, that is, within the household in partic-ular—terms amply defined in the Halakhic context.

In the cases provided in these pages, particularly in chapter 5, readers have seen how Israel relates to God in the encounter of enlandisement, where Israel takes its place in the Land of Israel and confronts its relation-ship with God in the very terms of the creation, when Adam take his place in Eden, with catastrophic results. Israel in the land reconstructs Eden by recapitulating creation and its requirements. All of this takes on detail and forms a cogent and compelling statement through the Halakhah.

Accordingly, the Aggadah describes exteriority, the Halakhah, interiority. The intangible of theology expressed through narrative and the tangible of theology expressed through concrete action intersect. The Aggadah answers the questions posed to justice by Israel's relationships with the world beyond. To complete the theological account, Aggadah having accomplished its task, the logic of a coherent whole requires that the Halakhah describe interior Israel. That logic must answer the questions posed to justice by Israel's rela-tionships within itself.

When the Aggadah's account of the exteriority of matters and the Halakhah's of the interiority ultimately join, then readers may indeed see the coherence of that one whole Torah of Moses, our Rabbi, oral and written, Aggadic and Halakhic, the unity of which defines as unique the hermeneu-tics of the sages. So my account of the theology that imposes upon monothe-ism the logical requirements of justice in the formation of world order by nature deals with the public issues: God and humanity, the Torah to remedy the flaw of creation in humanity, Israel and the nations.

How Christianity differs from Judaism in the matter of the law of the Torah requires attention. It is not because Christianity presents a superior account of life under the law. It is because Christianity rejects the law as medium of grace now that (in its language) Christ has risen from the dead. Paul marks the starting point of Christianity's departure from the Torah: its exit at the outset from Judaism, the religion of the Torah (however defined and interpreted).[12]

That is because Paul insisted that gentiles could enter "Israel after the spirit" without adopting the disciplines of the Torah. What is at stake has already come to light in chapter 1: Israel and the idolaters. Christians no less than Israelites rejected idolatry and accepted the revelation at Sinai. But at issue is whether God is known through the Torah or through some other medium. Peter and Paul reinterpreted who and what is "Israel" to make a place within the Torah, among the children of Abraham, for gentiles who had not the slightest intention of making a pilgrimage to the Jerusalem

Temple, circumcising their sons (or themselves), or accepting the dietary taboos of the Torah, to name three significant indicators of entering into holy Israel, God's people. What did Paul in particular do in defining this world's Israel as an ethnic group, "Israel after the flesh," as distinct from the "Israel after the spirit" that belonged to God beyond the bounds of the Torah's law? Bruce Chilton answers that question:

> Paul popularized Jesus' message . . . he also changed the message, shifting emphasis of Jesus' movement away from realizing the kingdom of God along with Jesus and toward realizing Jesus himself as the Christ within one's being. Every believer was animated with the Spirit that came from Jesus.. . . . Jesus is Christianity's founder, but Paul is its maker—he focused the elements of faith on the formation of Christ within . . . Baptism turned people into the Israel of God, transformed by the Spirit within them . . . by baptism the believer becomes . . . a helpful familiar in the kingdom of Christ that is coming to transform the world.

To be a Christian involved personal religious encounter:

> Knowing God's son meant realizing that his dying and rising again awakened the resurrection principle within every believer . . . the way Jesus found to eternal life was open to anyone who accepted his spirit.[13]

The issue is not improving on Judaism's alleged legalism. The issue is how God proposes to correct the condition of humanity, flawed from Eden and the fall, just as the Rabbinic narrative maintains. Christianity emerges not as an excuse for envious pagans to get the blessings promised to Israel without keeping the Torah but as a source of religious experience autonomous of the Torah. It is not a revision of Judaism, understood as the realization of the Torah of Sinai, but a distinct way of knowing God. To that path to God, covenantal conduct is monumentally irrelevant.

That is why most first-century Israelites and all generations to follow would reject Christianity in favor of the Torah of Sinai and the covenanted life with God nurtured by the commandments or *mitzvot*. For us who form Israel, "Israel after the flesh" and "Israel after the spirit" are, and always will remain, one and the same under the aspect of Sinai (flesh and spirit, the Halakhah and the Aggadah, law and narrative) forever form a single, coherent account of God, made known by God's own grace shown to Israel.

Notes

1   Maren Niehoff, *Philo on Jewish Identity and Culture* (vol. 86 of *Texts and Studies in Ancient Judaism*; ed. Martin Hengel and Peter Schaefer. Tuebingen: Mohr Siebeck, 2001).

2   In Chapter 2, I translate as "idolater" all references to "gentiles," since that is the intent throughout.

3   The advent of a *tertium quid*—not Israelite, not idolate—would pose a considerable problem for the Rabbinic theologians, both exegetes and lawyers. The Tosefta's famous passage represents the first documentary articulation of the problem presented by Christianity to the Rabbinic paradigm of the nations = idolaters. The issue is how on the Sabbath day one deals with saving from a fire the holy books belonging to minim, here clearly meaning, Christians, whose writings will include the Holy Name of God. Tarfon's statement, T. Shab. 13:5Dff., shows the unresolved dilemma presented by gentiles who were not idolaters, and who, in the very centuries of the writing down of the Mishnah and the Tosefta, were martyred for their faith in the one, unique God made known in the Torah.

      T. 13:5   A.   The books of the Evangelists and the books of the minim they do not save from a fire. But they are allowed to burn where they are,

              B.   they and the references to the Divine Name which are in them.

              C.   R. Yosé the Galilean says, "On ordinary days, one cuts out the references to the Divine Name which are in them and stores them away, and the rest burns."

              D.   Said R. Tarfon, "May I bury my sons, if such things come into my hands and I do not burn them, and even the references to the Divine Name which are in them.

              E.   "And if someone was running after me, I should go into a temple of idolatry, but I should not go into their houses [of worship].

D. Said R. Tarfon, "May I bury my sons, if such things come into my hands and I do not burn them, and even the references to the Divine Name which are in them.

E. "And if someone was running after me, I should go into a temple of idolatry, but I should not go into their houses [of worship].

F. "For idolators do not recognize the Divinity in denying him, but these recognize the Divinity and deny him.

G. "And about them Scripture states, 'Behind the door and the doorpost you have set up your symbol for deserting me, you have uncovered your bed' (Isa 57:8)."

H. Said R. Ishmael, "Now if to bring peace between a humanity and his wife, the Omnipresent declared that a scroll written in a state of sanctification should be blotted out by water, the books of the minim, which bring enmity between Israel and their Father who is in heaven, all the more so should be blotted out,

I. "they and the references to the Divine Name in them.

J. "And concerning them has Scripture stated, 'Do I not hate them that hate thee, O Lord? And do I not loathe them that rise up against thee? I hate them with perfect hatred, I count them my enemies' (P 139:2122)."

K. Just as they do not save them on account of fire, so they do not save them from a ruin, or a flood, or anything which will turn them to rubble.

4   On that matter, see the fundamental work of Ithamar Gruenwald, *Rituals and Ritual Theory in Ancient Israel* (Leiden: E. J. Brill, 2003). He focuses on rituals "as behavioral expressions of the human mind, regardless of any ideology or pre-existing symbolism . . . rituals in their own performative content." He sidesteps "the usual textual, historical, or theological perspective." He argues that rituals are autonomous expressions of the mind, focusing attention on what is done. The results set forth here conform to that theory of matters.

5   Alan J. Avery-Peck, tr. *The Talmud of the Land of Israel. Tractate Shebi'it* (vol. 5 of *Talmudi Yerushalmi*. Chicago: University of Chicago Press, 1991), 2.

6   Louis E. Newman, *The Sanctity of the Seventh Year. A Study of Mishnah Tractate Shebi'it* (no. 44 of *Brown Judaic Studies*. Chico: Scholars Press, 1983).

7   Avery-Peck, *Talmud*, 6.

8   Ibid., 3.

9   Ibid., *Talmud*, 4.

10 Newman, *Sanctity*, 15.

11 The sages maintain, as noted earlier, that had Israel not sinned, the Torah would have contained only the Pentateuch and the book of Joshua, a neat way of stating in a few words the conviction that permeates the Aggadic reading of the

land as counterpart to Eden, Israel as counterpart to Adam. It is on that basis that I see the wilderness as I do: the interval between death in Egypt and eternal life in the land.

12 Bruce D. Chilton, *Rabbi Paul. An Intellectual Biography* (New York: Doubleday, 2004).

13 Ibid., 264.

Index of Ancient Sources

Index of Subjects